Income Inequality and Poverty in Eastern and Western Europe

Contributions to Economics

Peter R. Haiss
Cultural Influences on Strategic Planning
1990. ISBN 3-7908-0481-9

Manfred Kremer/Marion Weber (Eds.)
Transforming Economic Systems: The Case of Poland
1992. ISBN 3-7908-0585-8

Marcel F. van Marion
Liberal Trade and Japan
1993. ISBN 3-7908-0699-4

Hans Schneeweiß/
Klaus F. Zimmermann (Eds.)
Studies in Applied Econometrics
1993. ISBN 3-7908-0716-8

Gerhard Gehrig/
Wladyslaw Welfe (Eds.)
Economies in Transition
1993. ISBN 3-7908-0721-4

Christoph M. Schneider
Research and Development Management: From the Soviet Union to Russia
1994. ISBN 3-7908-0757-5

Bernhard Böhm/
Lionello F. Punzo (Eds.)
Economic Performance
1994. ISBN 3-7908-0811-3

Michael Reiter
The Dynamics of Business Cycles
1995. ISBN 3-7908-0823-7

Michael Carlberg
Sustainability and Optimality of Public Debt
1995. ISBN 3-7908-0834-2

Lars Olof Persson/Ulf Wiberg
Microregional Fragmentation
1995. ISBN 3-7908-0855-5

Andreas Foerster
Institutional Analysis of Development Administration
1995. ISBN 3-7908-0853-9

Ernesto Felli/Furio C. Rosati/
Giovanni Tria (Eds.)
The Service Sector: Productivity and Growth
1995. ISBN 3-7908-0875-X

Giuseppe Munda
Multicriteria Evaluation in Fuzzy Environment
1995. ISBN 3-7908-0892-X

Boris Maurer
R & D, Innovation and Industrial Structure
1996. ISBN 3-7908-0900-4

Giovanni Galizzi/Luciano Venturini (Eds.)
Economics of Innovation: The Case of Food Industry
1996. ISBN 3-7908-0911-X

David T. Johnson
Poverty, Inequality and Social Welfare in Australia
1996. ISBN 3-7908-0942-X

Rongxing Guo
Border-Regional Economics
1996. ISBN 3-7908-0943-8

Oliver Fratzscher
The Political Economy of Trade Integration
1996. ISBN 3-7908-0945-4

Ulrich Landwehr
Industrial Mobility and Public Policy
1996. ISBN 3-7908-0949-7

Arnold Picot / Ekkehard Schlicht (Eds.)
Firms, Markets, and Contracts
1996. ISBN 3-7908-0947-0

Karin Peschel (Ed.)
Regional Growth and Regional Policy Within the Framework of European Integration
1997. ISBN 3-7908-0957-8

Thorsten Wichmann
Agricultural Technical Progress and the Development of a Dual Economy
1997. ISBN 3-7908-0960-8

Notburga Ott
Gert G. Wagner (Eds.)

Income Inequality and Poverty in Eastern and Western Europe

With 10 Figures

Springer-Verlag Berlin Heidelberg GmbH

Series Editors
Werner A. Müller
Peter Schuster

Editors
Priv.-Doz. Dr. Notburga Ott
University of Frankfurt
Department of Economics
Senckenberganlage 31
D-60054 Frankfurt, Germany

Professor Dr. Gert G. Wagner
German Institute for Economic Research
Königin-Luise-Straße 5
D-14191 Berlin, Germany

ISBN 978-3-7908-0974-9 ISBN 978-3-642-50003-9 (eBook)
DOI 10.1007/978-3-642-50003-9

Die Deutsche Bibliothek – CIP-Einheitsaufnahme
Income and poverty in eastern and western Europe / Notburga Ott; Gert G. Wagner (ed.). – Heidelberg: Physica-Verl., 1997
(Contributions to economics)

NE: Ott, Notburga [Hrsg.]

SPIN 10551744 88/2202-5 4 3 2 1 0 – Printed on acid-free paper

Preface

The contributions of this collected volume are the result of a call for papers. The authors met and discussed their drafts at the workshop „Inequality in Europe", organized by the editors.

The workshop was sponsored by the „Population Economics" section of the German Association for Demography („*Deutsche Gesellschaft fuer Bevoelkerungswissenschaft*" - *DGBw*) and by the „Josef-Popper-Naehrpflicht" Foundation. The aim of this foundation, located at the Johann-Wolfgang-Goethe-University of Frankfurt am Main, is to support research dealing with problems of achieving a „reasonable" standard of living. Originally the aim of the foundation was to further the notion of a guaranteed minimum income („*allgemeine Naehrpflicht*"). The publication of this book is also sponsored by this foundation.

The workshop was held at the „*Evangelische Akademie Arnoldshain*", near Frankfurt am Main. The helpful discussions during the workshop benefitted greatly from the friendly atmosphere of the academy.

Some of the articles were financially supported by the „Panel Comparability" Project (PACO), located at CEPS (*Centre d'Etudes de Populations, de Pauvreté et de Politiques Socio-Economiques*) in Luxembourg. PACO is a joint activity of the German Institute for Economic Research (DIW) in Berlin, CEPS and some other institutions in European countries. It is sponsored by grant No. ERBCHRX-CT92-0037 („European Network on Longitudinal Household Panel Studies Meeting Technology Requirement for Comparative Research") of the „Human Capital and Mobility" program of the Commission of the European Community.

The editors would like to thank all contributors and discussants at the workshop. Special thanks go to Daniel J. Schmidt (Ruhr-University of Bochum) and Janet Yates (Free University of Berlin) who did the English language editing for the volume, and to Irmingard Wuehler and Susanne Krugel for editorial management of the manuscripts.

Notburga Ott and Gert G. Wagner
Berlin and Bochum

May 1996

Contents

Competitive or Cooperative Welfare Policies in Europe?

Georg Meran and Aloys Prinz

1 Introduction

The transition to a "European Monetary Union" (EMU) is not only of relevance for enterprises and workers, but also for social policy.[1] Within the EU, there has been a long standing discussion on which level of government should be responsible for the "fight against poverty": national or supra-national authorities?[2] Some authors argue for a total harmonization ("unification") of welfare policies, whereas others prefer national policies against poverty; two views which are in conflict to each other. Although there have already been several EU programs to fight poverty and there are structural, social and regional EU funds that are at least partially used to reduce poverty,[3] there are only few theoretical and empirical investigations on the effects of supra-national welfare policies.[4] In addition, it seems even unclear what the best *national* welfare policy would be if it were to compete with the policies abroad.

In this paper, we will attempt to fill some of these gaps in theoretical literature. We start off with a two-country-model in which the countries have a common currency but are differ in their productivity.[5] We allow costly migration between

---

1 See, for instance, Berthold (1993a,b).
2 See Schulte (1991) and Kuhn (1991).
3 See Paqué (1992).
4 The relevant studies are Brown & Oates (1987), Wildasin (1991), Crane (1992) as well as Kumar (1977), Ladd & Doolittle (1982) and Southwick (1981).
5 An approach for analyzing regional differences in migration models is offered by Bell (1991).

Aloys Prinz is Associated Professor of Economics at Johannes Gutenberg-University of Mainz / Germany.

Claus Schäfer is Senior Research Fellow at the WSI within the Hans Böckler-Foundation, Düsseldorf / Germany.

Johannes Schwarze is Senior Research Fellow at the German Institute of Economic Research. In 1995 he was Visiting Assistant Professor in the Department of Economics at Syracuse University, New York / USA; in 1996/97 he is Visiting Professor of Public Admistration at Ruhr-University of Bochum / Germany.

Zsolt Speder is Assistant Professor of Economics at the Budapest University of Economic Sciences / Hungary.

Alexander Surinov is Deputy Director of the "Center for Economic Analysis" in Moskow / Russia.

Heinz Stapf is Managing Director of the Luxembourg Income Study at Walferdange / Luxembourg.

Irena Topinska is Assistant Professor of Economics in the Department of Economics at Warszaw University / Poland.

Karel Van den Bosch is researcher at the Centre for Social Policy, University of Antwerp / Belgium.

Bernhard M.S. Van Praag is Professor of Economics at the University of Amsterdam, and Director of the SEO-Institute at this university / The Netherlands.

Gert G. Wagner is Professor of Public Administration at Ruhr-University of Bochum, and Director of the German Socio-Economic Panel Study at the German Institute for Economic Research (Berlin) / Germany. In 1995 he was Visiting Professor of Economics at Syracuse University, New York / USA.

Income Inequality and Poverty in Eastern and Western Europe: An Introduction

Notburga Ott and Gert G. Wagner

1 Aims of this Volume

Issues of economic inequality and poverty have been of interest for many decades. There are at least three reasons why inequality and poverty is currently a growing "branch" of scientific research.

- The monitoring of inequality, poverty and their impact on society is no longer a research question only for economists, but social sciences are also analyzing these topics.
- In Western Europe, or more precisely, within the European Union, the "War on Poverty" is an official topic for the Commission of the European Union. In Eastern Europe, growing inequality and the development of poverty are crucial issues resulting from the transition process of the old "socialist economies".
- The collapse of the Berlin Wall and the subsequent reunification of Germany are only part of a broader process of world-wide change. Other important patterns include the convergence of economic and social organization despite decades of historical differences. As a consequence comparative research in the social sciences is becoming more and more important.

Beside the substantial interest in inequality and poverty, there may be a simple methodology reason for the new interest in those questions: the availability of micro databases which allow flexible research based on theoretical grounds. These micro databases are not only available in just a few countries, but in most countries of the European Union and, what might be surprising from a Western point of view, they are also available in major Eastern European countries. Similarly, in some countries, not only in Western Europe but also in Eastern

Europe, there are longitudinal databases available which are necessary in order to analyse the "dynamics of poverty" (cf. Gustafsson 1995).

This volume brings together different approaches, which are looking at different countries. All papers are analyzing inequality and poverty mainly from an economic point of view. The content of this volume will be presented in the next section, followed by the third section which discusses some comparative thoughts on these issues.

2 Content of this Volume

The first contribution of this volume is purely a theoretical one. *Georg Meran and Aloys Prinz* deal with the long-standing discussion within the European Union of which is the proper level of government that should be responsible for the "War Against Poverty". Many authors argue for a total harmonization of welfare policies, which would be administered by a supranational authority, whereas others, mainly economists, would prefer to have national policies against poverty, which sets up competition between countries or regions. To deal with this question, the authors demonstrate the properties of the best national welfare policies under autarchy, as well as under costless and perfect mobility across national borders. Then they analyze the more realistic case of costly and imperfect migration between nations. They then evaluate the efficiency of uncoordinated welfare policies and show under which circumstances coordinated policies will improve welfare. Of particular interest is the result they show for diverse national styles of welfare policy, due to different attitude towards risks. Meran and Prinz are able to show that national policies are no longer efficient in this context. This means that there are allocative reasons for cooperative welfare policies in Europe and not only distributive ones.

The contribution from *Richard Hauser* is a blueprint for comprehensive empirical analysis of poverty in an international comparative context. Hauser argues that in many ways, economic and social measurements are based on assumptions i.e.value judgments. These are assumptions which a broad majority of scientists have agreed upon by convention. For example, many users of the national accountsfigures may not be aware of the inherent value judgments. In contrast to these established (and invisible) measurement procedures and accounting systems, it is not possible to measure poverty based on widely agreed conventions because a great divergence of opinions on the definition of poverty still exists. Hauser argues that such a divergence can only be reduced through discussion about the underlying ethical questions, and not by theoretical or empirical scientific analysis.

Given this conclusion, Hauser outlines what can be done in the field of scientific analysis of poverty. In order to highlight the much disputed range of possible poverty levels, he suggests a practical procedure of measuring and analyzing poverty on the bases of a number of different poverty lines. The use of a grit of poverty lines may also assist illustration of which level that effective national minimum income regulations provide sufficient income to avoid income poverty, as defined by national political decisions. When endeavoring to make conclusions about national policy, political value judgments cannot be avoided. At this point the scientist can no longer claim to speak with the backing of his scientific knowledge but only as an ordinary citizen who is expressing his political opinion.

All of the following contributions deal with distribution of income and poverty lines in different European countries. Most of the chapters analyze household incomes and poverty of persons within the context of the households in which they live. Only the paper by *Claus Schäfer* deals with the distribution of wages. He calls his research question the analysis of "inadequate" or "inequitable" wages, which could be judged as an "unfair compensation". He addresses German workers who hold a job but receive wages so low that their income is insufficient to make ends meet in the case that such workers are living alone. This research is part of the investigation by a crew of international experts who are working on inequitable wages on assignment from the Commission of the European Communities. When Schäfer uses 50 percent of the medium wage of full time workers as the line of "inequitable wage", analogous to the household poverty line, he gets around 6 percent of full time workers in Germany whose pay is "unfair". When he uses a threshold of 66 percent (according to a standard which was established in 1960 by the European Social Charter of the Council of Europe), he gets around 13 percent. Since Schäfer analyzed only full time workers, which means that the numbers do not include such groups as part-time employees or "marginalized women", he is surprised to find such big shares of "unfair paid workers". Schäfer also gives some figures on the extent of unfair paid workers in other countries of the European Union. Evaluated by the 50 percent-threshold, unfair paid full-time workers are negligible in Belgium and France; with the biggest shares being found in the United Kingdom, Italy, Spain and Ireland (10 percent). In his conclusion, he argues that a "national minimum wage" could be helpful in Germany.

The contribution by *Bernard M. S. van Praag*, together with *Erik J. S. Plug*, *Peter Krause* and *Gert G. Wagner*, is an example of his "subjective poverty concept", using the case of reunified Germany. Van Praag and collaborators compare the subjective poverty notion with various other poverty concepts. Their main conclusion revealed that in 1992, the poverty line, in the subjective context, did not differ dramatically between East and West Germany. A special feature of this contribution is the testing of whether the answer from one respondent in a household is representative of the whole household. This is a unique possibility which is provided the database used, the German Socio-Economic Panel Study (GSOEP), which interviews all adult members of each survey household. The result is that the differences between spouses are surprisingly small.

Two other contributions deal with Western Europe. The paper from *Herman Deleeck, Karel van den Bosch* and *Lieve De La Thouwer* provides an overview on poverty with a special emphasis on the role of social security transfers within seven countries and regions in the European Union (Belgium, Catalonia, Greece, Ireland, Lorraine, Luxembourg and the Netherlands). The data come from socio-economic household surveys. Deleeck et al. use different poverty lines and they break down their results by socio-economic characteristics of the population. As has been reported in other studies, the extent of poverty is much greater in the peripheral countries of the European Union (Catalonia, Greece and Ireland) than in the central ones (Belgium, Lorraine, Luxembourg and the Netherlands). However, there are also important differences in the characteristics of the poor across these countries. Very young households in the northern countries are at high risk of poverty, but not in the southern countries. An interesting finding reveals that a sizable minority among the poor in all countries consists of households where the head is working.

Old age poverty in selected countries of the European Union is the research issue that *Heinz Stapf* reports on. He uses the data from the famous Luxembourg Income Study (LIS). For Belgium, France, Italy, the Netherlands, United Kingdom and West Germany, Stapf concludes that at the moment in a life course when the system of old age security starts to work, a decrease of poverty rates and poverty gaps (intensity of poverty) can be observed. However, with regard to older people, poverty rates increase with their age, although this pattern cannot be found for the intensity of poverty. The poverty rate for single women is higher than the poverty rate for single men, and the poverty gap of poor single men is larger than the gap for poor single women.

The last five papers of the volume deal with economies in transition in Eastern Europe (the Czech Republic, Russia, Hungary, Poland and East Germany). *Jiri Vecernik* presents an overview, from 1990 to 1993, of the extent and the social structure of poverty in the Czech Republic, which is a successor of former Czechoslovakia. The Czech Republic, as well as Hungary are interesting from a statistical point of view because there is survey data available which was collected in the „socialist period" (the possibilities to look back in the socialist area are much smaller in the former Soviet Union, Poland and East Germany). For the former Czechoslovakia there are "economic attitudes and expectations surveys" available which contain not only objective indicators but also subjective ones. Thus the poverty rate could be seen from three very different alternative perspectives and measured by various kinds of indicators.

The main results from Vecernik's paper for the Czech Republic are as follows: the poverty measured with reference to the official poverty line, also conforms very well with the poverty line suggested by the Commission of the European Communities. It shows a poverty rates for households of about 2 to 4 percent and the main determining factor of poverty is the number of dependent children. The second point is the subjective poverty approach which indicates a poverty rate of about 30 percent, is much more affected by the number of adults in the household. The third approach is a simple declaration of "subjective poverty" by the respondents themselves, giving a level of about 10 percent which is less effected by demographic or social characteristics and much more by the wealth status of a household. All in all, the transition economy in the Czech Republic is doing quite well in terms of the limited increase in poverty and curbed increase in economic inequality.

Alexander Surinov and *Igor Kolosnitsyn* present indicators on social inequality and poverty in Russia which are based on official statistics for 1993 and the first half year of 1994. As the authors mention the major methodological complication of measuring inequality and poverty in Russia is the growth of unreported income.

There are several factors contributing to an underestimation of officially reported income: a decreasing government sector and growing small business sector, especially in retail trade; an increase in the number of tax laws and an increasing incentive to bypass them; an increase in unemployment creating an incentive to work in an informal sector. For instance, an estimate of household income based on banking statistics reported figures about 20 percent higher than the income average in 1992 that is reported by the statistical office "Goskomstat". This difference reached 70 percent in the middle of 1994. If hidden income would be included in the surveys, income distributions would become more unequal and poverty lines as well as poverty rates would increase because unreported incomes are much more frequent in the higher-income classes.

But Surinov and Kolosnitsyn deal with official income figures only, which show a poverty rate based on an "basket of minimum expenditures" which in 1993/94 was around 25 percent of the population. The authors improve this official poverty rate by calculating real incomes by regions which differ by the price levels. The authors come up with a "corrected poverty rate" of about 15 percent which is considerably lower than the official rate. The results show also that the poverty rates are very different in various regions of Russia: the poverty rate in Moscow is about 5 percent whereas rural areas have rates of about 50 percent.

For Hungary and Poland not only cross-sectional data is available but also longitudinal data bases. *Rudolf Andorka* and *Zsolt Spéder* present results of the first two waves of the Hungarian Household Panel Study. This longitudinal survey, together with the Eastern sample of the German Socio-Economic Panel Study, are the only longitudinal survey which cover the very beginning of the transition process as well as the ongoing transition process in an Eastern European country (the Polish longitudinal data cover three years only).

The results for Hungary under transition are comparable to the results for the Czech Republic. Evaluated by the 50 percent threshold of mean income, around 20 percent of the population were poor in 1992 and 1993. As in Western Europe, the elderly are not a population with an extraordinary high risk of poverty, but families with children are a group on high risk.

The longitudinal character of the Hungarian Panel Study allows estimation of a first indicator for the dynamics of poverty under transition. Between 1992 and 1993, around 50 percent of the poor population in the previous year were able to escape out of poverty. This indicates a considerable dynamic in income positions for the transition economy in Hungary which is surprisingly comparable with the dynamics of income positions in Western European countries.

Joachim Frick, Irena Topinska, Gert G. Wagner and *Klaus Mueller* deal with the same question as Andorka and Spéder: income inequality and poverty dynamics which are evaluated for both the Polish and East German economies before and under transition. For Germany the authors use the eastern sample of the German Socio-Economic Panel Study; for Poland they use an artificial longitudinal data set which is based on the "household budget surveys" that have been conducted by the Polish Central Statistical Office for many years. These budget surveys are sampled by means of a partial rotation method on a quarterly basis which give the opportunity to survey the same household for a maximum of four years. This kind of data is used to create the so called Polish Household Panel.

Frick et al. analyze the first panel which is constructed for the years 1987 to 1990. It turns out that inequality as well as poverty rates were much higher in Poland than in the German Democratic Republic (for the years 1989 respectively 1991). The poverty rate (evaluated by the 50 percent level of mean income) was around 4 percent in the German Democratic Republic and about 11 percent in Poland. A major source of the higher poverty in Poland stemmed from a much bigger rural sector in this society. Income of pensioners was the most equally distributed in both countries; but pensioners were also the group most affected by poverty.

Under transition inequality and poverty rates increased both in Poland as well as in East Germany. This is not surprising because one aim of the transition is to introduce market forces in both countries. But the pathways have been very different: While there are remarkable changes in the results for Poland over time, the figures for East Germany have not changed very much. Under transition, pension protection was improved in Poland, although not for long as the authors figured out. The opposite is true in East Germany where the people who were retired at the point when the transition started, are the group with the biggest permanent increase in income position. This is due to transfers which are paid by West Germany and the zero-risk of unemployment (by definition) for pensioners.

The last contribution of this volume also deals with the income distribution of East Germany, but it includes a comparison with the income distribution of West

Germany and that of a Unified Germany as a whole (based on GSOEP). *Johannes Schwarze* analyzes the income distribution of a Unified Germany by decomposable inequality indicators. After a short discussion of decomposable income measures he chose the Theil Index for his analysis. He points out that the advantage of the Theil measure is the possibility that changes over time in the overall income distribution can be analyzed within a consistent framework, together with its most important aspects: distributions within and between the two areas. Given the significance of transfers which are paid from West Germany to East Germany such analysis is of vital importance. As expected, increasing mean income in East Germany contributed most to reducing overall German income inequality. The increase of mean income overcompensated for the increase of income inequality within East Germany.

3 Some First Comparative Thoughts on the Conversion in Europe

Thinking about inequality and poverty overall in Europe will still be divided into thinking about Eastern and Western Europe. The only Eastern European „country“ which is approaching the Western income level is East Germany; the other Eastern European countries are a long way from reaching Western income levels.

The competition of the low-wage countries of Eastern Europe with Western European economies will bring some unemployment problems to Western Europe. But from the Western European point of view, a drastic reduction in wages cannot be a successful strategy to overcome the challenges of the low-wage economies of Eastern Europe. The answer to this challange for Western European economies lies in a high-technology strategy. Maybe not all economies will be successful in doing this but on the whole, the income gap between Western and Eastern Europe will not be closed by a rapid reduction of Western wages but by a slow increase of Eastern wages. However, it is to be expected that inequality will increase in Eastern Europe as well as in Western Europe.

For Eastern European countries which are analyzed in this volume, the picture is as follows (excluding Russia from this discussion because the data basis for Russia is not as good as those used for the former Czechoslovakia, Hungary and

Poland): for the countries under consideration that some similarities were revealed although they started from different points. Inequality and poverty are increasing but not in a dramatic way. All in all, inequality is growing faster in the former Czechoslovakia, Hungary and Poland than in East Germany. This may be surprising because a real shock therapy was applied in East Germany whereas in the former Czechoslovakia, Hungary and Poland the transition process has been much smoother.

A good indicator of the "amount of shock" is the change of the unemployment rate in the different economies. The dynamics of unemployment shows that in real terms the shock was much bigger in East Germany than in the other three countries which have been evaluated. But the dynamics of income inequality and poverty does not show up in East Germany because the shock of a common currency came together with a much more adequate social policy rules and subsidization for old industries which paints over the effect of the market forces.

In summary, the transition of East Germany is a unique economic event within Eastern Europe because it is a "transition with insurance" (cf. Schrettl 1992). In this context insurance simply means that West Germany is paying a big amount of transfers to the former German Democratic Republic, subsidizing old industries, partially financing unemployment benefits, creating job-programs and financing a good deal of the old age benefits. In the middle of the nineties, around one half of the "national income" of East Germany is still transferred from West Germany. This is the reason why the shock of the explosion of unemployment rates does not affect the welfare level (income and the inequality of household incomes) in the same manner. But the insurance provided by West Germany has a price: Most of the privatized firms in Germany are bought by Western companies (cf. Bruecker 1995). Such an "insurance contract" would be possible in the former Czechoslovakia, Hungary and Poland, too, but the price seems to be too high. Because the price would be the loss of economic independence and maybe the loss of political independence, too. No one in those countries is ready to accept such a „transition with insurance".

References

Gustafsson, Björn (1995): Assessing poverty - some reflections on the literature, in: Journal of Population Economics, 8 (4), 361-381.

Bruecker, Herbert (1995): Selling Eastern Germany, in: MOCT / MOST - Economic Policy an Transitional Economies, 5 (4), 55-77.

Milanovic, Branco (1995): Poverty, Inequality and Social Policy in Transition Economies, Research Project "Income Distribution during the Transition", Paper No. 9, World Bank, Washington, D.C.

Schrettl, Wolfram (1992): Transition with Insurance - German Unification Reconsidered, in: Oxford Review of Economic Policy, 8 (1), 1-12.

Contributors

Rudolf Andorka is Professor of Sociology and Rector of the Budapest University of Economic Sciences / Hungary.

Lieve De Lathouwer is Researcher at the Centre for Social Policy at University of Antwerp / Belgium.

Herman Deleeck is Emeritus Professor at the Universities of Antwerp, Louvain and Leyden / Belgium and The Netherlands.

Joachim Frick is Senior Research Fellow at the German Institute of Economic Research, Berlin / Germany.

Richard Hauser is Professor of Economics in the Department of Economics at the Johann Wolfgang Goethe University of Frankfurt am Main / Germany.

Jirí Veçerník, Institute of Sociology, Academy of Sciences, Praha / Czech Republic.

Igor Kolosnitsyn is Deputy Director for International Projects in the "Institute for the Economy in Transition" in Moscow / Russia.

Peter Krause is Senior Research Fellow at the German Institute of Economic Research. In 1995 he was Visiting Assistant Professor in the Department of Economics at Syracuse University, New York / USA.

Georg Meran is Professor of Economics in the Department of Economics at the Technical University of Berlin / Germany.

Notburga Ott is Visiting Professor of Economics at the Humboldt University of Berlin / Germany

Erik J.S Plug is Junior Research Fellow at the University of Amsterdam / The Netherlands.

the countries.[6] Furthermore, we assume the national governments intend to offer their citizens the highest possible welfare level through a public budget against unemployment and poverty. However, offering generous transfer payments may attract people from the other country. This raises some questions: what transfer level will national governments choose if discrimination against foreigners is not allowed and each country acts on its own? And how will the results be changed when side payments between countries are feasible?

We will proceed as follows. First, an analytical framework is to be constructed which incorporates characteristic facts from European countries. Next, we show the properties of the best national welfare policy under autarky as well as under costless and perfect mobility across national borders. Then we analyze the more realistic case of costly and imperfect migration between nations. After this, we evaluate the efficiency of uncoordinated welfare policies and show under which circumstances coordinated policies will improve welfare.

2 The Analytical Framework

Consider two countries L_i, $i=(1,2)$, with populations N_i. and GNP is exogenously given as Y_i.[7] In our context this is a reasonable assumption because we are interested in the allocation of poor and unemployed people[8] and not in the effects of transfer payments on labor supply.

The crucial assumption in our main model is that labor demand falls short of labor supply. We take note that this phenomenon is actual fact in most European labor markets. It means that each person in our model wishes to work the standard number of hours, but not all of them will find such a job. The number of employed is given by $n_i < N_i$; with one reason for this being that the labor market

6 Roemer (1983) considers migration as an indicator for 'unequal trade'. We do not follow this idea here since in our model, migration turns out to be caused by arbitrage of transfers. Therefore we do not judge migration itself as welfare reducing.

7 The construction of regional models with endogenous GNP is shown in Atkinson & Stiglitz (1980) and Wildasin (1986).

8 In this paper, we use the notions 'unemployed' and 'poor' synonymously.

is not fully competitive.[9] Consequently, there exists an employment lottery in which the employees are randomly selected. We assume that all persons are of identical skill; therefore, employers do not discriminate against them. The number of unemployed in each country is given by $N_i - n_i$.

Migration causes costs m whereby we suppose that these are psychic costs (e.g. loss of cultural identity, foreign language) rather than resource costs. The reasons for this are; (a) if costs of migration were resource costs, they would be incomes to others and, therefore, they had to be incorporated in the welfare analysis and would be unduly complicated, (b) costs of transport are rather low in the EU, and may, therefore, be neglected. We assume that migration costs are randomly and equally distributed on $[0,m]$ among the population.

Welfare policies (T_i,S_i) are described by tax-transfer-schemes which contain taxes on workers, T_i and transfers to the unemployed, S_i. The budget constraint for national welfare policy without migration is given by:

$$(1) \qquad T_i \cdot n_i \geq (N_i - n_i) \cdot S_i.$$

We suppose next that only unemployed people will migrate. The decision rule for the unemployed is as follows: migrate from country j to country i if transfers in j less costs of migration are higher than transfers in i.[10] In this way, we are able to calculate the number of migrants from one country to the other.

The *objective* of both countries is to maximize welfare of their own people whether they reside within or outside their home country. For country 1 (which is also analogously for country 2) the objective is:

$$(2) \qquad W_1(T_1,S_1) = \begin{cases} n_1 U(Y_1 - T_1) + (N_1 - n_1) \cdot \\ \quad \cdot [U(S_1)(1 - P(S_2 - S_1)) + \int_0^{S_2 - S_1} U(S_2 - m) f(m) dm], \\ \hfill \text{if } e_{12} > 0 \\ n_1 U(Y_1 - T_1) + (N_1 - n_1) U(S_1)(1 - P(S_2 - S_1)), \\ \hfill \text{if } e_{21} > 0 \end{cases}$$

---

9 There are several theories of the labor market which explain this phenomenon: efficiency wages, segmented labor markets, insider-outsider problems etc.

10 In formal terms: Migrate from j to i if $S_i - m \geq S_j$. This implies that migration occurs as long as $m \leq S_i - S_j$.

where e_{ji} means the number of migrants from i to j and $f(m)$ is the density function for m. Accordingly, $P(\ldots)$ is the distribution function of m, i.e.

$$P(S_2 - S_1) = \int_0^{S_2 - S_1} f(m)dm.$$

$U(\ldots)$ is a utility function for the citizens. Accordingly to this, national welfare is defined as the weighted sum of utilities of employed and unemployed people residing within their home country and abroad. It is also assumed that country 2 is more productive than country 1.

3 Welfare Policy under Autarky and Perfect Mobility

We will distinguish three different scenarios for mobility:

1. *Autarky*: there is no migration because national labor markets and transfer systems are supposed to be closed for foreigners.
2. *Perfect mobility*: labor markets and transfer systems are open to all and there are no mobility costs.
3. *Limited mobility*: labor markets are closed for foreigners, but transfer systems are open and migration is costly.

3.1 Autarky

The main result here is as follows:

Proposition 1 Autarky is Pareto-efficient.

In this case, Pareto efficiency requires; (a) that there are no externalities, and (b) that there is full coverage of the unemployment risk if citizens are risk averse.

(a) If it is impossible to leave a country, then it is also impossible that the national levels of benefits to the unemployed will have an effect on each other. This means that there is no externality due to the national welfare policy. Hence each national authority can choose that level of benefits which maximize national welfare.

(b) If there are no externalities and people are risk averse, a national unemployment insurance will emerge which is characterized by full coverage of the risk to become unemployed (*risk shifting*). Consequently, utility *and* income for all citizens of a country, be she/he employed or unemployed, will be the same, i.e. $S_i = Y_i - T_i$. This result follows immediately from the concavity of the national objective function and from the inelasticity of the labor supply.

Under autarky, it may very well be that there is a welfare differential between the countries which can cause distribution problems. The result obtained, however, will not change at all if the richer country pays *voluntarily* lump-sum transfers to the poorer one. This would be the only way for equalizing welfare differentials under these circumstances.

3.2 Perfect mobility

As said above, under perfect mobility all persons can move around without any restrictions. This implies the following effect:

Proposition 2 Perfect mobility does not require a coordinated welfare policy. National policies will lead to a Pareto efficient outcome.

The outcome of this effect is that perfect mobility gives rise to a second constraint[11] the problem of welfare maximization for both countries. This additional constraint requires that *the level of expected utility for all people in both countries must be the same.* The reason for this is that otherwise migration - which is supposedly costless - would still continue until the levels of expected utility, for workers and unemployed people alike, are equalized.[12] As can be shown, this equalization of expected utility requires:

$$S_i = Y_i - T_i,$$

i.e. an equalization of (after tax) work and transfer income. This means that the risk to become unemployed is completely covered by insurance.

---

11 The first constraint is one of the unemployment insurance budget.

12 This is a standard approach in regional economics; see e.g. Wildasin (1987) and Rubinfeld (1987).

A further implication of this result is that even ex post utilities in both countries are equal. *Voting by feet* renders it impossible to hold up any utility differential.

A comparison of autarky to perfect mobility leads to the following conclusion:

Corollary 1 Perfect mobility seriously changes the distribution of income in both countries. Therefore, compensations must be paid.

With this, note that the levels of utility and income solution under autarky and perfect mobility are different, though both are Pareto-optimal. This, in turn, implies a distribution problem which can be solved by compensation payments.

These results show the importance of the assumptions concerning the openness of labor markets and transfer systems in our analysis.

The arguments presented so far underline that there is no need for international cooperation in our model: Since production is exogenously fixed, there are no gains from trade. Because each country owns a risk neutral insurance agency, there is no reason for a reallocation of risk.

We now turn to restricted mobility.

4 Welfare Policy under Restricted Mobility

As already defined above, restricted mobility means that national labor markets are closed to foreign workers whereas national transfer systems are open to all. We suppose two countries which do not cooperate.

We assume further that in autarky the indirect expected welfare[13] in country 2, W_2^a, is higher than in country 1, W_1^a:

(3) $W_2^a > W_1^a$.

Since both countries have full insurance, this requires:

(4) $S_1^a < S_2^a$,

---

[13] See eq. (2). In the case of autarky all items due to migration vanish.

i.e., unemployment benefits in the richer country are higher than in the poorer one.[14] Note that neither the differences in the indirect levels of expected welfare nor the differences in levels of national outputs are sufficient to determine *a priori* the direction of migration because this depends on the *style of national welfare policy* which will be explained below.

Next, optimal national welfare policy will be determined assuming that country 1 is an emigration country and country 2 an immigration country.[15]

4.1 Welfare policy in an emigration country

The optimal welfare policy requires that a country maximizes the welfare function defined above, *taking into account the utility level of citizens who emigrated to country 2* with respect to national policy instruments (level of unemployment benefits, S_1 and taxes, T_1).[16] The constraint to the problem of maximization consists of the insurance system budget equation which also must incorporate the emigration effect (the more those who are unemployed emigrate the less people have to be assisted by unemployment benefits). Hence, the country of emigration pays benefits for the part[17] of 'its' unemployed only. Despite this, the emigrants are incorporated in the national welfare function with their net utilities in country 2.[18]

Solving this maximization program, one obtains the following condition which governs optimal independent national welfare policy:

$$(5) \qquad U'(S_1)(1-P(S_2-S_1)) - U'(Y_1-T_1)\left[(1-P(S_2-S_1)) + S_1 f(S_2-S_1)\right] - \varphi_1 = 0$$

14 As can be shown, $Y_1 < Y_2$ is not a sufficient condition for $S_1^o < S_2^o$, whereas (first and second order) stochastic dominance is sufficient, but not necessary.

15 Should the roles of the countries change, the labels will be changed accordingly.

16 The objective in formal terms is
$\max_{S_2,T_2} W_1(S_1,T_1)$ s.t. $n_1T_1 \geq (N_1-n_1)(1-P(S_2-S_1))S_1$, $S_2 \geq S_1$.
W_1 is defined in eq. (2).

17 The percentage is $1-P(S_2-S_1)$.

18 These utilities are given as $(N_1-n_1)\int_0^{S_2-S_1} U(S_2-m)f(m)dm$ in eq. (2).

Thereby $\varphi_1(\geq 0)$ means the Lagrangean for the constraint $S_2 \geq S_1$. Condition 5 describes implicitly the optimal policy of an emigration country.

4.2 Welfare policy in an immigration country

An immigration country has to take into account that its policy provides incentives to migrate for the unemployed of the other country. Its objective remains to maximize welfare for its own citizens, but it cannot block migration which is intended for collecting unemployment benefits.[19] The number of immigrants in the insurance's budget constraint is given by $S_2(N_1 - n_1)P(S_2 - S_1)$.

Solving the maximization problem leads to the following condition for an optimal welfare policy:

$$(6) \qquad U'(S_2) - U'(Y_2 - T_2)\left[\left(1 + \sigma P(S_2 - S_1)\right) + \sigma S_2 f(S_2 - S_1)\right] - \varphi_2 = 0$$

whereby $\sigma := {(N_1 - n_1)}/{(N_2 - n_2)}$. This condition gives implicitly the optimal policy of an immigration country.

5 Efficiency of Uncoordinated Welfare Policy under Restricted Mobility

In order to analyze the efficiency of national uncoordinated welfare policies, assumptions about the second derivative of the utility function are required. It is common in economics to associate $U'' = 0$ with *risk neutrality* and $U'' < 0$ with *risk aversion*. In our context, a different interpretation may be possible. We propose to label *styles of welfare policies* via the sign of U'' as follows: $U'' = 0$ is labeled as an *individualistic* policy style whereas $U'' < 0$ is called a *social democratic* style.[20] An individualistic policy style is characterized by the fact that

---

19 In formal terms, the maximization problem for an immigration country is as follows: $max_{S_I, T_I} W_I(S_I, T_I)$ s.t. $n_I T_I \geq (N_I - n_I)(1 - P(S_2 - S_I))S_I$, $S_2 \geq S_I$.

20 Leibfried (1991), pp. 15, characterizes policy styles of European welfare states in a different way. He distinguishes four areas: Scandinavian Countries, "Bismarck"

the income profile does not matter at all. It emphasizes the chance of getting a well-paid job in the employment lottery and ignores deliberately the risk of unemployment. A social democratic policy style is willing to sacrifice part of the income from well-paid jobs for a higher transfer income when unemployment occurs; which means that the income profile matters.

Accordingly, for two countries we have four possible combinations of individualistic and social democratic styles:

	Country 2	
Country 1	individualistic	social democratic
individualistic	I	II
social democratic	III	IV

Our main result in this section is:

Proposition 3 Let $\{S_i^{NC}, T_i^{NC}\}$ be the non cooperative Cournot-Nash solution for national welfare policies. Then one yields the following results for S_i^{NC}:

I $S_2^{NC} = 0$ $S_1^{NC} = 0$	II $S_2^{NC} \geq 0$ $S_1^{NC} = 0$
III $S_2^{NC} = 0$ $S_1^{NC} \geq 0$	IV $S_2^{NC} \geq 0$ $S_1^{NC} \geq 0$

Combination I is Pareto-efficient whereas combinations II and III are not.[21]

Countries, Anglo-Saxon Countries, and "Latin Rim" Countries. In this categorization, our individualistic style is probably comparable to the Anglo-Saxon, Latin Rim-style, and our social democratic style to the Bismarck, Scandinavian style.

21 The evaluation of combination IV follows, below.

A formal proof of the results can be found in Meran & Prinz (1993). Here, we want to make them plausible using economic intuition.

If both countries are individualistic, they are risk neutral and do not insure their citizens at all against the risk of unemployment. Then, there is no incentive to migrate from one country to the other, and the resulting allocation cannot be improved further.

If at least one country pursues a social democratic policy style then this country will pay unemployment benefits. Consequently, it will attract the *ex post* unemployed persons from the other country even if these persons are *ex ante* neutral to risk. This is the case because the *ex post* incomes of employed and unemployed vary in the individualistic country, and hence, transfers paid in the other country motivate the unemployed to migrate.

This migration causes an externality for both countries: the transfer paying, social democratic country is forced to pay its transfers to foreigners whereas the individualistic country can 'export' part of its unemployed.[22] In this way the decisions to establish an unemployment insurance are disturbed by migration. It can be shown that the social democratic style country *reduces* the transfers to its unemployed anticipating the migration it induces. Therefore, there remains an income differential between employed and unemployed people in the risk averse country. This is the reason why the combinations II and III are not Pareto efficient.

A further remark is important. If the poorer country is risk averse and the richer one is individualistic, then the richer country will be the emigration country.

The next question is, what will be the result when both countries are risk averse?

To answer this, it is necessary to know the properties of the *reaction function* of one country to the actions (levels of S_i) of the other. As can be shown, the slope of the reaction function is greater than zero:

$$\frac{dS_2^{NC}}{dS_1} > 0 \tag{7}$$

22 How strong the externality is, depends on the costs of migration. The lower they are the greater the externality will be.

Figure 1: Cournot-Nash and cooperative equilibrium in welfare policies between two countries

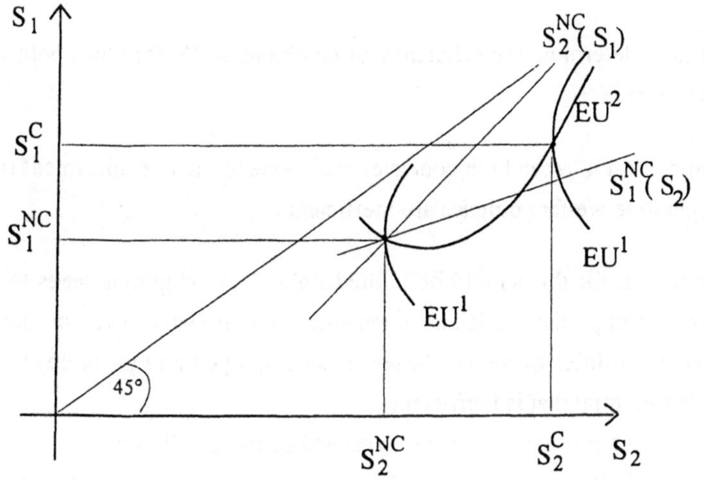

Figure 1 shows the Cournot-Nash equilibrium in unemployment benefits $\left(S_1^{NC}, S_2^{NC}\right)$ when both countries are risk averse. It is given by the intersection point of the reaction functions of the countries, $S_1^{NC}(S_2)$ and $S_2^{NC}(S_1)$. These reaction functions are defined as the maxima of the conditional indifference curves of both countries, EU^1 and EU^2, respectively.[23] Note that in thc non cooperative

---

[23] The indifference curve for country 1 (analogously for country 2) is given by:

$$n_1 U(Y_1 \frac{N_1 - n_1}{n_1}(1 - P(S_2 - S_1)) S_1) + (N_1 - n_1)\cdot$$

$$\cdot\left[U(S_1)(1 - P(S_2 - S_1)) + \int_0^{S_2 - S_1} U(S_2 - m) f(m)\, dm\right] = \bar{U}.$$

This yields:

$$n_1 U(Y_1 - \frac{N_1 - n_1}{n_1}(1 - P(S_2 - S_1)) S_1) + (N_1 - n_1)\left[U(S_1)(1 - P(S_2 - S_1)) + \int_0^{S_2 - S_1} U(S_2 - m) f(m)\, dm\right] = \bar{U}.$$

Using the second order condition, one obtains:

$$\frac{dS_1}{dS_2} = \infty \Leftrightarrow S_1 = S_1^{NC}, \quad \frac{dS_1}{dS_2} > 0 \Leftrightarrow S_1 > S_1^{NC}(S_2) \quad \frac{dS_1}{dS_2} < 0 \Leftrightarrow S_1 < S_1^{NC}(S_2)$$

Cournot-Nash equilibrium S_2^{NC} is larger than S_1^{NC} because we assumed that under autarky $S_2^a > S_1^a$.

We now determine the efficiency of combination IV for when both countries are risk averse.

Proposition 4 When both countries are averse to the unemployment risk, then non cooperative welfare policies are inefficient.

The reason for this should be immediately clear. Migration leads to externalities which change the decisions concerning the transfer level in both countries. Marginal utilities of income when those employed and unemployed differ; leads to a differential that is inefficient.

We can summarize the results reached so far as follows:

If one or both countries are risk averse to unemployment and labor markets are closed, but transfer systems are open, then noncooperative welfare policies are inefficient. The reason is that migration acts as a threat to countries with high national transfer levels and in this way influences national decisions. This is a Pareto relevant negative externality.

We now turn to the analysis of cooperative welfare policy.

6 Cooperative Welfare Policy

6.1 Allocative efficiency

In this section, it is assumed that both countries coordinate their welfare policies jointly.[24] In addition to that we suppose that both countries are risk averse.

Formally, country 1 is to solve the following program:[25]

---

24 Compare Boadway (1982) as well as Mintz & Tulkens (1986) and Oates & Schwab (1988) for analyses of the advantages or disadvantages of competitive and cooperative fiscal policies.

25 We assume, as before, $S_2 \geq S_1$.

The first constraint in this program requires that the welfare level of country 2 cooperates at least as high as in the case of national policy. We call this the *participation constraint*. The second constraint says that the tax revenues of both countries, taken together, must be sufficient to pay unemployment benefits in both countries. We call this the *resource constraint*. Thereby it is implicitly taken into account that *there might be transfer payments between the countries.*[26]

(8) $$\max_{T_i,S_i} \; n_1 U(Y_1 - T_1) + (N_1 - n_1)\left[U(S_1)(1 - P(S_2 - S_1)) + \int_0^{S_2 - S_1} U(S_2 - m) f(m) dm\right]$$

(9) $$s.t. \; n_2 U(Y_2 - T_2) + (N_2 - n_2) U(S_2) \geq \overline{U}_2^{NC}$$

(10) $$\begin{aligned} & T_1 n_1 + T_2 n_2 \geq \\ & \geq S_1(N_1 - n_1)(1 - P(S_2 - S_1)) + S_2(N_2 - n_2) + S_2(N_1 - n_1)P(S_2 - S_1) \\ & \geq S_1(N_1 - n_1) + S_2(N_2 - n_2) + (S_2 - S_1)P(S_2 - S_1)(N_1 - n_1) \end{aligned}$$

(11) $$S_2 \geq S_1$$

Solving the program and rearranging terms gives the following central condition for our argument:

(12) $$\lambda U'(S_2) - \lambda U'(Y_2 - T_2)[1 + P\sigma + (S_2 - S_1)\sigma f] + \varphi = 0$$

whereby (as already defined above) $\sigma := {(N_1 - n_1)}\big/{(N_2 - n_2)}$.

We are now able to present our first main result for cooperative welfare policies.

---

26 Note that the migration effect can be recognized on the right hand side of the second constraint; it is given by $(S_2 - S_1)P(S_2 - S_1)(N_1 - n_1)$. It should be immediately clear that for $(S_1 \geq S_{21})$ only the indices in the equations above have to be relabeled.

Proposition 5 The level of unemployment benefits under cooperation is higher than in the Cournot-Nash equilibrium:

$$S_1^{NC} < S_1^C$$
$$S_2^{NC} < S_2^C$$

This result can be seen in Figure 1. The cooperative equilibrium is given in the tangential point of the indifference curves of the countries which fulfill the participation and the resource constraint. This point is reached in $\left(S_1^C, S_2^C\right)$ and it follows from construction that $S_i^C > S_i^{NC}$

How can this result be explained? In the non cooperative Cournot-Nash equilibrium, *risks* in the form of unemployed migrants are exchanged to provide an equilibrium. Migration is a threat to countries with relatively high benefits because it takes place if there is a large enough benefit differential between the countries. This externality is to be reduced through cooperation where one country can pay transfers to the other to stop migration. In this way, money instead of persons will be transferred. This allows an overall increase in unemployment benefits. The question is, however, whether the externality will be completely removed.

The following proposition gives the answer:

Proposition 6 If both countries are risk averse and $S > 0$, then;

1. *It is optimal that migration occurs even with cooperation* (*i.e.* $S \neq S$), *and*
2. S *is not the first-best-optimal.*

This result seems rather strange since one is tempted to conclude that cooperation will lead to a first-best-optimum. The key to the understanding of our conclusion is that risk aversion on both parts is crucial here. This can be shown as follows. Imagine that country 2 is risk neutral whereas the other country remains risk averse. Then it can be shown that $S = S$ and no migration takes place.

Why?

For country 2, welfare maximization is identical to income maximization because it is risk neutral. Its national income is maximized when $S_2^{NC} = 0$, because the income profile in country 2 is of no importance at all for national welfare. But this is different for the risk averse country 1. It would like to have complete coverage of the unemployment risk, i.e., $S_1 = Y_1 - T_1$. This is only feasible when country 1 can compensate country 2 in such a way that country 2 voluntarily chooses $S_2 = S_1$. Under such circumstances, no migration will take place and the resulting allocation would be first-best.

What are the conclusions for the case where both countries are risk averse? The insurance parameters, taxes and benefits, are required to internalize the externality through cooperation. But then there is no other instrument to stop migration which will come up again if one country tries to insure the unemployment risk *completely*.

Therefore, unemployment benefits remain too low for a first-best allocation. This result shows the *importance* of cooperation for a better welfare policy. The more the countries are interested in securing their unemployed (or poor), the more cooperation is necessary. But cooperation is not enough; international transfer payments are necessary to reach a Pareto improvement.

6.2 Transfer payments

We now turn to the determination of the transfers between countries with a cooperative welfare system. To simplify the analysis, throughout this section it is assumed that country 1 is risk averse and country 2 risk neutral.

First, we specify a *minimum transfer* which is to be paid by country 1 (at least) to guarantee that country 2 will agree on a cooperative welfare policy.

Proposition 7 Assume that country 1 is risk averse and country 2 is risk neutral. A minimum transfer from country 1 to country 2 is given by

$$\tau = [S_1^{NC} P(S_1^{NC}) - \int_0^{S_1^{NC}} mf(m)dm](N_2 - n_2).$$

The rationale behind this result is that country 2 claims a payment which is *at least* as high that the country will be indifferent to cooperative and non cooperative policies, i.e.:

$$EU_2^C = EU_2^{NC}$$

This implies that an increase in unemployed benefits in country 1 must be compensated for by a transfer to country 2 which exactly offsets the anticipated decrease in EU_2^C in comparison to EU_2^{NC}.

This monetary compensation consists of two parts: (i) the loss of unemployment benefits of citizens from country 2, formerly received in country 1 (after migrating there); this 'loss'[27] occurs because there is no migration in the cooperative equilibrium, and (ii) the saved costs of migration of unemployed persons who formerly migrated from country 1 to country 2.[28] The necessary minimum transfer is, then, determined by (i) minus (ii).

It can be shown that under these conditions all gains in welfare will go to country 1 - despite the fact that it is this country which pays the compensation. It is even possible to make *both* countries better off because there are no costs of migration in the cooperative equilibrium.

There is an *upper limit* for the inter-national transfer payment. This is shown in Figure 2.

In this figure, y_1 is represented on the abscise and S_1 on the ordinate. The outer line is determined by total income (of the employed and unemployed) in country 1 under national welfare policy.[29] The national optimum is reached in the under-insurance equilibrium $\left(y_1^{NC}, S_1^{NC}\right)$. The resulting income profile is Pareto improvable because unemployment is not completely covered by an insurance. The Pareto optimum lies in $\left(y_1^*, S_1^*\right)$). This point is only feasible if $S_1^* = S_2^*$. (Note that country 2 suffers no loss if both levels of S_i are increased at the same time because its expected utility level remains unchanged).

---

27 The loss is given by $S_1^{NC} P\left(S_1^{NC}\right)\left(N_2 - n_2\right)$.

28 These costs are given by $\left(\int_0^{S_1^{NC}} m f(m) dm\right)\left(N_2 - n_2\right)$.

29 Numerically, it is given by $n_1 y_1^{NC} + \left(N_1 - n_1\right) S_1^{NC}$.

Figure 2: Determination of the upper limit for inter-national transfers

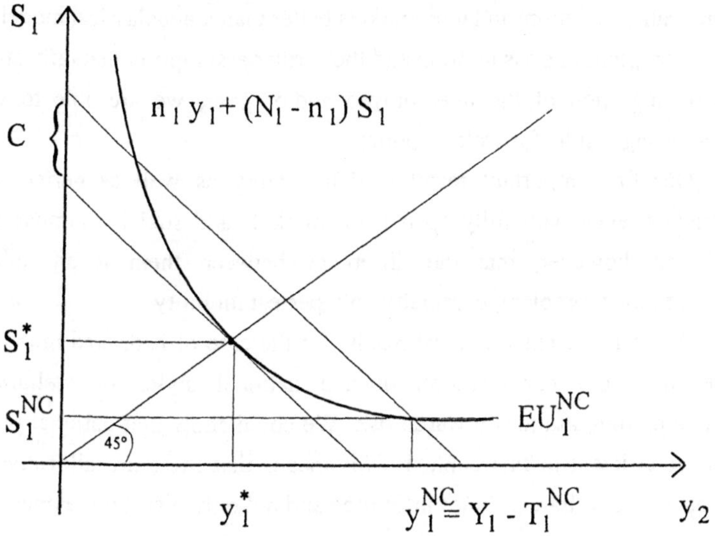

Starting from a state $S_1 = S_2 < S_2^*$[30] and augmenting, S_1 and S_2 simultaneously increases welfare in country 1 (because of risk aversion), but leaves welfare in country 2 unchanged (because of risk neutrality). Therefore, country 1 can implement full coverage of the unemployment risk. S_1^* and can afford to pay maximally the amount C as a pure income transfer to country 2. The monetized welfare gains C can be transmitted to country 2 without distorting the allocation. However, all gains would go to country 2.

7 Concluding Remarks

It should be emphasized again that our results depend on the crucial assumption that the labor markets within the countries are not flexible in the sense that they do not react to migration. A fully competitive neoclassical labor market would destroy nearly all of our main results. With fully flexible labor markets, there is

30 Note that a precondition for any $S_1 = S_2$ is the payment of the minimum transfer from country 1 to country 2.

neither a need for coordination of welfare policies nor a need for limiting migration. We think, however, that our model reflects - at least in the short run - the reality of European labor markets better than a neoclassical model.

Accepting this assumption and the further assumption that only cultural factors limit migration of the unemployed and/or poor, we are able to show several interesting results for welfare policy.

Our first important result is that autarky as well as perfect mobility are efficient, even with fully open labor markets and social insurance systems. We showed, however, that the difference between them is an indicator for a distributional problem, especially with perfect mobility.

We then presented several results for the case of restricted mobility. Thereby, we took into consideration diverse national styles of welfare policy by reinterpreting attitudes towards risk. We could show that national policies are no longer efficient in this context. This means that there are allocative reasons for cooperative welfare policies in Europe and not only distributive ones.

As we further showed, this cooperative welfare policy does not bring us back to a first-best-optimum. If both countries are risk averse, complete coverage of the unemployment risk is not feasible. As a consequence, there is migration in equilibrium. A different result is to be obtained when one country is risk averse whereas the other is risk neutral. Under these circumstances, both countries will cover the unemployment risk completely when they cooperate. There will be no migration in equilibrium.

Our results are, without major changes, transferable to the case of several countries. An extension of our approach, however, could be to endogenize national behavior, i.e. to give up the idea of a national welfare function. The goals of different groups within society would then be given a different weight. Another extension might be the endogenization of labor market regulations. Following these lines, we could reach a more realistic version of our model.

References

Atkinson, A.B. & Stiglitz, J.E. (1980), Lectures on Public Economics, Maidenhead.

Bell, C. (1991), "Regional Heterogeneity, Migration, and Shadow Prices", in: Journal of Public Economics, Vol. 46, pp. 1 - 27.

Berthold, N. (1993a), "Sozialunion in Europa - Notwendig oder überflüssig?", in: Wirtschaftsdienst, Jg. 73, pp. 414 - 418.

Berthold, N. (1993b), Sozialunion in Europa - Integrationsfaktor oder Sprengsatz einer Wirtschafts- und Währungsunion?, Tübingen.

Boadway, R. (1982), "On the Method of Taxation and the Provision of Local Public Goods: Comment", in: American Economic Review, Vol. 72, pp. 846 - 851.

Brown, C.C. & Oates, W.E. (1987), "Assistance to the poor in a federal system", in: Journal of Public Economics, Vol. 32, pp. 307 - 330.

Crane, R. (1992), "Voluntary income redistribution with migration", in: Journal of Urban Economics, Vol. 31, pp. 84 - 98.

Hercowitz, Z. & Pines, D. (1991), "Migration with Fiscal Externalities", in: Journal of Public Economics, Vol. 46, pp. 163 - 180.

Kuhn, B. (1991), "Sozialunion in Europa", in: Aus Politik und Zeitgeschichte, B3-4/91 vom 11. Januar 1991, pp. 40 - 46.

Kumar, R. (1977), "More on non-white migration, welfare levels, and the political process", in: Public Choicc, Vol. 32, pp. 151 - 154.

Ladd, H.F. & Doolittle, F.C. (1982), "Which level of government should assist the poor?", in: National Tax Journal, Vol. 35, pp. 323 - 336.

Leibfried, St. (1991), "Towards an European Welfare State? On Integrating Poverty Regimes in the European Community", Zentrum für Sozialpolitik, ZeS - Arbeitspapier Nr. 2/91.

Meran, G. & Prinz, A. (1993), "Nationale oder gemeinsame Mindestsicherung in Europa?", Discussion Paper, Freie Universität Berlin.

Mintz, J. & Tulkens, H. (1986), "Commodity Tax Competition between Member States of a Federation: Equilibrium and Efficiency", in: Journal of Public Economics, Vol. 29, pp. 133 - 172.

Oates, W.E. & Schwab, R.M. (1988), "Economic Competition Among Jurisdictions: Efficiency or Distortion Inducing?", in: Journal of Public Economics, Vol. 35, pp. 333 - 354.

Paqué, K.-H. (1992), "Der europäische Sozialstaat. Eine Zwischenbilanz", in: WiSt, 21. Jg. pp. 627 - 630.

Roemer, J.E. (1993), "Unequal Exchange, Labor Migration, and International Capital Flows: A Theoretical Synthesis", in: Desai, P. (Ed.), Marxism, Central Planning, and the Soviet Economy: Economic Essays in Honor of Alexander Erlich, MIT Press, Cambridge, Mass., pp. 34 - 60.

Rubinfeld, D.L. (1987), "The Economics of the Local Public Sector", in: Auerbach, A.J. & Feldstein, M. (Eds.), Handbook of Public Economics, Vol. II, Elsevier Science Publishers B.V., pp. 571 - 645.

Schulte, B. (1991), "Das Recht auf ein Mindesteinkommen in der Europäischen Gemeinschaft. Nationaler Status quo und supranationale Initiativen", in: Sozialer Fortschritt, pp. 2 - 23.

Southwick, L. (1981), "Public welfare programs and recipient migration", in: Growth and Change, Vol. 12, pp. 22 - 32.

Wildasin, D.E. (1986), Urban Public Finance (Fundamentals of Pure and Applied Economics 10), Harwood Academic Publishers, Chur u.a..

Wildasin, D.E. (1987), "Theoretical Analysis of Local Public Economics", in: Mills, E.S. (Ed.), Handbook of Regional and Urban Economics, Vol. II, Elsevier Science Publishers B.V., pp. 1131 - 1178.

Wildasin, D.E. (1991), "Income Redistribution in a Common Labor Market", in: American Economic Review, Vol. 81, pp. 757 - 774.

The Main Problems of International Comparative Poverty Research

Richard Hauser

1 Questions of International Comparative Poverty Research

International comparative poverty research is part of international comparative social policy research, which has increased in importance in recent years. A quote from the English researcher Catherine Jones (1985, p. 4) shows why scientists are interested in international comparative social policy research:

> "... the necessity for it rests on three grounds: comparative study promotes a better understanding of the home social policy environment; it helps broaden ideas as to what may be done in response to particular issues or problems and may even suggest 'lessons from abroad'; it opens the doors to a greater breadth and variety of case material, such as may further the development of theoretical constructs about social policy formation and development to an extent that could not be possible on the basis of home country experience and material alone."

Further impetus came from the attempt to give the process of European union a social as well as an economic dimension. This requires scientifically founded knowledge of social security systems and labour market regulations in all member states and countries who may join in the future on the one hand, and of the social situation of the economically and socially weaker groups of the population on the other. I would like here to mention the "Common Charter on the Social Basic Rights of Employees" of 1989 and the recommendations of the Council of Ministers of 1992 on "Harmonisation of objectives and policies in the area of social protection" and on "Common Criteria Concerning Sufficient Resources and Social Assistance in the Social Protection Systems"[1].

International comparative poverty research is confronted with all those questions with which poverty research in one particular country is confronted as well as facing problems of comparison.

The main questions for an individual country are the following ones:

1) The theoretical question: "How should poverty be defined and how should the poor be identified?" requires a normative answer involving a value judgement.
2) A number of questions to which empirical, descriptive answers must be given:
   - What share of the total population is poor and how is it subdivided according to socio-demographic characteristics? Which groups are affected more or less than average?
   - Are there particular groups with minority, race and other discrimination problems?
   - Are there regional variations in the poverty ratios or local concentrations of poor people in ghettos?
   - Is there "hidden poverty" and does it vary between groups?
   - Are there differences between the poor as to the degree of poverty?
   - What dynamic of poverty development can be observed on the macro and micro levels? On the macro level, questions must be asked about trends in the share of poor people and possible shifts between groups, and on the micro level, the emphasis should be on the duration of individual poverty situations (poverty spells) and the distribution of the duration of phases of poverty (short-run versus long-run) as well as the problem of multiple periods of poverty. Furthermore, we wish to know from which class the poor come, how great their fall was, how great the climb is of those who leave poverty and for which groups of poor people the chances are high to leave poverty.
3) Questions which ask for an explanation:
   - How can the extent of, the composition of, the individual duration of, and changes in poverty over time be explained? What influence do the following issues have?
     - Economic development, especially unemployment

[1] See Europäische Gemeinschaften (1992a and 1992b); Kommission der Europäischen Gemeinschaften (1981, 1991, 1992, 1993a, 1993b, 1993d).

  - Socio-demographic changes, such as family split-ups, marriage, and birth behaviour
  - Migration
  - Social security regulations and other institutional conditions
- What events and processes lead to falling into poverty on the individual level, what constellations lead out of it, and which cause lasting poverty?

4) Questions which aim to analyze social policy:
   - Which regulations and instruments are used in the fight against poverty, which are not used, and what suggestions for reform are discussed? Is a specific policy to combat poverty being pursued or is there a reliance on more general policies which also benefit the poor?
   - Is poverty policy organised and financed centrally or decentrally and does this influence its success?
   - Is there a systematic compilation of reports and control of the success of poverty policy?
   - Are there influential organisations which act as the voice and political advocate of the poor?
   - What is the attitude of individual parties and leading associations (such as trades unions, employers' associations and churches) towards poverty?
5) Questions which require predictions:
   - How will the main influencing factors which lead to poverty develop in the foreseeable future and what influence will they have on the extent and structure of poverty?
   - What social policy reactions to the poverty problem are foreseeable?
6) A final group of questions is concerned with social psychology:
   - How do the poor see themselves? Do they organise themselves?
   - What is the attitude of the population towards poverty?
   - What is the attitude of the media? Are there typical allocations of blame?
   - Are there basic religious values or traditions which dominate attitudes towards poverty?

This, perhaps slightly long, list of questions outlines the field of poverty research on a country level. International comparative poverty research can analyse all these problems focusing on the differences and similarities between countries. The final scientific objective of comparative research is to arrive at generalised statements on the determinants of poverty and ways to combat it.

2 The Main Problems of International Comparative Poverty Research

2.1 Selecting the countries to be compared

If I now turn to the main problems of international comparative poverty research, I must greatly restrict myself in this paper. I will mainly look at the choice of countries and the various methods of determining poverty.

The choice of countries is the first problem of comparative studies. If this choice is not predetermined by exogenous restrictions - for example, that all EU or OECD member states are to be examined or that the relevant statistics are only available for certain countries - then the so-called "most similar cases approach" would seem to be the most fruitful one[2]. This method states that one should select countries, the basic structures of which (i.e., cultural traditions, political systems, educational systems, economic systems, levels of economic development, integration in the world economy) are as similar as possible in order to reduce the otherwise enormous number of possible determinants of poverty. The differences between the countries with respect to poverty can then be put down to differences in demography, the phases of the business cycles, the regulations determining the functioning of the labour market, the systems of social protection, the tax systems, etc.. On the other hand, this means that comparisons of poverty between very different countries, such as between industrialised nations and developing countries or between EU countries and the transforming countries of Central and East Europe are much more difficult and possibly even meaningless if only simple indicators are used that have a different meaning in the various national contexts.

2.2 Alternative concepts of poverty

If one wishes to scientifically examine questions of poverty, then one is confronted with the problem of accurately distinguishing the subject or population group to be investigated. This is a far more difficult problem than distinguishing other groups relevant to social policy, such as single parents, pensioners, the

---

2 See Wilensky et al. (1987); Heidenheimer et al. (1993).

handicapped and the homeless. Although distinguishing all these groups is based on normative judgements, consensus amongst scientists, society and politicians seems to be far smaller on those value judgements made implicitly about the definition of the poor than on those relating to distinguishing other groups with problems. This may be related to the fact that detecting poverty is a stark contradiction of the aims of a welfare state and signalizes a need for direct social policy action. The concept, therefore, gains the character of a social policy objective in the sense that with its help the undisputed aim of avoiding poverty can be stated more precisely and the success or failure of a specific policy to combat poverty or even of the complete social policy can be measured in terms of the extent of poverty remaining. Although science is free in establishing its concepts, it must not ignore this relationship if it wishes to aid practical social policy or if its results are used against its will in the political process. The scientist can, however, specify explicitly the individual value judgements which go into his formation of the concept, or he can work simultaneously with several concepts of poverty which are based on different value judgements. This is a research strategy which leaves politicians a limited amount of freedom to decide - especially with empirical and quantifying analyses - which of the derived results are based on normative decisions closest to their own political value judgements.

There are several basic types of concepts of poverty[3]. On the one hand one finds the concept of "absolute poverty", which implies that those concerned do not have the essentials for long-term survival and/or lack sufficient health care. On the other hand there is the concept of "relative poverty", which means that the socio-cultural minimum of subsistence is not reached - i.e., the standard of living of those concerned is too far below the societal average and they are consequently deprived and marginalized from society. This difference was already noted by Adam Smith more than two hundred years ago:

> "By necessities I understand not only the commodities which are indispensably necessary for the support of life, but what ever the custom of the country renders it indecent for credible people, even the lowest order, to be without. A linen shirt, for example, is, strictly speaking, not a necessity of life. The Greeks and Romans lived, I

---

3 See Kakwani (1980, part VI); Sen (1981); Hauser (1984); Atkinson (1989); Ruggles (1990); Callan (1991); Sen (1992, ch. 7); Van den Bosch (1993); Whelan (1993); Muffels (1993); Bradshaw (1993).

> suppose, very comfortably though they had no linen. But in the present times, through the greater part of Europe, a credible day-labourer would be ashamed to appear in public without a linen shirt, the want of which would be supposed to denote that disgraceful degree of poverty which, it is presumed, nobody can well fall into without extreme bad conduct. Custom, in the same manner, has rendered leather shoes a necessary of life in England. The poorest credible person of either sex would be ashamed to appear in public without them"[4]

The physical minimum of subsistence is not the same in every country, being dependent on climate, the societal and economic system and the state of medical development. The physical minimum of subsistence cannot be completely objectively determined, but - if the economic, cultural and political conditions are accepted - the range of justifiable differences of opinion is far narrower than is the case for the socio-cultural minimum of subsistence.

The socio-cultural minimum of subsistence requires first of all recognition of the value judgement that marginalizing members of society ought to be avoided, or expressed positively, that social integration of all members of society is a desirable social and societal policy objective. Even if consensus could be reached on this, the further question of who should count as a member of society crops up. The main options to choose from are as follows:

- all people of the same nationality who live in the same national territory;
- all people of the same nationality irrespective of their domicile;
- the whole long-term resident population of a national territory;
- the whole long-term population of a national territory plus those temporarily resident;
- the population of a supranational territory consisting of more than one country, in the extreme the whole population of the EU or even the world population.

This question can be formulated differently: "How far should the solidarity reach, which forms the basis of social policy measures to combat poverty, and what is the decisive reason for raising the required funds from the wealthier members of society?

Both with the physical and the socio-cultural minimum of subsistence one can differentiate between a living condition definition, which focuses on the actual

---

4 As cited by Sen (1981, p. 18).

availability of goods and services to each individual in selected dimensions of its well-being, and a resource definition, which is based on the economic resources available - normally income and monetary and physical assets, and possibly earnings capacity.

A living condition definition requires a decision about which dimensions of the well-being of the individual are considered relevant (e.g., food, clothing, health care, housing, housing conditions, education, safety from social risks, transport and communications, legal security and protection from crime, and opportunities to participate in social, cultural and political activities in society). Here the physical minimum of subsistence differs from the socio-cultural minimum of subsistence in that it is restricted to a few dimensions of the well-being. I will not discuss the absolute minimum of subsistence or absolute poverty in more detail in the following, as they are barely of any significance to the industrialised countries of today to which I will limit myself here. But in a wider perspective, absolute poverty remains the irreducible core of the poverty concept[5].

With a resource definition it must be decided which economic factors should be considered. Although income and assets must unquestionably be included, questions requiring decisions crop up when determining the elements of income and assets. The relevant income period and the appropriate method of assessing assets and determining minimum necessary assets can only be decided qualitatively. A particularly controversial question is whether potential income, which could be earned by entering the work force, should be taken into account; in other words, who should be expected to undertake paid work, and how much? Another difficult problem arises when taking into account obligations for maintenance. On the one hand, one must find out which persons, who are related by blood, by law or by behaviour are mutually obliged to pay maintenance according to the law of the country, and whether maintenance obligations are in fact fulfilled. On the other hand, it must be decided to what extent differences in need between households of different size and persons of different age, sex and

---

5 Sen (1981, p. 17) is right in insisting that describing "the customs of the country" on which a relative poverty concept can be based has nothing to do with value judgements; but he concedes that this description usually remains vague and that often there is no consensus or dominating opinion. In these cases measurement of poverty is only possible by precisely specifying poverty criteria making additionally use of value judgements.

health condition should be taken into account. In other words, this is the problem of choosing the correct equivalence scale[6].

A resource definition is also based on the value judgement that responsibility for expenditure decisions should rest with those concerned. If a person has sufficient resources, he is not regarded as poor, even if he uses these resources inefficiently such that he seems to have serious shortages in individual dimensions of his well-being. In a similar way, a household is accorded the responsibility for ensuring a balanced fulfilment of needs of its members. Accordingly, one assumes that there can be no differences in welfare within a family. Even if this value judgement seems to be widely accepted in modern welfare states (if it were not, welfare payments would be made using goods and services and not money and they would be granted directly to each individual), restrictions on the individual's right to decide are sometimes accepted. I mention the discussion of payments in kind to asylum seekers and the measures to protect children and young people with extremely negligent parents.

The living condition definition of the socio-cultural minimum of subsistence requires the determination of minimum standards of provision in all dimensions of well-being that are considered relevant. These minimum standards which would be well below the average should be related to the threshold of marginalization, which itself is difficult to state precisely. With a living condition definition it is, therefore, also necessary to use value judgements to set minimum standards in every dimension; falling short of which is an indication of poverty. Furthermore, it must be determined whether poverty is confirmed by failing to reach the minimum standard in one dimension or whether only certain cumulative failures to reach several minimum standards should lead to poverty being established.

With the resource definition, a certain fraction of average resources (e.g., 40 % or 50 % or 60 %), is usually set as the poverty line. Because this is a much more abstract standard, it is more difficult to justify a certain percentage as the marginalization threshold.

The calculation of an average does, however, require a clear distinction of the people included. I will give just three examples. The average can refer to the populations of individual regions, then one obtains different poverty lines for each region, which could be justified by the fact that comparisons of standards of living

---

6 For an overview of many equivalence scales used in various countries and their influence on the calculation of poverty ratios see Buhmann et al. (1988).

and marginalization phenomena often refer to smaller geographical areas. The average could, however, include the whole population of a national territory. Such a decision could be justified with the oft-stated objective of achieving equal standards of living in the individual regions of a national territory and claiming the solidarity of all members of the society. Finally, the calculation of the average could be based on an even wider delimination of the relevant population (e.g., the population of all the member states of the European Union), arguing that the Economic Union has to be complemented by a Social Union. Each of these justifications requires a value judgement and each chosen course of action leads to different empirical results and different conclusions for social policy [7].

If real economic growth is achieved, the minimum standards, which serve to specify a living condition definition of the socio-cultural minimum of subsistence, must be adjusted over time in the same way as the level of real income and assets thresholds in a resource definition. Increases in the price level, however, only influence the level of the monetary socio-cultural minimum income on the basis of the resource definition, i.e., only a nominal adjustment is necessary. As long as poverty lines are related to regional or national averages, changes in exchange rates or the question to what extent exchange rates correspond to purchasing power parities for the cost of living of people in the middle or lower income bands do not play a role. This problem would, however, immediately crop up if one wished to define a common poverty line for different currency areas or if one wished to make international comparisons based on a poverty line of exactly the same level in real terms for all countries under consideration.

Many of these problems are easier to solve in a national context than on an international level because there may be a narrower range of accepted value judgements. In international comparisons one would have to base the concepts used on the same methods and value judgements in order to arrive at comparable empirical results, even if these do not receive the same recognition in each country. If one used poverty lines "according to the dominant opinion in each country", empirical results concerning the extent of poverty would be

---

7 This choice is particularly topical in Germany. If one considers the considerable differences between the old and new Länder and asks whether a poverty line should be the same everywhere taking an average for the whole country, or whether in view of the differences in average income in the Western and Eastern Länder different levels should be used.

incomparable in the strict sense. But the results could still be interesting in the following sense: If of two countries to be compared, the population of one were much more tolerant with respect to different attitudes and life styles, its poverty line based on the marginalization threshold could be lower, and therefore, even with the same distribution of income, its measured poverty.

2.3 Methods of calculating the poverty line

I would like now to briefly sketch out the methods used for calculating the poverty line and make a few observations on difficulties with them in international comparisons.

The first method can be described as a *political standard.* Parliament, government or the relevant authority sets the poverty line and adjusts it discretionary or regularly based on a formula. In setting it, they may use one or more methods; however, in the end setting it is a political decision. There are two types of politically set poverty lines. The first one is purely a measuring instrument, then it is not linked with income maintenance payments to all people below it. Such a poverty line exists in the United States, for example[8]. International comparative studies would only be possible on this basis if there were such measuring instruments in all countries under consideration. It would also be an interesting question how the official national poverty lines diverge as a percentage of average national income. Transferring one country's measuring instrument to another - whether it be on an absolute level using purchasing power parity or as a relative threshold, whereby one takes the same percentage difference between it and average income - is inconsistent with its character as a political decision in the relevant country. A second type can be called a political quasi-poverty line. Such a poverty line is derived from the level of minimum payments set in a country (e.g., minimum wage, minimum pension, level of welfare payments). In the end, these political quasi-poverty lines are always dependent on financial capacity, and typically fluctuate in relation to the average income. If it is used, then only those people receiving less than these minimum payments are classified as poor. The results would be distorted, since it is by no means certain

---

8 For a recent discussion of the American poverty line and its shortcomings see Ruggles (1990).

that these minimum payments should be granted to everyone. Only if those countries which have a welfare benefits system, and whose system every resident citizen can make use of were compared could such a comparison be meaningful. It would then provide information on "hidden poverty" according to each country's definition and make a comparison of the non-take-up rates possible. But it would remain open as to whether the level of benefits does or does not avoid poverty - compared with a relative poverty line of the same level for all countries. The use of political poverty lines is based in the end on the adjudged position: "Who is poor is determined by the government of each country, and all that is checked is to what extent each country carries out a successful policy to combat poverty as defined by its own standards".

The same arguments are relevant if one uses minimum standards in the various dimensions of the living conditions of individuals in each country for a comparison.

The second method can be described as an *expert standard* [9]. National experts set a basket of goods containing all those goods in the appropriate quantity for the given time period (week or month). This is the basket the experts consider to be necessary to reach the socio-cultural minimum of subsistence. The goods in this basket are then given prices in order to arrive at the necessary monetary amount. As the experts have a great deal of scope here and may be exposed to many different cultural and political influences, one cannot expect that this method will give rise to internationally comparable poverty lines. Only if the methods for choosing the basket of goods were uniform and exhaustive could one see this method as a real option, but such methods which can be applied in different countries have not yet been developed. The same is true for setting minimum standards for various dimensions of the living conditions of individuals.

The third method can be described as a *relative income standard* or *a relative consumption expenditure standard*[10]. Since it can be set by political bodies or by the researcher, it comes either close to a political standard or to an expert standard. With this standard a certain percentage of average net income or average consumption expenditure is set as the poverty line. A level of 50% is most often

---

9 See Ruggles (1990) and Bradshaw (1993); until the end of the eighties this method was used for decades to determine social assistance benefits in Germany.

10 A consumption expenditure standard is used by Eurostat to obtain comparable poverty figures for the member states of the European Union; see Ramprakash (1994).

used, but so are 40% and 60%. The plausibility of this threshold can be checked by calculating what basket of goods one can buy for the resultant sum in each country. Comparisons with results from expert standards and the two methods still to be described could be made. This method, which is the one used most often in international comparative poverty research, aims to consider and examine a poor part of the population which is relatively far from the average in each country. The results are also comparable in this precise sense as long as the conditions mentioned below are adhered to. With this relatively uniform measuring instrument one can also compare the national minimum standards properly. Such a poverty threshold is, however, somewhat arbitrary, and it remains open as to whether tendencies to marginalize people actually start here. In order to obtain a more complete picture, different percentages could be used.

Choosing the average to be used is also by no means easy. The alternatives are the following ones:

- the arithmetical mean of net income or consumption expenditure from a survey;
- the survey median of net income or consumption expenditure;
- the arithmetical mean of the personal disposable income or consumption of the household sector taken from the national accounts.

The advantages of the arithmetical mean based on the survey under consideration are better comparability with other arithmetical means, often provided with other statistics, and easier calculability. The disadvantage is that unrepresentative samples with too few high income earners or underreporting of income categories that mainly occur with high earners and with certain types of income (income from self-employment, farming and capital) can distort the result.

The advantage of the median is its lower dependence on the higher income groups, which are often badly recorded in surveys; its disadvantage is that there are fewer possibilities to compare it with other averages which are published. One must, however, remember that with typical distributions which are steep on the left hand side the median is always less than the arithmetical mean, so that when changing from the arithmetical mean to the median, the percentage used for fixing the poverty line must be increased. The same is true for changing the reference value from net income to consumption expenditure.

An arithmetical mean, which is derived from national income figures, benefits greatly from being based on an internationally standardized method of calculation and, therefore initially, seems to have advantages. Since, however, surveys typically underrepresent income and consumption, the threshold based on the national income accounts is too high if the same percentages are used (as in sample surveys), and poverty is, accordingly, overestimated. This is especially problematic if the surveys in the countries being compared are of varying quality, or if they exclude parts of the population (e.g., foreigners and farmers). Then one can only use the survey means. If the population group excluded is sizeable, doubts begin to arise, however, as to whether such surveys can be used at all.

The calculation of the average requires a decision about the unit of reference. It is now widely believed that this should be the individual and not the household or the nuclear or extended family. However, with a resource definition of poverty, the mutual obligations among the members of the nuclear or wider family to pay maintenance cannot be denied. Economies of scale resulting from living together in a household and the differing needs of adults and children have to be taken into account by using an equivalence scale which gives the head of household a weight of 1 and each member a weight of less than 1.

There are no objective methods for determining these equivalence scales. When choosing a scale, another value judgement must be made. The question also arises as to whether the same scale should be used for all countries in the comparison or whether - as far as is possible - national scales should be used.

When using an equivalence scale, the household's net income is divided by the sum of the weights of the members of the household, thus arriving at a level of welfare that is assigned to each member of the household. The arithmetical mean or the median is then determined from these individual levels of welfare. The chosen equivalence scale, therefore, has an effect both on the level of the poverty line and the position of each individual in the distribution, be it below or above the poverty line. Both the level of the calculated poverty rate and the structure of the poor population, therefore, depend on the equivalence scale used.

In my view, the use of a uniform equivalence scale is preferable in international comparisons (For example, the OECD scale old was 1.0, 0.7, 0.5; the new is: 1.0, 0.5; 0.3). The alternative is determining a method of deriving equivalence scales with which the appropriate scale can be empirically determined in all countries being compared. These country-specific scales would then be used in comparative studies of poverty. Such methods are available, but the value judgement problem is only pushed back one stage[11].

When using equivalence scales an unequal distribution of consumption amongst members of a household, which could lead to poverty for individuals, is obviously not taken into account. This is a grey area.

With a living condition definition, on the other hand, the situation of each individual is directly considered thus avoiding problems of the distribution of welfare within the household.

As well as distinguishing the poor population using a poverty line and calculating its share of the total population, the degree of poverty is also important. This problem can be dealt with using the resource definition with the concept of the poverty gap or special measures of distribution among the poor[12]. In theory these measures can also be applied with a living condition definition if the various dimensions are measured using indicators which can be interpreted as cardinal numbers. Slight poverty can then be differentiated from extreme poverty.

I would also like to mention that deciding on the relevant net income or consumption throws up problems, which I will cover here with the key words 'assessment of imputed rent' and 'domestic production'. Deciding on the period (weekly or annual net income) is also significant.

The problem of how assets should be taken into account is also important. To what extent ought assets be exhausted, i.e., sold and the revenue spent for consumption? There is a value judgement here, too, because the maximum permissible amount of assets has to be defined. One will probably have to work with limits on the amount of assets allowed in relation to the poverty line. In this way many people who are poor in terms of income, though not in terms of assets, will be excluded from the poor population.

A further problem, serious in international comparisons, is posed by different real transfers in different countries. If, for example, one country has a free state health care system, and in another one some or all of the people must pay for health care, then the net incomes are no longer comparable. The same is true for real transfers in the form of subsidised public services, such as public housing or food stamps.

---

11 This approach was used to derive equivalence scale for Germany and the US in: Merz et al. (1994).

12 For a short discussion and references to the literature see Sen (1992, chapter 7).

In international comparisons of poverty, it must, therefore, always be checked as to whether such differences exist for the group of people initially identified as being poor, and if necessary additional assessments must be made. This can also affect the calculation of the average.

A final general problem with resource definitions is that they are always geared towards the needs of "normal people". The long-term special needs of certain groups (e.g., the handicapped or those requiring care), which may not be covered by the social security system, are not taken into account. This can only be solved by specifically identifying such groups and adjusting their poverty lines.

Despite these problems, which for the most part can be resolved as long as a good statistical base is available, the relative income standard or the relative consumption standard are currently the best and most often used approaches for international comparative studies of poverty.

The fourth method can be described as a *behavioral mixed citizen-expert standard.* It was developed by the English poverty researcher Townsend[13]. It uses living condition elements to determine the poverty line in the sense of a resource definition, that is, the lowest level of income at which there is no marginalization. It defines a number of indicators, about 60 to be precise, which should indicate whether one still leads a typical life at a modest level. Examples of the proposed indicators are the following ones:

- whether one has an apartment of adequate size and with a heating system and the necessary facilities indoor,
- whether one's children can occasionally invite schoolfriends home;
- whether they can take small gifts with them when invited to other people's houses;
- whether one can go on holiday for at least a week;
- whether one can afford to be a member of a club, etc.

Using a representative sample survey, it is shown that on average there exists an income threshold; if income falls below this threshold, many of these activities quickly cease and marginalization begins. This income threshold is called the poverty line.

This approach obviously requires experts - Townsend was the expert himself to choose the indicators - and it is based on the actual behaviour of the

---

13 See Townsend (1979); non-monetary indicators are also broadly discussed in Whelan (1993).

respondents. Furthermore it is highly country-specific because different indicators may be relevant for participation and marginalization in different countries. It also requires a great deal of statistical information. So far only a few steps have been taken to provide similar information for other countries (see Muffels 1993). International comparative investigations would require similarly constructed surveys in all countries; even if judgements by experts cannot be completely avoided, such an approach would be a great step forward in international comparative poverty research. The result could be called a resource based poverty line derived from living conditions.

The fifth method could be described as a *pure citizen's standard*, since it uses the citizen's evaluation of their own income as a basis. In the literature, this standard is usually refered to as the "subjective standard"[14].

With this method, a resource based poverty line is derived by asking a well-defined question to a representative sample of the population. Three variants of this question are distinguished[15]:

The so-called Subjective Poverty Line is derived from a minimum income question which reads: "What is the minimum amount of income that your family, in your circumstances, needs to be able to make ends meet?" The so-called Leyden Poverty Line is based on answers to an income evaluation question which reads: "In the circumstances of your household, which monthly disposable income would you regard as 'very bad', 'bad', 'insufficient', 'sufficient', 'good', 'very good'". The so-called CPS-method uses also the minimum income question and in addition the following question: "With your current income, can you make ends meet: 'with great difficulty', 'with difficulty', 'with some difficulty', 'fairly easily', 'easily', 'very easily' ".

The answers to these questions are used in different ways to finally derive the respective poverty line. At this point value judgements of the researcher enter into the analysis, since he has to aggregate in some way the answers and/or to choose a minimum welfare level that characterizes the poverty threshold.

---

14 See Van den Bosch (1993); he distinguishes three different approaches resulting in the "Leyden Poverty Line", the "Subjective Poverty Line" and the "CSP-Poverty Line". (See also Plug et al. in this volume).

15 See Van den Bosch (1993, pp. 11-13); there the wording of the three different income questions can be found with further explanations. The subjective methods were pioneered by van Praag, Hagenaars, Kapteyn, Deleeck in the Netherlands and Belgium.

For international comparisons, this method has the advantage to take differences in publicly provided transfers in kind into account. On the other hand, it can be doubted whether the questions asked have the same meaning for the respondents in the various countries, and whether the possibility of different levels of aspiration in various countries can be and should be excluded. Comparative studies that are already available raise some doubts as to the plausibility of the results[16]. But this obviously is a criticism that can only be supported if results based on other methods are accepted as more plausible. Additionally, this approach, which leads to a resource based poverty line, cannot avoid criticism based on the living condition concept, which is geared towards the individual.

Another variant of the citizen's standard is theoretically less well-developed but seems to me another approach with potential for further development, especially because it could form the basis of national consensus building. It circumvents income as an aggregate indicator of resources, and eventually poverty, and aims directly at some indicators of living conditions. This method presupposes a representative survey with a wide range of questions about the availability of consumer goods and activities. In addition to that, each person would be asked which of these items his household should have or be able to use in order not to be poor. Compared to the behavioral mixed citizen-expert standard, this approach would avoid the necessity that indicators of poverty are predetermined by experts, and from that an income threshold is calculated. On the other hand, it has to be decided by a value jugdement which and how many basic goods, consumer durables, facilities and activities that are not available to a respondent constitute living conditions that are so bad that they can be termed poverty[17]. This could also be a matter of political debate.

From this approach, a connection to a resource based poverty line can easily be made if individuals or households, to whom a certain number of items (e.g., three) are not available, are defined as living in poverty. Based on this value judgement, the incomes of these poor people can be compared to national averages. Rainwater (1992) mentions interesting American investigations, the

---

16 See Van den Bosch (1993, pp. 13-15).

17 The approach by Sen who distinguishes between capabilities and income is - roughly speaking - close to using a relative living condition definition of poverty; although he contributes to the theoretical foundation of this concept he cannot solve the problem of the necessity of value judgements.

result of which was that the net income calculated in this way was around 45% to 50% of the median over a long period. This indirectly supports the relative income standard and even helps to decide on the adequate percentage.

Finally, it has to be emphasized that all the variants of the citizen's standard are even more relative than the relative income standard, since each country's poverty is determined exclusively by the country-specific answers and estimates, similarly to a comparison of country-specific minimum standards set by political bodies. This can be seen as an advantage or as a disadvantage.

This is the range of approaches available for identifying the poor in international comparisons. It ought to have become clear that there is no scientifically objective measure of poverty. The analysis has always to be based on value judgements which have to be inserted into the analysis - at least as hypotheses. But these value judgements have to be emphasized and stated explicitly.

3 Concluding Remarks

The fact that the measurement of poverty cannot avoid value judgements is not unique. Economic and social measurement are in many ways based on value judgements. But these are value judgements on which a broad majority of scientists and politicians have agreed by convention. Many users of figures from the national accounts - to mention only one example - may even not be aware of the value judgements implied. In contrast to these established measurement procedures and accounting systems, the measurement of poverty cannot be based on widely agreed conventions. There still is a great divergence of opinions as to what constitutes poverty. This divergence can only be reduced by discussions about the underlying ethical questions, but not by theoretical or empirical scientific analyses. Given this conclusion, what can be done in the field of scientific analysis?

For descriptive analyses, the best solution in practice seems to be to measure and to analyse poverty on the basis of a number of different poverty lines in order to highlight the much disputed range of possible poverty situations. The use of a grid of poverty lines can also serve to show at which level effective national minimum income regulations provide income to avoid income poverty as defined by national political decisions. For the questions aiming to provide explanations for the persistence of income poverty it may not be so important whether poverty is believed to set in at 40%, 45% or 50% of average net income; in my opinion the analysis should focus on the whole range of low income.

When aiming at political conclusions - whether they be controlling success or judging and adjusting the level of minimum standards - political value judgements cannot be avoided. At this point the scientist cannot claim to speak with the backing of his scientific knowledge but only as an ordinary citizen who expresses his political opinion.

References

Atkinson, Anthony B. (1989), How should we measure Poverty? Some conceptual issues, in: Atkinson, A. B., Poverty and Social Security, Hemel Hempstead, pp. 7-24 (Harvester Wheatsheaf)

Atkinson, Anthony B. (1993), The Institution of an Official Poverty Line and Economic Poverty, Discussion Paper Suntory-Toyota International Centre for Economics and Related Disciplines, London School of Economics, WSP/98, London

Berghman, Jos/Cantillon, Bea (eds.) (1993), The European Face of Social Security, Essays in honour of Herman Deleeck, Aldershot (Avebury)

Bradshaw, Jonathan (1993), Rediscovering budget standards, in: Berghman, Jos/Cantillon, Bea (eds.), pp. 60-76.

Buhmann, Brigitte/Rainwater, Lee/Schmaus, Günther/Smeeding, Timothy M. (1988), Equivalence Scales, Well-Being, Inequality and Poverty, in: The Review of Income and Wealth, vol. 34, pp. 115-142.

Callan, Tim/Nolan, Brian (1991), Concepts of Poverty and the Poverty Line, in: Journal of Economic Surveys, vol.5, no.3, pp. 243-261.

Deleeck, Herman/Van den Bosch, Karel (1992), Poverty and adequacy of social security in Europe in a comparative analysis, Journal of European Social Policy, vol.2, no.2 pp.107-120

Dierckes, Meinolf/Weiler, Hans N./Berthoin Antal, Ariane (eds.) (1987), Comparative Policy Research, Learning from Experience, Aldershot (Gower)

Döring, Diether/Hanesch, Walter/Huster, Ernst-Ulrich (eds.) (1990), Armut im Wohlstand, Frankfurt a.M. (Suhrkamp)

Europäische Gemeinschaften (1992a), Council Recommendation of 24 June 1992 on common criteria concerning sufficient resources and social assistance in social protection systems (92/441/EEC), in: Official Journal of the European Communities No. L 245/46 of 26.8.92

Europäische Gemeinschaften (1992b), Council Recommendation of 27 July 1992 on the convergence of social protection objectives and policies (92/442/EEC) in: Official Journal of the European Communities, No. L 245/49 of 26.8.92

Glatzer, Wolfgang/Hübinger, Werner (1990), Lebenslagen und Armut,in: Döring, Diether/ Hanesch, Walter/Huster, Ernst-Ulrich , pp. 31-55 (Suhrkamp).

Hauser, Richard (1984), Problems of Defining a Poverty Line for Comparative Studies, in: Sarpellon, Giovanni (ed.) Understanding Poverty, Milano, pp. 329-355 (Franco Angeli)

Hauser, Richard, Neumann Udo (1992), Armut in der Bundesrepublik Deutschland. Die sozialwissenschaftliche Thematisierung nach dem Zweiten Weltkrieg, in: Leibfried, S. Voges, W., pp. 237-271.

Hauser, Richard (1993), Approaches to comparative social policy analysis, in: Berghman, Jos/Cantillon, Bea., pp.79-93

Haveman, Robert H. (1993), Who Are the Nation's "Truly Poor"?, in: The Brookings Review, Winter, pp. 24-27.

Heidenheimer, Arnold J./Heclo, Hugh/Teich Adams, Carolyn (1983), Comparative Public Policy, The Politics of Social Choice in Europe and America, 2nd.ed. London (Macmillan)

Jones, Catherine (1985), Patterns of Social Policy, An Introduction to Comparative Analysis, London and New York.

Kakwani, Nanak C. (1980), Income Inequality and Poverty, Methods of Estimation and Policy Applications, Oxford (Oxford University Press)

Kohl, Jürgen (1992), Armut im internationalen Vergleich. Methodische Probleme und empirische Ergebnisse, in: Leibfried, S./Voges, W., pp. 272-299.

Kommission der Europäischen Gemeinschaften (1981), Schlußbericht der Kommission an den Rat über das erste Programm von Modellvorhaben und Modellstudien zur Bekämpfung der Armut, Brüssel KOM(81) 769 endg. bzw. KOM(81) 769 endg./2

Kommission der Europäischen Gemeinschaften (1991), Schlußbericht des Zweiten Programms zur Bekämpfung der Armut 1985 - 1989, Brüssel KOM(91) 29 endg.

Kommission der Europäischen Gemeinschaften (1992), Auf dem Weg zur Europäischen Solidargemeinschaft, Den Kampf gegen die Soziale Ausgrenzung intensivieren, die Eingliederung fördern. Mitteilung der Kommission, Brüssel,KOM(92) 542 endg.

Kommission der Europäischen Gemeinschaften (1993a), Soziales Europa, Zweiter Bericht über die Anwendung der Gemeinschaftscharta der sozialen Grundrechte der Arbeitnehmer, Beiheft 1/93, Brüssel

Kommission der Europäischen Gemeinschaften (1993b), Mittelfristiges Aktionsprogramm zur Bekämpfung der Ausgrenzung und zur Förderung der Solidarität: ein neues Programm zur Unterstützung und Anregung der Innovation (PROGRESS) 1994-1999 und Bericht über die Durchführung des Gemeinschaftsprogramms zur wirtschaftlichen und sozialen Eingliederung der am meisten benachteiligten Gruppen (1989-1994), Brüssel KOM(93) 435 endg.

Kommission der Europäischen Gemeinschaften (1993d), Grünbuch über die europäische Sozialpolitik, Weichenstellung für die Europäische Union, Brüssel KOM(93) 551

Leibfried, Stephan/Voges, Wolfgang (eds.) (1992), Armut im modernen Wohlfahrtsstaat, Kölner Zeitschrift für Soziologie und Sozialpsychologie, Sonderheft 32

Merz, Joachim/Garner, Thesia/Smeeding, Timothy M./Faik, Jürgen/Johnson, David (1994), Two Scales, One Methodology - Expenditure Based Equivalence Scales for the United States and Germany, Discussion Paper no. 8 of the University of Lüneburg, Forschungsinstitut Freie Berufe.

Muffels, Ruud J. A. (1993), Deprivation standards and style of living indices, in: Berghman, Jos/Cantillon, Bea, pp. 43-59.

Muffels, Ruud/Berghman, Jos/Dirven, Henk-Jan (1992), A multi-method approach to monitor the evolution of poverty, in: Journal of European Social Policy, vol. 2, no. 2 pp. 193-213.

Piachaud, David (1992), Wie mißt man Armut?, in: Leibfried, Stephan/Voges, Wolfgang , pp. 63-87.

Rainwater, Lee (1992), Ökonomische versus soziale Armut in den USA (1959 - 1990), in: Leibfried, Stephan/Voges, Wolfgang, pp. 195-220.

Ramprakash, Deo (1994), Poverty in the Countries of the European Union: A Synthesis of Eurostat's Statistical Research on Poverty, in: Journal of European Social Policy, vol. 4, no. 2, pp. 117-128

Room, Graham (1990), 'New Poverty' in the European Community, London (Macmillan)

Ruggles, Patricia (1990), Drawing the Line, Alternative Poverty Measures and Their Implications for Public Policy, Washington D.C. (Urban Institute Press)

Sen, Amartya (1981), Poverty and Famines, An Essay on Entitlement and Deprivation, Oxford (Clarendon Press)

Sen, Amartya (1992), Inequality reexamined, Oxford (Clarendon Press)

Statistisches Amt der Europäischen Gemeinschaften (Eurostat) (1990), Armut in Zahlen: Europa zu Beginn der achtziger Jahre, Studie des Instituts für Sozialstudien (ISSAS) im Auftrag von Eurostat, Luxemburg

Townsend, Peter (1979), Poverty in the United Kingdom: A Survey of Household Resources and Living Standards, London (Allen Lane and Penguin Books)

Townsend, Peter (1993), The International Analysis of Poverty, Hemel Hempstead (Harvester Wheatsheaf)

Van den Bosch, Karel (1993), Poverty measures in comparative research, in: Berghman, Jos/Cantillon, Bea , pp. 3-23.

Whelan, Brendan J. (1993), Non-monetary indicators of poverty, in: Berghman, Jos/Cantillon, Bea, pp. 24-42.

Wilensky, Harold L./Luebbert, Gregory M./Reed Hahn, Susan/Jamieson Adrienne M. (1987), Comparative Social Policy: Theories, Methods, Findings, in: Dierkes, Meinolf/Weiler, Hans N./Berthoin Antal, Ariane (eds.) pp. 381-457

Working Poor: "Inequitable" Wages in Germany and in Europe! - (Higher) Minimum Wages as an Instrument of Justice?

Claus Schäfer

The subject of this survey is the "working poor" phenomena. We address workers who hold a job but receive wages so low that their income is insufficient to make ends meet. We adduce them as "working poor". There is a marked difference between our approach, which focuses on individuals, and conventional poverty research, which is based on families. Extreme cases aside, it is evident that individual poverty is qualitatively less severe than the type of poverty which afflicts unemployed people and their families. Therefore, the recently revived European discussion pertaining to the poverty issue refers to "inadequate" or "inequitable" wages in order to distinguish between "working poor" and conventional poverty. These terms indicate that the poverty of the working poor is a relative concept and that "inequitable" wages are seen in relation to "equitable", "ordinary", or "sufficient" wages[1]. This should be taken into consideration when these terms are used throughout this paper without quotation marks.

The concept of the working poor is also meant to instigate discussion and is a means of drawing attention to a problem which the industrialised countries - or at least the whole of Western Europe - believed to have mastered a long time ago. The concept also points to another aspect which has probably been neglected up to now; i.e., the connection between social policy where the debate about poverty usually takes place, and the domain "preceding" it, of employment and labour policy. The latter has also recently become known as the primary labour market. These areas are connected on several different levels. If wages are inequitable, wage-earners and their dependants need supplementary transfers of public funds

---

1 For a topical survey of this debate since 1990 see Equitable wages and minimum pay setting, in: Income Data Service, London, November 1993, pp. 9.

in order to secure for them a decent standard of living. In Germany, this income supplement is granted under the welfare system. Furthermore, inequitable wages create even more injustice when a person becomes unemployed or retires, because in Germany - and many other countries - income transfers, like unemployment benefits or pensions, are largely determined by previous individual wages.

Occasionally, it seems we need to be reminded that primary distribution comes before secondary distribution or, to put it differently, that a good employment policy very often constitutes the best social policy and is best suited to combat poverty as it creates jobs and income and makes transfer payments superfluous[2]. Supplementary to that, it should be pointed out that employment policies can achieve such targets only when wages are equitable and adequate. Therefore fighting the phenomenon of the working poor may also help to fight conventional family poverty.

The discussion about equitable wages[3], restricted to developing countries until recently, has now been revived and refocused in the industrial countries by none other than the Commission of the European Union[4]. In 1990, when the Single Market was drawing nearer though its social aspects were still underdeveloped, the Commission began to fear that tougher competition would lead to social dumping and especially wage dumping in some member states or individual branches of industry. In late 1990, the Commission entrusted a group of international experts with a survey on "inequitable wages" in the countries of the European Union in order to underpin these apprehensions with facts[5].

This group of experts, of which the "Institute for Economic and Social Studies of the Confederation of German Trade Unions" (WSI) was a member, first developed joint criteria and parameters for their respective national reports in order to make them comparable at the EU-level. First equitable wages and thresholds of justice had to be defined. In this context the group of experts

2 Hauser (1993) stresses the precedence of employment over welfare as the first of 10 priorities for a reform of the welfare system.

3 ILO/Bureau International de Travail (1992).

4 See Commission of the European Community, Opinion of the Commission on adequate wages, Commission Document SEK (1991) and Opinion of the Commission on adequate wages in: Bulletin of the European Communities No. C 248, 11.9.1993, pp. 7.

5 Working methods and results of the international group of experts are summarised in an EC document of CERC (1991).

rediscovered a standard laid down in the 1960 European Social Charter (ESC) of the Council of Europe which says that wages in the signatory states - among them all EU members - should not drop below 68% of the national average income. It seems that the signatory states, their governments, as well as the social partners made light of this standard. They either forgot it or pushed it to the back of their minds - so much so that no one noticed or contradicted a statement contained in the biannual implementation report to the European Council in which the government claimed it was not possible to do empirical checks whether wages dropped below that standard or not. The international group of experts drew some inspiration from that ESC-standard but did not adopt it as a sole guideline. Their empirical survey of inequitable wages was based on three different threshold values that indicate injustice: 50%, 66% and 80% of the respective national average income, i.e., the median income.

The range of these threshold values reflects different ideas and codifications of justice; they may be either explicit or implicit, national or international in character. Here are some examples:

- The 50% threshold value corresponds to the legal minimum wage level in France; at the same time it is not very different from the actual level of welfare benefits in Germany which - housing benefits included - amounts level to 40-45% of the average wages.
- The 66% threshold value is almost identical with the above mentioned ESC-standard of 68%; it also corresponds fairly well with Germany's unemployment benefits, which the law defines as a certain percentage of the last monthly wages.
- The 80% threshold value is close to the 75% mark, which until a few years ago, was the basis for the German "minimum-wage-linked pension" provisions - according to which, even part-time workers were entitled to 75% of an average worker's pension; internationally, this value is comparable to the EU's Regional Aid I provisions in which a region qualifies for support if its gross domestic product is below 75% of the national average. In Norway, outside today's EU borders, there are collective agreements , even in the metal industry stipulating that wages must not be lower than 90% of the average wage of that particular industry.

Figure 1

Proportion of low-paid workers among full-time workers within the European Union

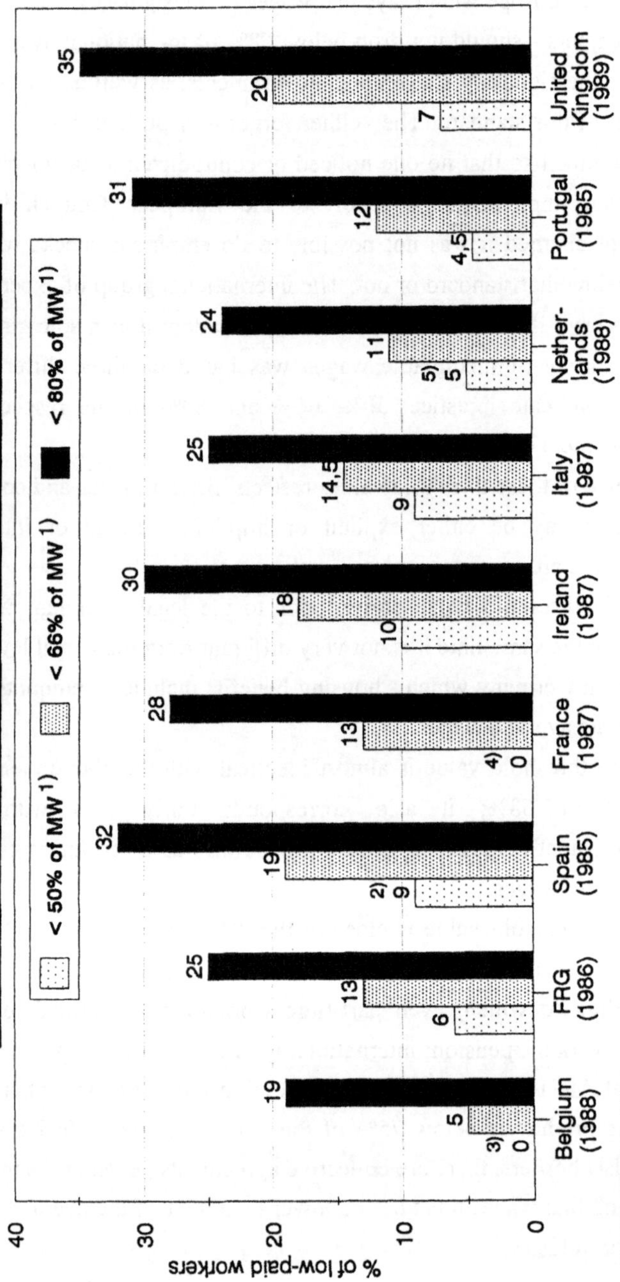

1) MW: Median Wage
2) More exactly, the percentage of wages less than 40% of the MW
3) Negligible
4) Negligible
5) Gross wages. Proportions for wages net of taxes are as follows: 3%, 8%, 21%

Source: **CERC 1991**

All German standards of justice, however, are linked with social policy or transfer payments calculated on the basis of wages. Oddly enough, there is no valid comparable standard that applies directly to income from work.

The international group of experts used these threshold values to assess the income of full-time workers on the basis of gross wages in order to exclude national differences. Incomes of part-time workers, persons employed for a minimum of hours per week, and social benefits financed by rates, taxes or other sources were left out for the same reason. National currencies and their purchasing power were not compared; instead, the thresholds were related to the respective national average wage. The remaining empirical task was then to find and evaluate wage data which could be used for wage stratification. This wage pyramid was subsequently "cut" at the three points which correspond to the above mentioned thresholds in order to determine the population of workers with inequitable wages, define their characteristics, and evaluate these results. This task could not be fully accomplished in all countries of Europe, not all methods could be used throughout and the study could not be conducted at the same depth everywhere. Therefore, the results must be viewed with certain restrictions. (See Table 1 and Figure 1).

In Germany, the income data of the SOEP survey (Socio-Economic Panel) - which are otherwise widely applicable - could not be used for comparison this time, though they usually provide a satisfactory stratification of incomes. In the SOEP, however, the cases of low-wage earners, i.e., those with wages below 80% of the national income median, are so small that the sampling error of incomes projected on this basis is not small enough to satisfy the criteria of the Federal Statistical Office. The total number of worker households contained in the SOEP data is too low to establish a descriptive connection between low wages and deeply disaggregated industries, or to clearly identify which wages are paid in which industry[6]. None of these sampling problems occur in the employment statistics of the Federal Statistical Office, which also uses random sampling and regularly publishes the effective wages of workers subject to statutory social insurance up to the upper earnings limit valid for the pension insurance (see Statistisches Bundesamt 1993).

6 These two disadvantages of SOEP are also mentioned in Berntsen (1989, pp. 32).

Table 1: Proportion of low-paid workers among full-time workers within the European Union[5]

Country (Year of inquiry)	Wage less than 50 % of the	66 % Median	80 % wage	Statutory minimum wage[4] in % of the Median wage	Percentage of full-time workers within the workforce
Belgium (1988)	neg.[1]	5	19	66	90.5
FRG (1986)	6	13	25	-	87.5[6]
Spain (1985)	9[2]	19	32	60	94.5
France (1987)	neg.[1]	14	28	61	89.0
Ireland (1987)	10	18	30	-	92.5
Italy (1987)	9	14,5	25	-	94.0
Netherlands ('88)	5[3]	11	24	77	70.0
Portugal (1985)	4,5	12	31	74	94.0
U.K. (1989)	7	20	35	-	79.0

Source: Centre d'Etude de Revenues et des Coûts (CERC) 1991

[1] Negligible

[2] Percentage of wages less than 40 % of the median wage

[3] Gross wage. Proportions for wages net of taxes are as follows: 3%, 8% and 21%

[4] The minimum wage taken into account is the wage for industry in Portugal and the wage for adults aged 23 and over in the Netherlands. In Luxembourg and Greece there is also a minimum inter-occupational wage; however, we have been unable to determine the relationship of this minimum wage to the median wage.

[5] We have been unable to acquire data on wages and their distribution in Luxembourg. Data from Greece relate to annual wages for all workers regardless of whether they have worked a few hours per month for part of the year only or full-time throughout the year. The only statistics available for Denmark do not provide data on wage distribution.

[6] Including trainees

Even a 1% random sample of full-time workers employed throughout the year and liable for statutory social security contributions (exempting trainees) still covers more than 150 000 persons. It contains data on wage level and other combinable characteristics (age, qualification, branch of industry, gender, status in working life etc.). These statistics include data from 300 different industries, which is as many as the absolute number of all blue-collar (300) and white-collar (400) worker households below the 80% threshold that are contained in the SOEP. The employment statistics, however, have some disadvantages. They are not very up-to-date, so the latest wage and income data available to the international group of experts dates from 1986. Established civil servants (Beamte), usually employed on a full-time basis, are not included as they are exempted from statutory social insurance.

Also, the income group brackets used for income stratification by the Federal Statistical Office are relatively coarse, so the position of the three thresholds of justice within the income pyramid of salaried employees had to be determined by interpolation. The same applies to the median income as a point of reference for the three thresholds. In spite of these and other methodical problems encountered in some EU-countries, the empirical results can give an indication of the extent of inequitable pay in Germany and elsewhere in the European Union (see Tables 1 and 2)[7].

The extent of inequitable pay is surprisingly high, though Germany is found "merely" in the middle bracket of the European Union as a whole. The figures would be even higher if - instead of using the median income of all full-time employees independent of gender as a point of reference - the experts had restricted their study to the median income of male full-time workers. In this case, the assumed discrimination of women who receive lower pay for equal work or have restricted access to jobs would probably have been much more discernible. If these calculations were solely based on the median income of male full-time workers, the populations of "working poor" in Germany could be up to 50% higher than those shown in Tables 1 and 2. Irrespective of this particular aspect, the empirical results indicate a need for remedial action especially in certain groups of workers and certain branches of industry where poverty is strongly concentrated (Table 2).

7 For a detailed description see Schäfer (1991, pp. 711).

Table 2: Groups of full-time employees[1] with low pay in the FRG 1978 and 1986 in percent (thresholds of low pay: percent of the median of male and female pay[2])

Groups/ Characteristics	Thresholds 50 % 1174 DM/m 1978	50 % 1671 DM/m 1986	66 % 1549 DM/m 1978	66 % 2205 DM/m 1986	80 % 1878 DM/m 1978	80 % 2673 DM/m 1986
Employees in total						
- percentage	6,8	6,3	14,1	13,3	26,0	24,6
- persons in mio.	1,2	1,1	2,4	2,3	4,4	4,2
among them: concentration of low pay in high risk groups[3] in percentage:						
1. Sex						
Female employees	82,1	94,6	78,3	81,7	66,8	71,5
- blue collar	46,0	40,0	45,6	39,4	39,0	39,0
- white collar	38,3	42,7	35,5	41,6	29,9	34,2
2. Age						
Less than 20 years	22,0	10,8	17,0	7,5	10,8	4,9
20 - 30 years	23,4	31,7	32,6	42,0	36,6	43,8
60 and more years	0,4	0,3	0,4	0,3	0,3	0,2
3. Education						
Elementary school without finals	36,7	25,3	40,4	28,5	40,4	21,1
4. Professions						
in agriculture ...	3,5	4,1	2,6	2,9	1,9	2,3
in private and public services	72,4	73,5	66,6	68,1	57,0	61,7

When the lowest threshold of 50% is used as a basis, the group of full-time workers with wages categorised as "too low" totals 6.3% or 1.1 million persons. Significantly, more than 90% of these workers are women, 73% work in the service sector and 65% hold jobs in only 11 different sectors of economy with trade, accommodation and catering business, health service, food, textile and clothing industries heading the list. If the middle threshold of 66% which is almost identical with the ESC-standard is applied, there are as many as 13% or 2.3 million persons in the low-income group. Eighty percent are women, 68% work in the service sector and there are still 55% who work in the same eleven sectors of economy mentioned above. If "inequitable pay" groups consisting of established civil servants (Beamte), part-time workers liable for social security contributions

Table 2 continued

Groups/ Characteristics	Thresholds 50 % 1174 DM/m 1978	50 % 1671 DM/m 1986	66 % 1549 DM/m 1978	66 % 2205 DM/m 1986	80 % 1878 DM/m 1978	80 % 2673 DM/m 1986
5. Branches[4]						
agriculture ...	-	3,0	-	2,0	-	1,5
textile, leather ...	-	5,0	-	6,1	-	5,4
food, drink, tobacco..	-	6,3	-	5,7	-	4,6
installation and building completion	-	2,2	-	1,5	-	1,5
wholesale distribution	-	5,5	-	4,8	-	4,8
distribution services	-	1,0	-	0,9	-	0,8
retail distribution	-	14,5	-	14,5	-	11,7
hotels and catering	-	7,8	-	6,3	-	4,7
laundries ... beauty parlours	-	6,3	-	4,3	-	2,6
medical ... veterinary services	-	9,3	-	6,0	-	6,1
legal services, accountants ...	-	3,9	-	3,4	-	2,8
total	-	64,8	-	55,5	-	46,5

[1] Without part time workers, trainees and civil servants.

[2] The median and the groups are derived (by interpolation) from the income distribution (in income classes) of employees, who are employed the whole year. Their yearly income is split into a twelfth to define a monthly income. (And this one can be divided by the factor 4,33 to define a weekly income). This monthly (or weekly) income is more or less also representative for employees, who did not work the whole year.

[3] Percentage of low pay earners in groups with a high risk for low pay within the low paid full-time employees in total.

[4] For 1978 income distribution data are not available.

Source: Statistisches Bundesamt - own calculations.

and persons with hours of work below liability for social security were added to "low- pay" full-time workers liable for social security contributions, the number of those with "unjust wages" would probably rise by another 3.5 million.

The high occurrence of "inequitable pay" is quite surprising, but empirical studies show that the assumed causes of inequitable pay - discrimination of women denied access to higher income brackets or equal pay for equal work, lack of social recognition and ensuing bad pay for jobs in the service sector as well as the "structural weakness" of certain branches of industry - still seem to have a great deal of influence - much more than trade unions, for instance, would have believed or expected after all the time and effort invested into fighting these causes.

It is also surprising that this could happen in spite of the existence of unions. Even in industrialised countries, unions seem unable to prevent inequitable wages. The fact that countries with "weak" trade unions like France need a statutory minimum wage to prevent inequitable pay has been accepted for several years. Now that an international group of experts has submitted its findings to the EU Commission, we can safely assume that even trade unions as strong as Germany's cannot stop inequitable pay.

The EU Commission, for one, realised that the findings of the international group of experts definitely called for action. Consequently, the Commission recommended that the national governments take adequate steps to fight inequitable wages by introducing statutory or collectively agreed minimum wages or a combination of both[8]. The recommendation implicitly demands an increase for wages which are inadequately low and assigns the responsibility to the national governments or the partners of collective agreements. It is hardly surprising that this recommendation, however moderate, sparked off a heated public debate, which started at a Brussels conference of the EC Commission for members of governments, trade unions and employers in October 1991 and is still raging. Politics and science are equally involved and opinions are quite divided[9].

This division is most apparent on the political level: On the one hand, an increasing number of governments, especially Germany's, are now convinced that it is the general wage level which causes the crisis and weakens their international competitiveness. Their conclusion however is that wages must be reduced, especially in the lower wage bracket. The nation-wide debate in Germany clearly reflects this attitude. Some suggest that "wages below the minima of collective agreements" should be paid from the publicly subsidised secondary labour market and the regular, so-called primary labour market; others support the introduction of "entrance wage rates" for beginners, former unemployed persons etc. The European Parliament, on the other hand, took international politics one step further than the Commission when, in spring 1993, it demanded that a statutory or

8 See above (5) Opinions of the European Commission.

9 Some of these views are contained in Bazen and Benhayoun (1992, pp. 623), Department of Employment (1990), Wilkinson (1992).

collectively agreed minimum wage should be set within only two years, or, alternatively, an EU-guideline should be submitted at the end of these two years[10].

The intentions of the two supranational institutions - the EU Commission and the European Parliament - are clearly opposed to the wishes of several European governments. Some governments have indeed raised their statutory minimum wage over the last few years, but it seems doubtful that this increase can even compensate national inflation rates. What is more, the statutory minimum wages in the European Union are usually not above but rather below 50% of the national median wage, i.e., below what the international group of experts regards as the lowest threshold of justice - the adequacy of this threshold is debatable in itself. Governments which raise minimum wages hesitatingly or inadequately may also be influenced by the tendency mentioned above. They use low wages and wage groups as an instrument for securing their position in the race for international competitiveness, and prepare the ground for those wage-dumping policies that the European Commission was worried about in the first place.

Opinions of employers and trade unions are divided along similar lines both on a national and an international level[11]. Employers advocate "wage cost reduction" and support governments promoting such strategies; they criticise the European Parliament and Commission when they make recommendations and demands for "just" wages as this would lead to higher wages, and subsequently raise their costs. Trade unions have not yet taken a clear stand, though they vehemently scold national governments and employers whenever they attempt to reduce wage costs - the German controversy about the so-called secondary labour market and its discussion about wages below collective agreement minima are a case in point. Statutory or collectively agreed minimum wages that would raise the wage levels of whole groups of workers or even industries to a greater or lesser extent are an issue about which trade unions are caught between scepticism and approval. Scepticism is rampant in Germany, a country with no statutory or collectively agreed minimum wage, i.e., no national minimum wage valid for all branches of industry. Both options, however, are possible under the Collective Bargaining Act. This scepticism may be rooted in the fact that unions in Germany

10 See European Parliament (1993, pp. 44).

11 Discussions in the Economic and Social Committee of the EC, where the European Confederations of Trade Unions and Employers are represented, merely hint at the controversial and violent nature of this issue; see again note 5 above.

and several other countries are organised by branches and have learnt to cherish the advantages and benefits of this system.

A national minimum wage for all industries would force unions to admit that, for all its benefits, there are limits to what the principle of "one industry - one union" can do. "Fair wages", for instance, cannot be implemented everywhere due to branch-specific conditions.

In spite of these possible implications, the collective bargaining committee of the German Confederation of Trade Unions, which discusses and, if necessary, co-ordinates the bargaining policies of all affiliates, decided to tackle the problem of inequitable wages on the basis of the results presented by the EU Commission's international group of experts. In November 1993, the committee decided to support a WSI research project that will collect empirical data on the extent of inequitable wages in Germany and study the various aspects of the minimum wage issue in order to provide concepts for decision-making. Empirical research on the extent of inequitable pay in Germany will be based on the latest available data and guided by the threshold values used by the international group of experts. The study will cover both full-time workers and part-time workers. As far as possible, data will be broken down by branch of industry and region as well as by urban and rural areas in order to achieve the highest possible differentiation. The Federal Statistical Office will conduct a detailed study on the basis of original data, where available, so that inequitable pay-populations do not have to be determined by estimates any more.

Another part of the research project will deal with remedies for the problem and compare the possible advantages and disadvantages of statutory or collectively agreed minimum wages. Due attention will be paid to the Europe-wide debate of the issue and the controversy caused by the argument that "fair wages", i.e., higher wages cause additional unemployment. Furthermore, the project will focus on the discussions and experiences of two European countries where unions' opinions on minimum wages are very clear but differ from each other significantly: In Britain, the TUC has been demanding a statutory minimum wage based on the male workers' wage median for quite some time, and the Labour Party even made this a demand in their electoral campaign. In Austria, the OGB and its affiliates have also demanded a national, collectively agreed minimum wage of 10.000 Austrian Shillings, and have, meanwhile, translated this demand into collective agreements which are now valid in some industries.

Encouraged by their success and the apparently great popularity of the minimum wage, the unions now aim at the 12.000 Austrian Shillings mark. Moreover, the strategy employed by the Austrian trade unions proves that a uniform national wage can be successively achieved through the branch agreements still common in Austria, and that a national minimum wage does not necessarily have to be laid down in a collective agreement at national level.

WSI and the Hans-Böckler-Foundation have scheduled a research project on this issue and plan to present results in 1995. Even now, however, we can safely assume that the European debate about inequitable wages will continue irrespective of WSI's research project or its possible implementation in German collective bargaining. In its latest "Opinion on Equitable Wages" the European Commission not only advocates more empirical transparency and comparability of wage structures in the whole of the European Union but also announces that within three years of the publication of this opinion the commission will issue a report on "progress and impediments" in this area to the Council of Ministers, the Economic and Social Committee and the European Parliament and that such progress shall be reviewed "every other year"[12]. In its recent "Resolution on Social Marginalisation", the European Parliament demanded that the right to "equitable wages" be included in the Maastricht treaty when it comes up for revision in 1995; and elsewhere in the document, Parliament specifies the "need for a minimum income and a minimum wage in every member country"[13].

National minimum wages could doubtlessly create more justice on the labour market and reduce poverty in the conventional sense of the word, i.e., poverty of households with no income - which brings us back to our original point. In 1993, for instance, 200.000 Germans registered as unemployed had to apply for welfare benefits in order to supplement insufficient wage-related unemployment benefits. The German government's decision to cut unemployment benefits is sure to boost these figures in 1994. The group of people who are gainfully employed and receive welfare benefits supplementary to their wages does not seem to be quite as large. In two recently published studies on the area where welfare benefit levels and low-pay ranges overlap, the authors agree that only a few thousand families

---

12 See EC Commission (1993, p. 9).

13 See European Parliament (1992).

with more than three children fall into that category and that this overlap is due to insufficient child allowances rather than to low wages[14].

The study, however, makes one important point which needs to be stressed: The provision of the Federal Public Assistance Act which says that welfare benefits must not be higher than a person's former wages is based on a comparison between welfare benefit levels and the earnings of the lower wage groups, i.e., the average earnings of a larger group of persons. Both aforementioned studies also equate this average to the average earnings of blue- and white-collar workers in the lower wage range of the wage statistics of the Federal Statistical Office. If we base this comparison on individual wages and household incomes of wage earners rather than on the provisions of the Federal Welfare Act, the area of overlap will probably turn out to be somewhat larger. The WSI research project on inequitable pay may be able to find some evidence for this assumption.

References

Bazen, S., Benhayoun, G. (1992), Low pay and Wage Regulation in the European Community, in: British Journal of Industrial Relations, Vol. 30.

Berntsen, R. (1989), Einkommensanalyse mit den Daten des Sozio-ökonomischen Panels unter Verwendung von generierten Einkommensdaten, Arbeitspapier Nr. 291 des Sonderforschungsbereich 3 der Universitäten Frankfurt und Mannheim, Frankfurt.

Breuer, W., Engles, D. (1993), Der Abstand zwischen dem Leistungsniveau der Hilfe zum Lebensunterhalt nach dem Bundessozialhilfegesetz und dem verfügbaren Arbeitnehmer-Einkommen unterer Lohn- und Gehaltsgruppen im Juli 1992, Gutachten des Instituts für Sozialforschung und Gesellschaftspolitik, im Auftrag des Bundesministeriums für Familie und Senioren, Köln.

Centre d'Etudes des Revenues et des Coûts (CERC) (1991), Les Bas-Salaires en Europe, EC-Document V/1018/91-FR, Brussels.

Department of Employment (1990), Estimating the Effect of a National Minimum Wage (in the United Kingdom), London.

European Parliament (1992), Resolution on Social Marginalisation, 28.10.1993, in: Bundestags-Drucksache 12/6235, 23.11.1993.

---

14 See Hanesch et al. (1993); Breuer and Engles (1993).

European Parliament (1993) Resolution A 3-0060/93 from 9.3.1993 (Resolution on the Commission's Draft Opinion on Adequate Wages), in: Bulletin of the European Communities, 26.4.1993, No. C 115.

Hanesch, W., Bäcker, G., with Steffen, J. Schäfer, C. (1993), Sozialhilfeniveau und untere Arbeitnehmer-Einkommen - Eine Untersuchung im Auftrag des Ministeriums für Arbeit, Gesundheit und Soziales des Landes Nordrhein-Westfalen, Mönchengladbach und Düsseldorf.

Hauser, R. (1993), Verteilungsgerechtigkeit im Vordergrund - Ökonomische und politiche Bedingungen zukünftiger Sozialpolitik, in: Soziale Sicherheit 5.

ILO/Bureau International de Travail (1992), Conférence International du Travail 1992: Salaires Minima - Méthodes de fixation, application et contrôle, Geneva.

Schäfer, C.(1991), Europa sucht einen gerechten Lohn, in: WSI Mitteilungen 12.

Statistisches Bundesamt (1993), Fachserie 1: Bevölkerung und Erwerbstätigkeit, Reihe 4.2.2: Entgelte und Beschäftigungsdauer der Arbeitnehmer, last edition: Wiesbaden 1993

Wilkinson, F. (1992), Why Britain Needs a Minimum Wage, Institute for Public Policy Research, London.

Measurement of Poverty - Examplified by the German Case

Erik J. S. Plug
Peter Krause
Bernard M. S. Van Praag
Gert G. Wagner

1 Introduction

In the last decades, economists have taken a renewed interest in the poverty phenomenon (e.g. Atkinson 1974, Sen 1976, 1983, Hagenaars 1986). In the European policy context the European Commission took the lead in the European Poverty Program which first focused on action programs to alleviate poverty. The statistical agency of the EU (EUROSTAT) has also commissioned research to estimate poverty in the member states according to various poverty definitions (see Van Praag, Hagenaars and Van Weeren, 1982).

Since poverty is a metaphysical notion, we have at first to conceive of an acceptable definition which provides a measurement formula, in order to quantify the concept with reference to a specific population. There is no universally accepted poverty definition. Usually definitions are either of an objective or a subjective nature. In the objective tradition poverty is defined by experts, politicians etc. exogenously. Subjective poverty, on the other hand, is not exogenously defined but derived from stated opinions within the population on what the poverty situation stands for.

Within the objective approach one distinguishes between the relative concepts, where poverty is identified by a specific position in the relative income distribution, and the objective concepts, where poverty is identified by a specific level of command over commodities.

As there is no uniformly agreed upon definition of poverty; we compare two objective relative notions with two subjective variants. We do not consider the objective absolute variant (cf. Hauser in this volume), mainly as we do not have sufficient data for it. We follow the EUROSTAT-studies where objective absolute concepts are not used either.

An additional requirement is to be able to compare households of different sizes. Also here there is no uniformly accepted way to establish equivalence scales. In this paper we use for comparison the rather arbitrary Oxford scale, which assigns a weight of 1.0 to the first adult and 0.7 to each other adult in the family and 0.5 per child under 18 years, and the subjective scale which is derived from the data itself (cf. OECD 1976).

The unification of Germany generates unique research questions. In October 1990, the FRG had to be redefined because of the reunion. For the old GDR, even less information is available. In this paper we attempt to provide poverty estimates for the old and the new part of the FRG, based on data collected in 1992 by the German Socio-Economic Panel (GSOEP). Clearly we will be especially interested in the differences between the East and West.

In Section 2 the various poverty concepts are defined. In Section 3 we consider the results in terms of poverty lines (threshold-incomes) and resulting poverty ratios for various concepts. One of our conclusions is that in 1992 the meaning of poverty in a subjective context, i.e., the poverty line, did not differ dramatically between East and West Germany and due to a lower income level the poverty ratio referring to the East German population is about three times as high as that for the Western population[1].

In Section 4 we look at the question of how representative the answers of one respondent are for the whole household. This is a special possibility provided by GSOEP which interviews all adult members of each survey household. Thus, one of the subjective questions has been answered by male and female. Finally Section 5 concludes.

---

1 The result relates to nominal income figures. The real poverty rates in East Germany are lower according to a somewhat lower price level. But we have no exact numbers about the price differences between East and West Germany. Thus we use nominal figures.

2 Poverty Concepts

In recent years, it has become a regular idea that poverty is, at least partially, a relative phenomenon. It is argued that standards differ from society to society. This is the reason why poverty should be connected to some kind of *standard of living index* of the society. Then the linkage of poverty to the income distribution seems an obvious one. In line with Runcimans Relative Deprivation theory (1966) several poverty lines can be constructed. Given the income distribution function $F(y)$, well-known poverty lines are the *First Decile* - and the *Half Mean* poverty line.

In case of the First Decile approach, the poverty line is positioned at the lower first decile in the income distribution. It follows that ten percent of the population is considered poor by definition. The poverty line y_{FD} is defined by $y_{FD} = F^{-1}(0.1)$. The Half Mean method is based on a somewhat different idea. In this case the poverty line y_{FD} equals 50% of the average household income or in formula:

$$y_{HM} = \frac{1}{2}\int_0^\infty y dF .$$

Here the mean income reflects the standard of living within a society.

In contrast to the former methods, where the expert determines whether one is poor or not, the alternative approaches applied in this paper make use *of stated preferences* of society itself. A subjective poverty approach is embodied by the Leyden Welfare function of Income introduced by Van Praag in 1968. This function, which measures utility derived from income directly, can be regarded as an indirect utility function. The Income Evaluation Question (IEQ) developed by Van Praag (1971) presents a method to identify this Welfare Function. It makes use of the idea that different income levels can be connected to the *verbal labels* "very bad", "bad", ... , "very good" which are assumed to be representative for different welfare levels. This attitude question has the following form:

"Which monthly household after tax income would you in your circumstances consider to be very bad? Bad? Insufficient? Sufficient? Good? Very good?

About \$.........very bad.
About \$.........bad.
About \$.........insufficient.
About \$.........sufficient.
About \$.........good.
About \$.........very good."

The answers of the IEQ, denoted by c_1, c_2, c_3, c_4, c_5 and c_6, may be interpreted as realizations of points on a household cost function, see Danziger, Van der Gaag, Taussig and Smolensky (1984), Van Praag and Van der Sar (1988).

Using the Equal Interval Assumption the verbal welfare qualifications are transformed into numbers between zero and one[2] in order to come to the welfare parameters μ and μ of the Welfare Function of Income. The welfare parameters, μ_n and σ_n, of household n are defined and estimated according to:

$$(1) \qquad \mu_n = \frac{1}{6}\sum_{i=1}^{6} lnc_{in}$$

and

$$(2) \qquad \sigma_n^2 = \frac{1}{5}\sum_{i=1}^{6}\left(lnc_{in} - \mu\right)^2.$$

This function can be regarded as an indirect utility function and has the log normal shape. The household cost function equals to:

$$(3) \qquad lnc = \mu + \Phi^{-1}(u)\sigma$$

where u stands for the utility level. If utility level $\underline{u}$ represents the feeling that there is not enough to get along, someone is considered poor whenever his welfare derived from income falls below $lnc \leq \mu + \Phi^{-1}(\underline{u})\sigma$. The Leyden approach uses

2 These numbers partition the [0,1] interval in equal intervals, see also Van Doorn and Van Praag (1988), Van Praag (1991).

different welfare levels for identification of the poor. In these cases $\underline{u}$ equals to 0.4 and 0.5.

The parameter μ is best explained by the family size fs and the current net-household income y_c according to the equation:

(4) $$\mu = \beta_0 + \beta_1 \ln fs + \beta_2 \ln y_c + \varepsilon$$

where ε has the well-known econometric properties. This leads to the Leyden Poverty Line (LPL) first given in Goedhart et. al. (1977):

(5) $$\ln y_{lpl} = \frac{\beta_0 + \beta_1 \ln fs + \Phi^{-1}(\underline{u})\sigma}{1-\beta_2}.$$

Another subjective poverty approach is the Subjective Poverty Line (SPL). This method is also first proposed in Goedhart et. al. (1977), albeit under another name. In this case the poverty analysis is done based on the Minimum Income Question

> "Which monthly household after tax income would you, in your circumstances, consider as absolutely minimal? That is to say that with less you could not make ends meet.
>
> About \$.........to make ends meet."

As in the case of the Leyden method, this MIQ answer, y_{min}, may be regarded as the realization of a point on a household cost function immediately related to the poverty welfare level y_{min}, which may be described as "absolutely minimal". As in the Leyden method, the variation in y_{min} is best explained by:

(6) $$\ln y_{min} = \alpha_0 + \alpha_1 \ln fs + \alpha_2 \ln y_c + \varepsilon .$$

Similar as in equation (5), the SPL poverty line becomes:

(7) $$\ln y_{spl} = \frac{\alpha_0 + \alpha_1 \ln fs}{1-\alpha_2}.$$

We notice that the SPL is actually a simplified version of the more general LPL. Its simplicity lies in the fact that the MIQ is an easier question than the IEQ.

Household cost functions, see equation (5) and (7), do depend on the composition of the household *fs*. Using an economic point of view to explain this phenomenon, a family increase at a given income would result in a welfare decrease, as the income has to be spread over more family members. The effect of different household sizes on poverty, a state of welfare deprivation, can be expressed by household equivalence scales. Most of these equivalence scales make use of household cost functions. Given an arbitrary cost function $c_n = c(u, fs_n)$ for household fs_n, the household equivalence scale becomes:

$$(8) \qquad m_n(u, fs) = \frac{c(u, fs_n)}{c(u, fs_r)}$$

where fs_r is the reference household. For specification (5) this boils down to

$$(9) \qquad m_n(u, fs) = \left(\frac{fs_n}{fs_r}\right)^{\frac{\beta_1}{1-\beta_2}}$$

We notice that this specific scale does not depend on the utility level u. For the SPL we derive a similar scale as in (9) where the βs are replaced by αs. This exponential scale is extensively studied by Buhmann et. al. (1988).

In the next Section the empirical analysis will be presented. German data, gathered after the transition in early 1992, will be applied on the poverty concepts above.

3 Results

Data

In 1984 the German Socio-Economic Panel (GSOEP) started with a national representative sample of West Germany, using a yearly interval (cf. Wagner et al. 1993). In 1990 the panel included for the first time East Germany as well. In this paper, the questions of interest deal with subjective poverty. In the panel of 1992

Table 1: Number of households and the IEQ response

Missing levels	0	1	2	3	4	5	6	Total
East	1140	79	24	10	25	29	27	1334
West	1493	160	45	12	29	37	52	1828

the Minimum Income Question as well as the Income Evaluation Question were posed. For that reason only the information from 1992 is used.

In this first study we restrict ourselves to "standard" households. From the sample all single parent-families and one person households are excluded.

Furthermore, we notice that the investigation only concerns households where the oldest household member is younger than 66 years. From the remaining households, a number of observations had to be removed for the analysis due to (partial) non-response on the IEQ and/or the MIQ. Concerning the IEQ, Table 1 presents the number of items missing. We see that in the East 85.5%, (1140/1334), of the panel answered the IEQ fully, while 2.0% did not respond at any level. For the West these figures equal 81.7% and 2.8% respectively.

Table 2: IEQ/MIQ response rates

	Total	(West)	Response Rate
IEQ	1828	1698	92.8
MIQ_{Male}	1828	1640	89.7
MIQ_{Female}	1828	1541	84.3
	Total	(East)	Response Rate
IEQ	1334	1243	93.2
MIQ_{Male}	1334	1210	90.7
MIQ_{Female}	1334	1193	89.4

Concerning the IEQ, we applied a screening technique that allowed for some degree of incompleteness. The six IEQ answers were screened according to three criteria. The first requires that the answers are increasing, the second allows at most two answers to be missing and the third criterion states that neither the first two nor the last two answers should be missing. For a more detailed description of the screening technique, we refer to Van Praag, Flik and Stam (1992). The number of observations that is kept in the sample after screening is presented in Table 2, accompanied with the response rates. In addition to IEQ screening results, Table 2 shows also the response rates of the MIQ. Conform experience shows that the IEQ response rates are rather high. In general these rates are about eighty percent, while the German GSOEP offers response rates of above ninety percent. The same story holds for the MIQ. It is interesting to note the small difference in the response rates of the attitude questions. It seems that the IEQ performs slightly better than the MIQ.

Before we turn to the estimation results one remark has to be made concerning the MIQ and the IEQ. The MIQ answers used for analysis are those remained in the sample after the "IEQ-missings" were excluded. The analysis is concentrated on two-adult households. For that reason the sample contains only those observations where *both* parents answered the MIQ. For the West the number of observations left for MIQ analysis equals 1393 where for the East this number equals 1085.

Results

We now turn to the estimation results for the equations (4) and (6). In Table 3 the Leyden results are presented for East and West Germany after the transition.

The same Table shows the estimation results of the SPL equation for the male and female within the household. Instead of estimating these equations one by one using Ordinary Least Squares, these two equations may also be estimated simultaneously using a Seemingly Unrelated Regression method[3].

---

3 Although this case will yield SUR estimates equal to OLS estimates, see Judge et. al. (1982), the SUR method reveals information on the distribution of the disturbances of equation (6) which will be fully discussed in Section 4.

Table 3

	The Leyden Method			The SPL Method			
				East		West	
	East	West		Male	Female	Male	Female
β_0	3.35	2.93	α_0	4.75	4.59	3.90	3.94
	(22.93)	(26.33)		(22.74)	(22.08)	(24.04)	(22.82)
β_1	0.10	0.08	α_1	0.13	0.11	0.14	0.15
	(4.31)	(5.04)		(3.86)	(3.40)	(6.81)	(6.05)
β_2	0.55	0.61	α_2	0.37	0.39	0.48	0.47
	(28.93)	(44.98)		(13.43)	(14.30)	(24.36)	(22.52)
R_2	0.46	0.57		0.19	0.20	0.34	0.30
N	1243	1698		1085	1085	1393	1393

Table 4: Family Equivalence Scales

			(East)		
Family size	lpl	spl_{Male}	spl_{Female}	Half Mean	First Decile
2	1.00	1.00	1.00	1.00	1.00
3	1.09	1.09	1.08	1.29	1.29
4	1.16	1.15	1.13	1.59	1.59
5	1.22	1.20	1.18	1.88	1.88
6	1.27	1.25	1.22	2.18	2.18
			(West)		
Family size	lpl	spl_{Male}	spl_{Female}	Half Mean	First Decile
2	1.00	1.00	1.00	1.00	1.00
3	1.09	1.12	1.12	1.29	1.29
4	1.16	1.21	1.21	1.59	1.59
5	1.21	1.29	1.28	1.88	1.88
6	1.26	1.36	1.35	2.18	2.18

Table 5: Poverty Lines

				(East)		
Family size	lpl04	lpl05	spl_{Male}	spl_{Female}	Half Mean	First Decile
2	1663	2134	2198	2146	1045	1259
3	1818	2333	2333	2309	1352	1629
4	1936	2485	2485	2433	1659	2000
5	2033	2610	2610	2533	1966	2370
6	2117	2717	2716	2618	2273	2741
				(West)		
Family size	lpl04	lpl05	spl_{Male}	spl_{Female}	Half Mean	First Decile
2	1707	2200	2255	2150	1655	1826
3	1858	2394	2520	2408	2142	2363
4	1973	2542	2724	2609	2628	2900
5	2067	2664	2895	2776	3116	3437
6	2147	2767	3043	2921	3602	3974

Concerning the results of the Leyden equation we see that there is a slight difference in the β-estimates between East and West. The same is observed for the α-estimates of the SPL method. Van Praag and Van der Sar (1988) might give an explanation of the difference in preference drifts between East and West. They argue that higher welfare is correlated to a higher preference drift. Another striking point is the fact that there is hardly any difference between the α-estimates for both respondents, male or female, *within* the household. This suggests that the *stated preferences* of the adults in the household are likely to be similar. However, this phenomenon will be scrutinized in Section 4.

In order to see the effect of family size on poverty lines, we calculated the household equivalence scales for the LPL and SPL method according to equation (8).

Table 4 shows the different outcomes due to different methods[4]. For former East and West Germany the equivalence scales derived from the two subjective

4 In contrast to the subjective poverty lines presented in this paper, the Half Mean- and First Decile poverty line are considered objective scales. For that reason objective equivalence scales are desired. Therefore we apply the Oxford scale. This an additive

approaches are much flatter than the so-called objective OECD (Oxford) scales. This seems to be a property of equivalence scales derived from the subjective methods described above in comparison with the OECD scales. Furthermore, note that the Leyden and SPL scales are almost similar in East and West except for the SPL scales in the West. The results from Table 4 are reflected in Table 5 where the poverty lines are calculated according to the methods of Section 2.

First of all, we see that all the calculated *subjective* poverty lines, except for the West German SPL, are almost equal. This is in contrast to the poverty lines based only on the Western and Eastern income distributions. In these situations the objective poverty lines of former West Germany are much higher than the objective lines of East Germany. The increase of these poverty lines with household size is also reflected by the steepness of the scales. Still, differences between East and West for the subjective poverty lines are smaller than the differences between the *Half Mean* and *First Decile* methods for both regions.

Given the outline of these poverty lines, the poverty ratios are presented in Table 6. We notice that the LPL case, despite the `equal' poverty lines, yields widely different poverty ratios between East and West. Almost similar results are found for the SPL approach. This suggests that the eastern part of the German population relates its own welfare situation to that of former West Germany where a comparison between the two income distributions shows that there is a significantly different income situation. This is reflected by the First Decile approach, where equal poverty ratios yield different poverty lines.

In order to gain more information about the poor, Table 7 and 8 contain information on the composition of the poor. These Tables present information on how specific socio-economic factors can influence the state of poverty. There is some misfortune that the results presented are somewhat ambiguous. Social-economic groups are not only accompanied with a high or low poverty risk due to characteristics but also through the poverty method applied. For instance, in contrast to subjective methods, objective variants have rather steep equivalence scales. Therefore small households are frequently poorer according to the subjective methods, whereas the objective approaches focus on large households.

---

scale, recommended by the OECD, where the first adult counts for 1.0, the other adults for 0.7 and children below 18 for 0.5 respectively.

Table 6: Poverty Ratios

	West	East
lpl04	2.72	15.01
lpl05	7.94	37.13
spl_{Male}	10.08	39.37
spl_{Female}	8,36	36.89
First Decile	10.00	10.00
Half Mean	7.39	5.04

This is reflected by the figures in Table 7 and Table 8. For all the subjective methods the poverty ratios for the two person households exceed the ratios presented in Table 6 as well for the East as for the West, while the objective methods show this feature for at least the five- and more-person households.

With respect to the age of the head of the household the Western age group 55-65 behaves like a group where poverty is relatively high, independent of the applied poverty approach. The same story holds for the twenty-five and younger age group in the East. If only subjective methods are applied, both groups are considered to have a relatively high poverty risk.

The situation where households consist of two adults working full time is much more commen in the East than it is in the West (40% compared to 20.1%). We might state that in the East the need to alleviate poverty through working is more urgent than in the West. This is also expressed by the results presented in Table 7 and 8. Here the conclusions are rather straightforward. In the Western situation households where both adults are unemployed belong to "poverty risk groups", while in the East the households where both adults are employed full time are the only ones who do not belong to "poverty risk groups".

Table 7: The Poverty Ratios (East)

	Total Sample	lpl04	lpl05	spl_{Male}	spl_{Female}	Half Mean	First Decile
Family size							
2	30.60	22.85	54.48	54.88	54.48	2.30	5.65
3	35.20	12.57	31.90	32.40	31.90	5.14	9.53
4	27.70	8.25	25.21	32.23	25.21	4.88	14.37
5	5.40	20.12	35.53	35.53	31.83	17.34	26.75
≥6	1.20	21.26	30.97	30.97	27.87	21.26	35.82
Age[1]							
≤25	9.90	23.01	62.32	65.50	62.32	11.91	20.18
25-35	29.80	12.67	31.58	35.55	30.88	5.89	13.86
35-45	22.90	8.82	22.68	25.01	22.56	5.00	9.37
45-55	23.20	12.54	31.91	32.27	31.91	1.05	5.23
55-65	14.30	28.35	62.94	63.78	62.94	5.00	9.96
Labor Participation							
none	16.70	40.69	75.29	77.40	75.29	11.72	21.07
one	43.30	15.31	44.05	46.34	43.50	5.55	13.83
both	40.00	3.96	13.70	15.94	13.70	1.65	3.04
Job Uncertainty[1]							
high	37.40	6.41	26.59	29.75	26.59	1.67	4.49
some	41.70	5.47	18.35	19.79	18.35	2.76	5.82
none	20.90	5.61	18.61	18.88	17.73	1.65	3.04

The first column represents the weighted Eastern sample.

[1] For these results we considered only the head of the household.

Table 8: The Poverty Ratios (West)

	Total Sample	lpl04	lpl05	spl_{Male}	spl_{Female}	Half Mean	First Decile
Family size							
2	35.40	3.66	10.22	10.22	8.82	3.35	3.66
3	29.40	3.77	8.61	12.78	9.82	8.04	10.19
4	23.20	0.57	4.52	7.60	6.73	7.57	11.55
5	9.10	2.10	7.59	8.56	8.14	16.48	23.64
≥6	0.90	0.00	2.32	6.32	1.76	22.61	34.64
Age[1]							
≤25	5.50	3.91	11.62	16.71	11.99	8.53	9.26
25-35	27.70	2.39	6.89	9.49	8.16	7.22	10.02
35-45	27.80	1.21	3.99	6.32	5.14	6.62	9.35
45-55	23.90	1.52	5.88	7.07	5.98	6.80	9.68
55-65	15.10	7.60	19.04	20.44	17.08	9.66	12.01
Labor Participation							
none	12.70	12.85	30.44	32.28	28.58	21.75	24.05
one	67.20	1.30	5.32	7.96	6.17	6.47	9.62
both	20.10	1.11	2.54	3.22	2.93	1.42	2.48
Job Uncertainty[1]							
high	6.70	3.48	5.12	13.19	9.68	4.13	11.33
some	23.40	4.20	6.52	6.52	6.04	5.34	5.78
none	70.10	0.81	3.80	4.74	4.13	3.26	4.43

The first column represents the weighted Western sample.
[1] For these results we considered only the head of the household.

Finally, on a related topic concerning the job uncertainty experience[5]. We notice that this feeling is more experienced in the East than in the West; great uncertainty (37.4% versus 6.7%) and some uncertainty (41.7% compared to 23.4%). However, the people who experience high job-uncertainty will have a relatively higher probability to be poor in the West, except for the Half Mean and the LPL05 approach. This feature might be explained by the fact that job-

5 In this group only the employed are considered.

uncertainty is a more accepted part of the daily life in East Germany and therefore less of a threat when poverty is considered.

4 Father and Mother

Dealing with subjective measures, we normally have to assume that the respondents' feelings towards income, operationalized through the discussed "attitude" questions, are representative of the family's welfare. Hartog (1988) considers this assumption as a major omission in the subjective approach. He wonders whether different members of the household agree on their evaluation of the household situation. As our German sample contains subjective information for different members within one household, it creates the possibility to test whether the *stated preferences* of different household members within one household are the same.

Turning to the equations in question, again the minimum income of the male is best explained by:

$$(10) \quad \ln y^m_{\min} = \alpha^m_0 + \alpha^m_1 \ln fs + \alpha^m_2 \ln y_c + \varepsilon^m$$

where a similar equation for the female reads

$$(11) \quad \ln y^f_{\min} = \alpha^f_0 + \alpha^f_1 \ln fs + \alpha^f_2 \ln y_c + \varepsilon^f$$

The disturbances ε^m and δ^f are assumed to follow a normal distribution with an expectation of o and covariance σ. This matrix is shaped such that:

$$(12) \quad \sigma = \begin{pmatrix} \sigma^2_m & \rho\sigma_m\sigma_f \\ \rho\sigma_m\sigma_f & \sigma^2_f \end{pmatrix}$$

In Table 3 the SUR estimates for the parameters of both equations are presented, while in this Section equation (12) is quantified through Table 9. This Table shows that the variance of the disturbances for man and women in the East are equal, where in the West the variance for women is a bit smaller. We note that the

Table 9: Covariance σ

	West	East
σ_m	0.30 (52.53)	0.31 (55.05)
σ_f	0.28 (52.10)	0.31 (46.61)
ρ	0.73 (57.82)	0.81 (79.06)

positive ρ indicates a positive linear relation between the disturbances ε^m and ε^f of the mother and father within the household.

The positive ρ in combination with the results of Table 3 suggests that there is only a slight difference in the α^m- and the α^f-estimates. In order to test whether the stated preferences of different genders within the household are equal we proceed as follows. Using equation (11), we find:

$$(13) \quad \ln y_{\min}^m - \ln y_{\min}^f = \left(\alpha_0^m - \alpha_0^f\right) + \left(\alpha_1^m - \alpha_1^f\right)\ln fs + \left(\alpha_2^m - \alpha_2^f\right)\ln y_c + \varepsilon^m - \varepsilon^f$$

Using reduced form coefficients we find:

$$(14) \quad \ln y_{\min}^m - \ln y_{\min}^f = \gamma_0 + \gamma_1 \ln fs + \gamma_2 \ln y_c + v$$

Table 10: The SPL Method

	West	East
γ_0	-0.04 (-0.28)	0.16 (1.30)
γ_1	-0.01 (-0.32)	0.02 (0.79)
γ_2	0.01 (0.55)	-0.02 (-1.25)
N	1393	1085

t-values in parentheses

where ν is normally distributed such that this equation can be estimated according to the Ordinary Least Squares (OLS) method.

If our hypothesis is true, we should find that $\gamma_0 = \gamma_1 = \gamma_2 = 0$. We now turn to the results. The OLS estimates for the parameters of equation (14) are shown in Table 10.

In view of the hypothesis posed, the most striking result is the insignificance of all the reduced form coefficients. Therefore we may assume that it does not matter if father or mother is the one who is interviewed. Father and mother share the same stated preferences with respect to the MIQ.

5 Concluding Remarks

In order to come to an operational concept of poverty we are using subjective approaches embodied by the Leyden method and the Subjective poverty method and relative methods embodied by the First Decile and Half Mean method.

During the last two decades, one major point of criticism had to do with the fact that subjective methods use data on hypothetical situations whereas the traditional economic methods use data based only on 'revealed preferences' or actual behavior. A drawback of using hypothetical information is considered to be that the assumed consistency; to what extent are the stated preferences of one member of the household representative for the *whole* family? The results imply that the representative assumption holds for the subjective analysis.

We applied the different approaches to German data after the transition. The analysis of poverty in the unified Germany is of special interest for two reasons. First, the unification of two societies with different welfare levels is of great interest for politicians as well as for scientists. Second, the German Socio-Economic Panel Study (GSOEP) provides data which makes possible the comparison of quite different poverty measurement methods.

As to be expected, different methods yield different poverty lines. However, it is interesting to see that the former East Germans use the former West as their point of reference with respect to their welfare perception. Among other methods, this is reflected by the LPL method. Despite the 'equal' poverty perception, the actual standard of living is different. Eastern Germans have less money income to spend than the Western Germans. Even if no distinction is made between the former East Germany and West Germany and feelings towards income are treated as equal, the poverty perception between the two parts of Germany reveals the difference.

Appendix

All the discussed information is based on two distinct data sets, namely one for the former East Germany and one for the former West despite the fact that the information has been gathered after unification. Therefore it is interesting to see what would happen if the analysis is done under the assumption that Germany is treated as one nation. In this situation the two separate data sets are transformed into one German data set containing 2941 observations.

Table A1 presents the estimates of the equations (4) and (6). If these estimates are compared with those from Table 3, we find that the results for the total sample are very similar to the results coming from theFamilysize analysis on Western data only. However, given the small differences between the estimates of Table A1 and Table 3, it is no surprise that the unified equivalence scales and poverty lines for the German sample calculated according the Leyden approach are about 'equal' to the scales and lines for West Germany only. The SPL results fall between the Western and Eastern SPL scales and lines. The equivalence scales and poverty lines are presented in Table A2 and A3.

Table A1

The Leyden Method		The SPL Method		
			Male	Female
β_0	2.98 (38.37)	α_0	3.98 (35.02)	3.99 (34.18)
β_1	0.08 (6.05)	α_1	0.12 (6.19)	0.12 (6.11)
β_2	0.61 (62.43)	α_2	0.47 (33.38)	0.47 (32.20)
ρ			0.78	0.78
R_2	0.59		0.34	0.34
N	2941		2478	2478

Table A4: The Poverty Ratios

	Germany	West	East
Total Sample		25.96	75.04
lpl04	5.74	64.90	35.10
lpl05	15.41	63.77	36.23
spl_{Male}	17.68	62.43	37.57
spl_{Female}	14.53	63.80	36.20
First Decile	9.98	59.63	40.37
Half Mean	8.42	61.36	38.64

Table A2: Family Equivalence Scales (Germany)

Family size	lpl04	lpl05	spl_{Male}	spl_{Female}	Half Mean	First Decile
2	1.00	1.00	1.00	1.00	1.00	1.00
3	1.09	1.09	1.10	1.10	1.29	1.29
4	1.15	1.15	1.17	1.17	1.59	1.59
5	1.21	1.21	1.23	1.23	1.88	1.88
6	1.25	1.25	1.28	1.28	2.18	2.18

Table A3: Poverty Lines (Germany)

Family size	lpl04	lpl05	spl_{Male}	spl_{Female}	Half Mean	First Decile
2	1685	2180	2235	2145	1503	1574
3	1826	2364	2443	2345	1945	2037
4	1933	2502	2602	2499	2387	2499
5	2021	2616	2733	2625	2829	2963
6	2096	2713	2844	2733	3271	3426

Even though the results are almost equal to the West German calculations, it is interesting to see what happens to the poverty ratios and composition of people who are considered poor with respect to one of the old "Bundesländer". Also in this case the poverty ratios show more affinity with the Western poverty ratios and as to be expected Table A4 shows that Germans who live in the East belong to a poverty risk group.

References

Atkinson, A. Poverty and Income in Britain. In Wedderburn, D., editor, Poverty, Inequality and Class Structure. Cambridge University Press, London, 1974

Buhmann, B., L. Rainwater, G. Schmauss and T.J. Smeeding, "Equivalence Scales, Well-Being, Inequality and Poverty: Sensitivity Estimates Across Ten Countries using the LIS Data Base", Review of Income and Wealth, 34, 115-142, 1988.

Danziger, S., J. Van der Gaag, M.K. Taussig and E. Smolensky, "The direct measurement of welfare levels: How much does it cost to make ends meet?", The Review of Economics and Statistics , 66, 500--505, 1984.

Goedhart, Th., V. Halberstadt, A. Kapteyn and B.M.S van Praag, "The poverty line: Concept and measurement", The Journal of Human Resources, 12, 503-520, 1977.

Hagenaars, A.J.M., The Perception of Poverty, Amsterdam: Noth-Holland, 1986.

Hartog, J., "Poverty and the Measurement of Individual Welfare", Journal of Human Resources, 23, 243-266, 1988.

Judge, G. G., R. Hill, W. Griffiths, H. Lütkepohl and T. Lee, Introduction to the Theory and Practice of Econometrics, Wiley: New-York, 1982.

Kapteyn, A., "The Measurement of Household Equivalence Scales: Revealed Preference versus Subjective Measures", presented at the ESPE conference in Budapest, 1993.

OECD, "Public Expenditures on Income Maintenance Programs", Studies in Resource Allocation, 3, 1976.

Pollak, R.A. and T.J. Wales, "Equity; the Individual versus Family. Welfare comparisons and Equivalence Scales", American Economic Review, 69, 216-221, 1979.

Runciman, W.G., Relative Deprivation and Social Justice, London: Rowledge and Kegan Paul, 1966.

Sen, A., "Poverty: an Ordinal Approach to Measurement", Econometrica, 44, 219-231, 1976.

Sen, A., "Poor, Relatively Speaking", Oxford Economic Papers, 35, 135-169, 1983.

Van Doorn, L. and B.M.S. Van Praag. The Measurement of Income Satisfaction. In Saris, W.E. and I.N. Gallhofer, editors, Sociometric Research. Mcmillan Press, Houndsmill, 1988.

Van Praag, B.M.S., Individual Welfare Functions and Consumer Behavior, Amsterdam: North-Holland, 1968.

Van Praag, B.M.S., "The Welfare Function of Income in Belgium: An Empirical Investigation", European Economic Review, 2, 337--369, 1971.

Van Praag, B.M.S., "Further Evidence on the Individual Welfare Function of Income: An Empirical Study in the Netherlands, European Economic Review, 4, 33-62, 1973.

Van Praag, B.M.S., "Ordinal and Cardinal Utility: An Integration of the Two Dimensions of the Welfare Concept", Journal of Econometrics, 50, 69--89, 1991.

Van Praag, B.M.S. and N.L. Van der Sar, "Household Cost Functions and Equivalence Scales", Journal of Human Resources, 23, 139-210, 1988.

Van Praag, B.M.S., R.J. Flik and P.J.A. Stam, "Poverty Lines and Equivalence Scales: A Theoretical and Empirical Evaluation". To be published in the proceedings of the Research Conference on Poverty and Distribution. Scandinavian University Press, Oslo, 1992.

Van Praag, B.M.S., A. Hagenaars and J van Weeren, "Poverty in Europe", The Review of Income and Wealth, 28, 345-359, 1982.

Wagner, G. G., R. V. Burkhauser and F. Behringer, The English Language Public Use Version of the German Socio-economic Panel, The Journal of Human Resources, 28, 329-333, 1993.

Poverty and Social Security Transfers - Results for Seven Countries and Regions in the EC

Karel van den Bosch, Lieve De Lathouwer and Herman Deleeck

1 Introduction

This paper presents comparative results on poverty and social security in seven countries and regions of the European Community (E.C.). The countries and regions are Belgium, The Netherlands, Luxembourg, Lorraine (region of France), Ireland, Catalonia (region of Spain) and Greece. We compare the incidence of poverty across countries, as well as the distribution of poverty across social and economic categories of the population within these countries. In addition, the impact of social security transfers on poverty is examined.

Previous studies have mostly used relative poverty lines, where both the level and the equivalence scale are essentially arbitrary. In addition to a relative standard, we have also applied subjective income thresholds, which are based on assessments of minimum income needs by the population itself, and the legal or official poverty standards, which are derived from the social security system.

The results in this paper have been collected in a collaborative project by researchers in the participating countries.[1]

---

1 The project, called EUROPASS (European Research On Poverty And Social Security), was conducted by research groups from seven countries: Centre for Social Policy (CSP), University of Antwerp (UFSIA), Antwerp, Belgium; Institute for Social Research (IVA), Tilburg, The Netherlands; Centre d'Etude de Populations, de Pauvreté et de Politiques Socio-Economiques (CEPS), Walferdange, Luxembourg; equipe de recherche pour l'Analyse Dynamique des Effets des Politiques Sociales (ADEPS), Université de Nancy II, Nancy, Lorraine; Economic and Social Research Institute (ESRI), Dublin, Ireland; Gabinet d'Estudis Socials (GES), Barcelona; National Center for Social Research (NCSR), Athens, Greece.
The project leaders in the respective countries were: Prof. Dr. H. Deleeck (Belgium), R. Muffels, Prof. Dr. J. Berghman, Prof. Dr. A. Kapteyn (The Netherlands), Prof. Dr.

The plan of the paper is as follows. After a brief discussion of the data and some important concepts in Section 2, we introduce the poverty lines in Section 3. In Section 4, we compare the incidence of poverty across countries and across social categories. Somewhat preliminary results on the mobility between poverty and non-poverty are presented in Section 5. In Section 6, we examine the impact of social security cash transfers on poverty. Section 6 concludes with a brief summary of the important empirical results.

2 Data and the Concepts of Household and Income

The data come from socio-economic household surveys in the several countries and regions. In Belgium, The Netherlands, Luxembourg, Lorraine and Ireland these surveys were part of household panels, of which two waves could be used for an analysis of poverty mobility. In the rest of the paper we use data only for a single year for each country, as the time between waves was too short to produce any interesting developments. The major topics of the questionnaires were income, labor market participation and demographic characteristics, while questions were also asked about subjective income evaluation and about the presence of some goods and conveniences in the household. Though sampling procedures varied across countries, all resulted in random samples of households. Appendix 1 provides some key information about methods used and characteristics of the samples.

Though the exact definitions of the concept of household are not the same in all countries (cf. Deleeck et al., 1992, Appendix C), they all boil down to the following: a group of related or unrelated persons who live in the same dwelling and share meals and/or a common budget. Probably the greatest difference occurs in the treatment of students who live in rooms, but come home regularly. In The

G. Schaber (Luxembourg), Prof. Dr. J.-C. Ray 5 (Lorraine), Prof. Dr. B. Whelan (Ireland), Prof. Dr. J. Estivill (Catalonia) and Prof. Dr. J. Yfantopoulos (Greece).
The Centre of Social Policy at the University of Antwerp coordinated the project. Funding was provided by the Commission of the EC, within the framework of the Second Community Action Programme to Combat Poverty, and by national funding. A full report of the study is contained in Deleeck et al. (1992). A methodologically oriented summary is in Van den Bosch et al. (1993).

Netherlands and Lorraine they are regarded as separate households; in the other countries they are treated as members of their parents' household.

The income concept in this paper is disposable household cash income, i.e. it includes social security transfers, and is net of taxes and social security contributions. Income in-kind is not included. For Lorraine, however, the income measure is household income before government taxes, but excluding social security contributions[2]. The household income variable has been built up from the answers to detailed questions about all possible sources of income of all persons in the household.

All income amounts in this paper are monthly amounts. The original income questions asked for weekly, monthly or yearly amounts, as seemed most appropriate in each country and for the kind of income concerned (e.g. yearly for interests, monthly for salaries). In many instances, the respondent could choose between several reference periods. All amounts have been recalculated to a monthly base, as this seemed to be the most common denominator. For more details on the income variables, we refer to Deleeck et al. (1992, Appendix C).

As in most poverty studies, we assume that the distribution of goods and services within households is such, that either all household members are poor, or none of them.

3 Poverty Lines

One of the most difficult problems in international comparative poverty research is how to set comparable poverty lines in the various countries. There are a number of different methods, which correspond to different concepts of poverty, and which imply different ways to translate a poverty line from one country to another. At the present moment, it seems premature to make a choice between the various methods. Callan and Nolan (1991, p. 258), in a review of poverty line methods, conclude that "each faces formidable problems and objections, at both conceptual and empirical levels", and that "nothing approaching consensus on the

---

2 The French tax system is so complex, that it does not make sense to ask people for their after-tax incomes, nor is it regarded as feasible to estimate after-tax incomes through micro-simulation.

measurement of poverty appears to be emerging". Given this situation, the best strategy appears to be to use several methods, so that any conclusions do not depend on a single approach. If several methods are in agreement, however, reasonably robust conclusions may still be drawn.

In this study we use a relative, an official, and two subjective poverty lines. *Subjective standards* are based on the views of respondents in a sample survey on minimum income needs. The method therefore takes account of the fact that poverty is a socially constructed category, and is not something that can be determined by an outside observer without regard to the circumstances and values in the surrounding society. Two specific subjective methods are applied. The first method is the one introduced by Goedhart et al. (1977), which we will call the SPL (Subjective Poverty Line), following Kapteyn, Van de Geer and Van de Stadt (1985). The other method has been developed independently around 1976 by the Centre for Social Policy at Antwerp University (Deleeck a.o., 1980; cf. Deleeck, 1989). Below, it will be referred to as the 'CSP-method'. The related but more complex Leyden Poverty Line (Van Praag, 1991, Van Praag et al., 1982, ; Hagenaars, 1986) is not used in this study. (For a methodological comparison of the SPL, the CSP-method and the LPL, see Flik and Van Praag, 1991.)

The SPL is based on survey responses to the Minimum Income Question (MIQ), which reads: "What is the minimum amount of income that your family, in your circumstances, needs to be able to make ends meet?" By estimating the parameters of an equation relating the answer to this question to household income and family size, minimum income thresholds can be derived. The CSP-standard also uses the Minimum Income Question (MIQ), and in addition the following question: "With your current income, can you get by: with great difficulty, with difficulty, with some difficulty, fairly easily, easily, or very easily?" The poverty lines is calculated as the average of the answer to the MIQ or actual household income (whichever is smaller), across those households (differentiated by type) who have answered "with some difficulty" to the above question. For further details we refer to Deleeck et al. (1992) or Van den Bosch et al. (1993).

The *relative standard* is defined, following O'Higgins and Jenkins (1990), as 50% of average equivalent income. This is the poverty line for a single person; the amounts for other household types are calculated on the basis of the following equivalence factors recommended by the OECD (1982): 1.0 for the first adult, 0.7

Table 3.1: Geometric means of social subsistence minima in ECU in prices of Jan. 1988, monthly amounts

		CSP-standard	SPL-standard	EC-standard	LEGAL-standard
Belgium (B)	1985	767	801	547	457
Netherlands (NL)	1986	708	764	645	681
Luxembourg (L)	1986	996	932	852	693
Lorraine (Lor.)	1986	835	855	599	430
Ireland (IRL)	1987	552	570	418	376
Catalonia (Cat.)	1988	764	956	552	-
Greece (GR)	1988	607	669	366	-

for each additional adult and 0.5 for each child (i.e. each person below 18 years *or* in full-time education); in Greece however, the factor of 0.7 was also used for children. Because this standard is an elaboration of the one used in the first Programme to Combat Poverty of the European Community, we call it the EC-standard, without implying that it is any way an official standard of the EC. The *legal or official poverty line* is defined as the level of income guaranteed in social security or social assistance to all or almost all citizens in each country. For further details we refer to Deleeck et al. (1992), and Appendix D.

To compare the resulting poverty thresholds, we discuss first the overall levels of the poverty lines, and then the equivalence scales. To represent the overall *level* of a poverty line, we have used the geometric mean of the amounts[3] (Table 3.1). In all countries, the subjective standards are the most generous ones. The legal standard is below the relative EC-standard, except in The Netherlands. In

[3] The amounts are expressed in constant European Currency Units (ECUs) of January 1988. Adjustments for differences in price levels between countries have been made using unpublished purchasing power parities for household consumption provided by Eurostat (for further details see Deleecket al., 1992, Appendix B). The geometric mean is used, because the proportional difference between two geometric means can be interpreted as the average proportional difference between the two series from which the means are computed.

Table 3.2: The steepness of the equivalence scales: elasticities of poverty lines with respect to household size

		CSP-standard	SPL-standard	EC-standard	LEGAL-standard
B	1985	0.40	0.27	0.71	0.42
NL	1986	0.29	0.27	0.71	0.36
L	1986	0.38	0.28	0.71	0.36
LOR.	1986	0.49	0.30	0.71	0.54
IRL	1987	0.64	0.44	0.71	0.67
CAT.	1988	0.55	0.36	0.71	-
GR	1988	0.29	0.44	0.82	-

Catalonia and Greece, no national guaranteed minimum income exists, so the official poverty line is not defined.

The EC-standard, being relative by definition, is lowest in Greece and Ireland, highest in Luxembourg, and at an intermediate level in Catalonia, Lorraine, The Netherlands and Belgium. The average levels of the subjective poverty lines follow a roughly similar pattern across countries. Nevertheless, the difference between the highest and lowest values is smaller than with the EC-standard, suggesting that the subjective poverty lines are only partly relative (i.e. an increase in the average living standard results in a less than proportional increase in the subjective standards). There are some deviations from this general trend: the relatively high level of the SPL in Catalonia, and the relatively low level of the CSP and SPL poverty lines in The Netherlands. There is no ready explanation for this.

As an indicator of the steepness of the *equivalence scales*, the elasticities of the poverty lines with respect to household size[4] are used (Table 3.2). The

[4] These are estimated using the equation: log (poverty line$_i$) = a + e*log (household size$_i$) + U_i , where e is the elasticity of the poverty line with respect to household size, U_i is the error term, and i is a subscript that runs across the types of household mentioned in Table 1. For the CSP poverty lines, a dummy variable, indicating

equivalence scales of the subjective standards are much flatter than the scale build into the E.C.-standard, which has an elasticity of 0.71. The equivalence scale implicit in the guaranteed minimum incomes also tends to be steeper than the subjective scales. This finding is typical of scales based on subjective income evaluations, as Buhmann a.o. (1988) show in a review of a large number of equivalence scales.

4 The Incidence and Characteristics of Poverty

In this section results are presented on the incidence of poverty, as defined by the various standards, for the countries and regions as a whole, and disaggregated by a number of variables. We also discuss the characteristics of the poor, i.e. the social composition of the group of households below the poverty line. The legal standard is not used for the disaggregated results on poverty, because it is not defined for all countries, and in other countries the number of households below the legal poverty lines is sometimes too small to get meaningful results. The disadvantages of the "headcount" measure of poverty are recognized (it does not take into account how far people are below the poverty line, cf. Sen, 1976), but it seems unlikely that the results would be very different if a more sophisticated measure of poverty had been used. Perhaps a more serious shortcoming is that households are counted, instead of individuals. There seems to be no good reason why the poverty measure should increase more when two poor single persons enter poverty, than when a couple with two children does so.

On the basis of the 'EC'-standard, the countries and regions can be divided into two groups: on the one hand the Benelux countries, with a relatively low poverty rate, and on the other hand Catalonia, Ireland and Greece, where the poverty incidence is at least twice as high (Table 4.1). Lorraine is situated in between these groups. These results are broadly in agreement with studies by Eurostat (1990) and by O'Higgins and Jenkins (1990), who present estimates for all EC-countries. It is noteworthy that, although only half of all EC-countries are

---

whether the head of household is elderly, was added to the equation (results for this term not shown).

Table 4.1: Proportion of all households in poverty

		CSP-standard	SPL-standard	EC-standard	LEGAL-standard
B	1985	21.4	24.9	6.1	2.9
NL	1986	10.9	15.9	7.2	7.2
L	1986	14.5	12.5	7.6	5.0
LOR.	1986	30.8	26.5	10.8	4.0
IRL	1987	29.6	31.6	17.2	8.1
CAT.	1988	31.3	37.3	15.1	-
GR	1988	42.6	42.0	19.9	-

represented in this study, these include some of the 'richest' as well as some of the poorest ones.

The estimates based on the SPL and CSP standards are much, often very much, higher than those obtained with the EC-standard. Roughly, they follow the same pattern: the southern countries, Greece and Catalonia, and Ireland have the highest rates of poor households, while the Benelux countries have the lowest ones. But within the Benelux countries, the subjective poverty rates are much higher in Belgium than in The Netherlands and Luxembourg, while the poverty rates based on the EC-standard are virtually the same for all Benelux countries. This is, of course, mainly a result of the differences in the levels of the subjective standards.

The poverty rates produced by the legal standard follow a rather different pattern. Ireland has the highest poverty rate, followed by The Netherlands, Luxembourg, Lorraine and Belgium. Except perhaps for Belgium, these percentages might appear rather high, considering that it involves a guaranteed minimum income. In the case of Luxembourg and Lorraine the probable explanation is that in both countries the guaranteed minimum income was not yet in effect in 1986. In Ireland, some groups are not covered by the guaranteed income scheme, such as students, some self-employed persons and some full-time employees. Most of the households below the legal minimum, however, do not take up support to which they are entitled, possibly because of lack of information

(Callan, Nolan a.o., 1989, p. 151). In The Netherlands, the guaranteed minimum income covers the whole population. Reasons for households falling below the official minimum could include punitive cuts in benefits and non-take up of certain small extra allowances.

We now turn to the question, which are the groups at high risk of poverty? There is unfortunately no simple answer to this question, not only because the characteristics of the poor vary considerably across countries, but also because there are important differences according to the poverty standard used. These differences depend in particular on the equivalence scale of the standard. The poverty risks for a selected number of interesting categories are reported in tables 4.2-4.4. In the discussion we will mainly consider *relative* risks: poverty risk in a category, compared with the average risk for the sample of that country as a whole.

A consistent finding by all standards and for all countries is that households where the head is *unemployed* face a very high risk of poverty. When the head is *sick or disabled*, the risk is lower, though still considerable above average. The results for households where the head is *retired* are rather mixed: using the EC-standard, these households are at relatively high risk of poverty only in Catalonia, while their risk is considerably below average in Ireland and The Netherlands. By the subjective standards, especially the SPL, their relative risk of poverty is much higher, and only in Ireland and Lorraine by the CSP-standard does it not exceed the average risk.

Similarly inconsistent results are found in general for households where the head is *elderly* (65+) and/or *widowed*. Nevertheless, it appears that in Ireland the elderly are no more than at average risk, while in Catalonia, and also in Belgium, a large proportion of these households is in poverty, relative to the overall poverty rate. The discrepancy in the results of the different standards is particularly striking for The Netherlands. Similar patterns are found for *female-headed* households, probably because many of these females are in fact widows.

Looking at the non-elderly, we find that in Belgium, The Netherlands, Luxembourg and Ireland, *single persons* are at relatively high risk of poverty by the subjective standards, but not by the EC-standard. In the northern countries the poverty rate among *very young householders* (16-24 years) is relatively high by all standards. *Divorced or separated* heads of household are in most countries at relatively high risk of poverty, except in Lorraine and in Luxembourg by the

Table 4.2: The incidence of poverty in a selected number of social categories by the CSP-standard

% in poverty	B 1985	NL 1986	L 1986	LOR. 1986	IRL 1987	CAT. 1988	GR 1988
all households	21.4	10.9	14.5	30.8	29.6	31.3	42.6
head of household is:							
employed	11.6	3.4	9.5	26.1	20.0	23.7	39.7
retired	29.8	16.4	15.0	29.1	18.1	40.3	46.5
unemployed	61.4	42.9	61.9	64.3	74.7	63.4	72.7
sick/disabled	38.0	28.6	40.0	46.9	61.1	63.4	-
farmer	21.3	25.4	16.4	47.6	42.6	36.5	56.6
16-24 years	32.4	20.3	32.3	45.3	42.5	27.2	46.5
65-74 years	25.9	14.4	18.0	21.2	20.7	33.2	47.7
75+ years	38.0	16.7	16.3	39.3	13.9	51.9	48.4
widow/widower	33.0	23.4	19.1	42.0	23.5	47.0	57.1
divorced or separated	30.3	16.9	13.9	25.4	53.4	33.6	51.4
female	33.7	20.6	24.1	44.3	26.5	40.6	54.5
Type of household[1]:							
single elderly person	36.7	22.8	25.7	41.9	27.0	46.2	55.9
two elderly persons	27.3	8.1	13.3	23.3	14.7	38.4	51.0
single adult	29.9	23.0	20.8	29.7	44.4	27.9	45.1
single adult, one child	51.7	3.3	47.0	38.1	45.6	42.9	45.5
single adult, two children	24.6	8.0	28.2	41.2	59.6	36.4	33.3
two adults, three children	12.5	4.3	5.5	32.2	39.0	40.5	42.6
only one income provider	33.3	14.9	20.7	40.5	39.5	48.1	47.5
no persons at work	40.7	27.1	26.4	42.1	51.7	57.8	53.1

[1] adult = non-elderly adult

Table 4.3: The incidence of poverty in a number of social categories by the SPL-standard

% in poverty	B 1985	NL 1986	L 1986	LOR. 1986	IRL 1987	CAT. 1988	GR 1988
all households	24.9	15.9	12.5	26.5	31.6	37.3	42.0
head of household is:							
employed	9.4	4.3	3.8	16.5	15.8	26.8	35.6
retired	47.2	29.0	16.5	35.9	35.2	58.6	54.2
unemployed	59.2	51.0	52.4	58.9	67.3	64.9	75.8
sick/disabled	34.6	28.4	25.1	31.2	57.0	61.0	-
farmer	21.3	23.7	6.3	37.5	38.5	38.9	53.4
16-24 years	40.1	40.9	26.7	42.8	38.6	33.3	50.0
65-74 years	46.1	25.6	30.4	36.4	40.3	53.6	39.5
75+ years	65.1	34.7	29.3	52.4	43.8	75.6	63.7
widow/widower	55.2	42.6	31.7	54.4	52.0	64.0	59.7
divorced or separated	34.4	32.8	12.4	34.5	58.6	44.3	49.1
female	51.9	39.2	33.2	57.4	50.0	56.2	56.9
Type of household[1]:							
single elderly person	67.7	47.8	46.0	72.6	70.2	85.9	70.5
two elderly persons	50.3	14.2	17.8	32.5	28.4	78.6	70.7
single adult	40.6	38.6	19.2	43.7	52.5	39.9	35.8
single adult, one child	54.0	33.9	47.0	52.4	67.6	52.4	44.1
single adult, two children	26.1	30.0	28.2	41.2	68.1	72.7	36.4
two adults, three children	6.2	5.9	0.9	18.2	36.1	50.6	47.5
only one income provider	40.7	23.5	19.5	39.1	45.1	60.5	48.3
no persons at work	55.8	41.7	33.6	50.6	68.2	77.0	62.8

[1] adult = non-elderly adult

Table 4.4: The incidence of poverty in a number of social categories by the EC-standard

% in poverty	B 1985	NL 1986	L 1986	LOR. 1986	IRL 1987	CAT. 1988	GR 1988
all households	6.1	7.2	7.6	10.8	17.2	15.1	19.9
head of household is:							
employed	2.9	5.2	5.5	6.8	11.9	9.0	19.1
retired	6.6	2.4	7.4	9.3	7.9	22.1	21.7
unemployed	26.2	19.4	40.9	41.0	58.9	43.5	36.4
sick/disabled	10.7	10.0	19.6	22.9	24.4	40.7	-
farmer	17.0	23.7	7.7	19.7	32.0	20.0	36.5
16-24 years	11.6	19.5	17.6	14.7	31.4	7.9	10.9
65-74 years	6.9	2.4	7.6	6.3	8.4	18.2	18.1
75+ years	9.2	2.5	7.8	18.6	4.1	36.9	29.0
widow/widower	4.6	2.3	5.3	15.4	6.6	27.3	22.0
divorced or separated	9.1	8.5	11.6	11.7	33.1	21.2	27.0
female	6.3	6.9	9.0	19.1	10.1	23.4	21.1
Type of household[1]**:**							
single elderly person	5.0	1.6	7.1	19.3	3.0	29.3	24.1
two elderly persons	11.3	3.2	11.5	9.2	8.4	30.2	33.7
single adult	5.8	8.5	7.0	12.5	20.3	10.1	7.4
single adult, one child	7.5	3.3	25.6	9.5	19.3	23.8	30.3
single adult, two children	13.0	14.0	32.9	23.5	61.0	18.2	24.2
two adults, three children	8.5	19.1	17.4	13.1	34.3	17.7	37.6
only one income provider	8.9	9.2	9.5	13.9	22.7	24.7	18.9
no persons at work	11.8	11.6	12.7	19.7	30.2	35.2	23.9

[1] adult = non-elderly adult

subjective standards. Very high relative poverty rates are also found for *one-parent families*, though there are several exceptions, notably in The Netherlands. In Ireland *two parent families with three or more children* are at high relative risk of poverty by all standards, while for The Netherlands, Luxembourg and Greece this is only true by the EC-standard.

A somewhat different perspective on poverty is provided when we look at the *composition of the population in poverty*. Some social categories are important among the poor, even though their risk of poverty is relatively low, simply because they form a large part of the population. Other groups with a high rate of poverty, but which are few in numbers, may form only a small minority among the poor. (The focus is here on the characteristics of the poor; to save space these distributions are not given for the non-poor, but the differences can to some extent be gathered from the poverty risk figures in Tables 4.2-4.4.)

In many cases, of course, the circumstances and characteristics mentioned only result in poverty if they occur in combination with each other. For a particular poor household, several of its characteristics could be designated as the cause of its poverty. Which factor is singled out then depends on the perspective taken. Nevertheless, these univariate results already provide some clues to the most important proximate causes of poverty in EC-countries.

The divergences between the standards used again make it difficult to obtain a clear picture of the characteristics of the poor. Nevertheless, the following observations seem to be warranted (Tables 4.5-4.7).

In very many poor households the *head of household is working*. By the strict EC-standard this is the case for around 40% of all poor households, except in Belgium where the proportion of working poor heads of household seems to be somewhat lower, and in Greece where it is considerably higher. By the subjective standards fewer among the poor households in Belgium, The Netherlands and Luxembourg have working heads. At this point it is unclear why so many households with working heads are in poverty. A large number of causes may be involved, and these need not be the same in all countries. We can identify two factors, however. First, because in the northern countries three-quarters or more of all poor households by any standard have only one, or no, income provider, it seems reasonable to assume that in the majority of working poor households the head is the only breadwinner. Cantillon (1991) has pointed out the problematic situation of one-income families in countries where double incomes are becoming

Table 4.5: The characteristics of the poor: percentage of poor households having selected characteristics, using the CSP-standard

% in poverty	B 1985	NL 1986	L 1986	LOR. 1986	IRL 1987	CAT. 1988	GR 1988
Head of household							
at work	32.7	20.0	41.0	52.1	39.1	51.6	65.4
(farmer)	0.7	3.0	1.8	2.9	17.3	3.3	26.0
retired	40.5	28.9	18.2	25.2	8.9	24.0	25.8
unemployed	15.8	18.1	3.0	8.4	26.8	8.9	1.9
65 years or older	29.5	22.1	26.2	18.8	14.5	21.6	22.7
Type of household							
One parent households	4.4	1.2	6.0	2.8	4.3	1.4	2.0
Two adults[1] + two children	10.4	6.8	8.6	13.2	14.0	12.0	11.9
Two adults[1] + three children	3.2	2.9	1.7	6.2	24.2	3.4	4.8
Number of income providers: 0 or 1	78.6	77.6	82.7	72.3	82.2	59.8	52.0

[1] adult = non-elderly person

the norm. Secondly, it is important to note that in countries where a large part of the population is employed in agriculture (here Greece and Ireland), many of the poor are in *farmer's* households.

In several countries, *unemployed* heads of household are an important group among the poor. This is true in particular for Ireland, to a lesser extent for Belgium, and also for The Netherlands, Lorraine and Catalonia. In all countries unemployment benefits seem to be inadequate for many, if not most unemployed heads of households. The variation across countries is mainly related to the varying proportion of these households in the entire population.

Households where the head is *retired* and/or elderly are in most countries an important group among the poor, though by no means a majority. Inadequate retirement and survival pensions for *some* elderly are still an important cause of poverty. In Ireland, however, the retired and elderly seem to form only a small minority among the poor. Using the EC-standard, this is also true for the

Table 4.6: The characteristics of the poor: percentage of poor households having selected characteristics, using the SPL-standard

% in poverty	B 1985	NL 1986	L 1986	LOR. 1986	IRL 1987	CAT. 1988	GR 1988
Head of household							
at work	22.8	17.3	19.0	38.3	28.9	49.6	59.5
(farmer)	0.6	1.9	0.8	2.7	14.6	2.9	24.9
retired	55.2	35.0	23.2	36.2	16.2	29.2	30.5
unemployed	13.1	14.8	2.9	8.9	22.6	7.7	2.0
65 years or older	44.4	28.7	22.1	32.3	9.5	28.1	29.2
Type of household							
One parent households	4.0	4.9	6.9	4.0	5.0	1.8	2.1
Two adults[1] + two children	6.4	6.4	1.9	7.9	9.4	12.5	8.9
Two adults[1] + three children	1.5	2.7	0.3	4.1	21.0	3.5	5.4
Number of income providers: 0 or 1	82.5	82.1	80.6	83.4	86.3	63.0	54.0

[1] adult = non-elderly person

Netherlands. In Belgium these households form a larger proportion of all poor than in other countries.

Even though the poverty rate among *one-parent families* is generally very high, they are few in number. Therefore, only a small proportion of all poor households are one-parent households. This is rather in contrast to the situation in the U.S.A. (Sawhill, 1988, p. 1084).

In Ireland, more than one-third of all poor households by the EC-standard, and about one-quarter by the subjective standards, are two-parent *families with three or more children*. By the EC-standard, but not by the subjective standards, almost half of all poor Dutch households are two-parent families with two or more children. In the other countries, these households are much less represented among the poor by all standards.

In the northern countries, around three-quarters or more of all poor households have only *one, or no, income provider* (i.e. a person with an income from earnings

Table 4.7: The characteristics of the poor: percentage of poor households having selected characteristics, using the EC-standard

% in poverty	B 1985	NL 1986	L 1986	LOR. 1986	IRL 1987	CAT. 1988	GR 1988
Head of household							
at work	28.7	46.2	45.3	38.7	40.0	40.7	67.4
(farmer)	2.0	4.3	1.6	3.5	22.3	3.7	36.0
retired	31.5	6.4	17.1	23.0	6.7	27.2	25.7
unemployed	23.6	12.5	3.8	15.2	36.3	12.7	2.0
65 years or older	26.4	5.4	22.1	21.8	9.5	27.6	29.2
Type of household							
One parent households	3.9	2.7	9.4	3.0	6.4	1.6	3.0
Two adults[1]	8.7	7.7	7.3	5.7	4.7	6.4	8.8
Two adults[1] + one child	11.5	6.3	7.6	10.2	7.7	3.3	4.2
Two adults[1] + two children	13.0	27.9	10.9	9.9	12.6	9.7	9.8
Two adults[1] + three children	8.4	19.4	10.3	7.2	36.7	3.1	9.1
Number of income providers: 0 or 1	73.7	74.5	74.4	78.2	86.8	64.0	44.3

[1] adult = non-elderly person

or social security). In Greece, and to a lesser extent in Catalonia, many poor households have two or even more income providers.

5 Panel Results on Mobility into and out of Poverty

Comparisons between subsequent cross-sectional surveys often show that there are few significant changes in poverty rates from one year to another. The impression of a stable situation could be misleading, if one would translate it from the macro-level to the micro-level. The result that the overall situation remains much the same from one year to the next does not imply that all or most households stay in the same position. In particular, a stable overall rate of poverty does not mean that the same households are poor in both years. Until recently, this was a blind spot, at least in European poverty research, as panel data, which are needed to analyse this issue, were not available. The data that have come available, in some European countries, have shown that, as in the USA (Duncan, 1984), changes at the micro-level are unexpectedly large and frequent (for Germany: Rendtel and Wagner, 1991; for The Netherlands: Muffels, Berghman and Dirven, 1992; for Belgium: Deleeck, Cantillon, Meulemans and Van den Bosch, 1992; for a comparative analysis: Duncan et al., 1993).

In this part of the paper some panel results on poverty are presented for five countries for which data of two waves of the household panel surveys are available: Belgium 1985-1988, The Netherlands 1985-1986, Luxemburg 1985-1986, Lorraine 1985-1986 and Ireland 1987-1989. Unfortunately, the time-gap between two waves is not the same for all countries: in The Netherlands, Lorraine and Luxembourg it is one year, in Ireland two years, and in Belgium three years. This obviously detracts from the comparability of the results. Furthermore, the panel results are somewhat limited in scope, because of the availability of only two waves. Nevertheless, they constitute one of the first comparative studies of transitions into and out of poverty in Europe.

The panel results are on the household level. Households were linked across waves if they had the same head in both years, or if the head had deceased and the partner had become head of household. This implies that certain wave-2 households that have split off from other wave-1 households, such as children who left their parent's home and women divorced from their husbands, are not included in the analysis. This is of course unfortunate, and it is certainly very much preferable to analyse mobility in poverty status on the individual level, where linking can be complete and unambigous. Due to technical problems, not all countries were yet able to produce results on the individual level. However, after only one or three years, the number of split-off households will be rather small, (1 to 3%)[5]. Not all wave-1 households are included either, because some have left the population through death or emigration, and others are lost due to non-response. For these reasons the figures for wave 1 given here are sometimes sligthly different from those given in section 4.

---

5 Results for Belgium on the individual level were virtually the same.

Table 5.1: Proportion of all households in poverty in the first wave, that are still poor in the second wave

		CSP-standard	SPL-standard	EC-standard	LEGAL-standard
B	1985-1988	62.9	60.8	42.0	24.2
NL	1985-1986	47.3	69.7	40.6	30.6
L	1985-1986	62.5	49.5	57.1	44.0
LOR.	1985-1986	73.6	73.9	56.9	42.9
IRL	1987-1989	71.2	84.1	63.8	26.2

The most interesting figure of the panel results is the *proportion of households insecure of subsistence in the first wave, that are still so in the second year* (and, of course, its complement, the proportion of these households that are not insecure any more) (Table 5.1). Interpretation of these figures is not alway easy. If the level of the poverty-line has fallen between two waves, as has happened in some countries, this will itself produce some apparent mobility in poverty-status even without there being any real change in any household's situation. If the poverty-line has risen, this will probably reduce the number of households who have left poverty. Moreover, there are the differences in the period of time between waves.

Nevertheless, it is clear from Table 5.1 that there is *substantial mobility* from insecurity to security of subsistence. On the basis of the EC-standard, between 34% to almost 60%, depending on the country, of all households financially insecure in wave 1, are *not* so in wave 2. Using the legal standard, the mobility appears to be even more substantial. The more generous subjective standards produce results that indicate less change in status. If we exclude cases where the poverty-rate in wave 2 diverges much from that in wave 1,[6] we find that generally 60% to 75% of households insecure in wave 1 remain in poverty. This is not true for The Netherlands, where the subjective standards are much lower.

These results seem to suggest an important methodological conclusion. It appears that in a given country, the higher the poverty rate, the lower the

6 These are: results with the SPL in Ireland, The Netherlands and Luxembourg, and with the CSP in Lorraine.

transition rate out of poverty. This also implies that estimated mobility will be lower if the poverty line is more generous (as there will be more households below it). Duncan, Gustafsson a.o. (1991, p. 9), also report "a marked inverse relationship between the estimated incidence of poverty and escape rates".

This tendency obviously affects comparisons across countries. Thus, using the EC-standard, we find that fewer households leave the state of insecurity of subsistence in Ireland than in the other countries. But it is difficult to say whether this is the result of less extensive income mobility in Ireland or of the fact that there are more households below the EC-line in Ireland. Changes in poverty status also seem less frequent in Lorraine and Luxembourg, where the number of households below the EC-standard is nearer to that of Belgium and The Netherlands. However, it must be kept in mind that the time-gaps between the two waves are not the same. It seems probable that after three years as many or more households would have escaped poverty in Luxembourg and in Lorraine as have done in Belgium. However, it is somewhat surprising that transitions are less frequent in Belgium, where three years have elapsed between the two waves, than in The Netherlands, where there is only one year difference.

Of course, there are not only households that escape poverty, but also a certain number that *become* poor or insecure of the means of subsistence, that were not so in the first wave. Using the EC-standard, between 3,3% in Luxembourg and 8,8% in Ireland of all households that were financially secure in the first wave, have become insecure in the second wave. On the basis of the subjective standards, the number of these households is much larger, from 16% in Ireland, to less than 6% in Luxembourg. These results are of course only the complement of those discussed in the previous paragraphs, and the same remarks apply, mutatis mutandis, to them too.

Another way to look at these figures is to see what proportions of all households are insecure of the means of subsistence in *both waves* (Table 5.2) Of course, these households cannot be equalled to the "permanent" poor in any sense of the word. Still, it would seem that these households are on average insecure or poor for a longer time than other households.

Because of the mobility in poverty-status, the figures in Table 5.2 are much lower than the single-year poverty-rates. Nevertheless, comparatively, conclusions drawn on the basis of cross-sectional analysis are mostly confirmed. In fact the differences across countries are reinforced. Using the EC-standard, we find that

Table 5.2: Percentage of all households that are poor in both waves

		CSP-standard	SPL-standard	EC-standard	LEGAL-standard
B	1985-1988	13.5	14.9	2.4	0.6
NL	1985-1986	5.3	5.3	2.6	2.2
L	1985-1986	9.4	9.8	4.4	2.8
LOR.	1985-1986	19.3	19.1	6.1	2.0
IRL	1987-1989	22.3	31.2	10.2	1.7

Ireland has the largest proportion of households insecure in both waves, followed by Lorraine. In Belgium and The Netherlands this proportion is less than 3%. In contrast to the single-year results, Luxembourg has more "longer-term" poor than the other Benelux countries. On the basis of the subjective standards, the relative positions of Ireland and Lorraine are similar. But in The Netherlands, the number of households with incomes below the subjective standard is much smaller than in other countries, while in Belgium it is now larger than in Luxembourg (despite the longer time-gap in Belgium). This is at least partly an effect of differences in the relative level of the subjective standards.

Of course, if, as has been argued above, the number of households that experience changes in poverty status depends partly on the level of the standard used, this is also true for the proportion of households poor in both waves. The comparisons must therefore be made with some caution.

However, even if the differences between countries could be wholly explained by the position of the standard within the income distribution, it would be wrong to regard them as only a statistical artefact. What one cannot do is conclude that there is less income mobility in Ireland. But, depending on the validity one is willing to grant to the various standards, one would still be justified in concluding that there is much more poverty of a longer-term nature in Ireland than in The Netherlands. In fact, it suggests that there are two types of gains in reducing inequality in the lower part of the income distribution: not only will there be at any given moment fewer households below any given poverty line, but in addition the average duration of poverty spells will probably be shorter.

What is interesting is not only to know how many households stay in poverty but also to know *which social categories* have a high probability of experiencing longer-term poverty vs. short term poverty.It appears that in most cases the panel results on longer-term poor confirm the cross-sectional results: categories of households that are at high risk of poverty at one moment in time are also at high risk of being in poverty in two consecutive waves. The social composition of the poor in the first wave is generally closer to that of the longer-term poor than to that of the entire population. This is an important conclusion, as it means that even though the population of poor at a certain moment may include many that are poor for only a short time, the results of cross-sectional studies are generally not very misleading as regards the *structure* of poverty, and provide adequate indicators of the categories of households that are at high risk of being in longer-term poverty.

6 Social Security Transfers and Poverty

In this section the role of social security cash transfers in reducing the incidence of poverty is examined. Social security transfers include social assistance payments and other means-tested benefits, as well as social insurance benefits. For a precise definition of social security transfers in the several countries, we refer to Deleeck et al. (1992, appendix C). The method used is that of calculating the number of poor households on the basis of pre-transfer and post-transfer incomes. Pre-transfer income is defined as actual disposable income less actual social security transfers received. Post-transfer income is equal to disposable income. In this procedure, the poverty lines remain unchanged. Pre-transfer income cannot be equalled to a hypothetical income in the absence of social security: social security contributions and taxes are not included in it, and behavioral changes are not taken into account. However, this relatively simple numerical exercise can serve as a first indication of the effect of social security transfers on poverty.

The procedure applied here differs from the method most often used (e.g. Ringen, 1989; Mitchell, 1991) in that both pre-transfer income (market income) and transfers are net of taxes and social insurance contributions. The reason for this is that for several countries no data on taxes and contributions were available, and all incomes were measured net of these deductions. This implies that we are

Table 6.1: Proportion of all households with pre-transfer incomes above the poverty line

		CSP-standard	SPL-standard	EC-standard	LEGAL-standard
B	1985	48.5	50.4	59.0	65.2
NL	1986	62.9	61.3	60.2	63.6
L	1986	56.7	64.0	61.1	68.3
LOR.	1986	43.3	50.3	60.6	71.3
IRL	1987	47.1	49.9	53.8	57.5
CAT.	1988	55.3	52.2	69.2	-
GR	1988	42.9	45.8	61.9	-

looking specifically at the impact of (net) transfers on poverty, *after* taxes and contributions have been paid. An assessment of the extent of redistribution is not intended.

Another limitation of this analysis is that only a partial evaluation of social security is carried out. Poverty relief (i.e. a minimum income guarantee) is certainly not the only aim of social security. Another important objective is the protection of accustomed living standards (cf. Barr, 1992). But combatting poverty seems important enough as a goal for the whole of social security transfers (not just of means-tested benefits) to justify analyzing the adequacy of social transfers in terms of a minimum income guarantee.

What are the results? In the first place, there are considerable differences in the proportion of households that would be non-poor on the basis of their pre-transfer-income alone (Table 6.1). Catalan households are the least dependent on social security. Using the EC-standard, almost 70% of all households in Catalonia would not be in poverty without social security. In Ireland, on the other hand, almost half of all households would be in poverty without social security transfers. In the other countries, this percentage is around 40%. Using the more generous CSP and SPL-standards, the proportions of households with incomes below the poverty line before social security transfers are generally higher. This is not true for The Netherlands, which, together with Luxembourg, has the highest proportion of households with pre-transfer incomes above the subjective poverty

Table 6.2: Proportion of pre-transfer poor households that are non-poor after social security transfers

		CSP-standard	SPL-standard	EC-standard	LEGAL-standard
B	1985	58.4	49.7	85.1	91.6
NL	1986	70.6	58.9	82.0	80.2
L	1986	66.4	65.6	80.5	84.2
LOR.	1986	45.7	46.7	72.6	86.4
IRL	1987	44.2	36.9	62.8	80.9
CAT.	1988	29.9	22.0	51.0	-
GR	1988	25.4	22.5	47.8	-

lines. By contrast, in Greece about 55% of all households have pre-transfer incomes below the subjective poverty lines.

Given these pre-transfer situations, a first measure of the effect of social security transfers on the extent of poverty is the number of households non-poor due to social transfers, as a proportion of all households with pre-transfer incomes below the poverty line (Table 6.2).

By all standards the effectiveness of social security, defined in this way, is highest in the Benelux-countries. Using the EC-standard more than 80% of the pre-transfer poor are not poor after social security transfers; using the subjective standards the percentages vary between 50% and 70%. In Lorraine the proportions are somewhat lower. In Greece and Catalonia the effectiveness is much lower; it is indeed very low. By the EC-standard only half of all households that would be poor without social security are non-poor thanks to it; only one-quarter of these households are lifted to the level of the subjective standards. Ireland occupies a position in between the Benelux countries and the southern countries.

The results based on the legal standard are particularly interesting. Because the legal standard is part of the social security system, we might say that using the legal minimum income is to evaluate the social security system by its own standard. In Belgium, 90% of all households whose income would be below the legal standard without social security, are brought above this level of income by

Table 6.3: The post-transfer poverty-gap as a percentage of aggregate income of all households

		CSP-standard	SPL-standard	EC-standard	LEGAL-standard
B	1985	2.6	3.0	0.5	0.2
NL	1986	1.0	1.6	0.9	0.9
L	1986	1.6	1.3	0.8	0.3
LOR.	1986	5.4	4.0	1.4	0.4
IRL	1987	5.0	4.5	2.7	1.7
CAT.	1988	5.3	7.0	1.8	-
GR	1988	N.A.	N.A.	N.A.	-

* figures calculated on the basis of average amounts

the social transfers, but in Ireland and in The Netherlands social security succeeds in making non-poor only 80% of the households that would be poor without it. The other countries are in between. The possible reasons why a significant group of households in several countries is below the legally guaranteed minimum income have been discussed in section 4.

To get a complete picture of the effect of social security on poverty, it is not enough to look only at the number of households below the poverty line before and after social transfers, but one must also take into account the amounts transferred.

An indicator of the extent to which social security fails to prevent poverty is the poverty-gap after social transfers are granted, which is equal to the total income deficit of all households (where the deficit is defined as the poverty line minus actual income). In order to facilitate interpretation, in Table 6.3 the poverty-gap is given as a percentage of aggregate income of all households. The poverty gap appears to be relatively large in Ireland, Catalonia and Lorraine (1,4 - 2,7% by the EC-standard, 4% to 7% by the subjective standards). In the Benelux-countries the poverty gap is a relatively small amount: less than 1% of aggregate household income by the EC-standard, between 1% and 3% of aggregate household income by the subjective standards. Unfortunately, there are no results on this point for Greece, but because both the number of poor and the average poverty-gap exceed those for any of the other countries, it seems likely that the poverty-gap in Greece is much larger - relatively - than in the other countries studied here.

To assess the adequacy of social security regarding poverty alleviation, the so-called Beckerman ratios (Beckerman, 1979) are used, through which we can evaluate the effectiveness and the efficiency of the social security system. By effectiveness we understand the extent to which social security succeeds in "relieving the poor", i.e. how far the poverty-gap before social transfers is eliminated by social security. The measure of efficiency, on the other hand, indicates what part of social security actually helps in making households non-poor, and what part does not help in the sense that it flows to households with pre-transfer incomes above the poverty line, or to pre-transfer poor households in excess of what they strictly need to reach the minimum income level. This is illustrated in figure 6.1. It has to be kept in mind that here we assess "efficiency" and "effectiveness" purely in terms of minimum income standards. Only a partial evaluation is carried out.

The shaded area (B+C) represents social security transfers. Area A is the poverty gap before transfers. Areas A and C together form the poverty gap before social security. Area B represents the part of social transfers that is received either by households that are non-poor before social transfers, or by pre-transfer poor households in excess of what they strictly need to get out of poverty. Thus we can measure effectiveness by C/(A+C) and efficiency by C/(B+C).

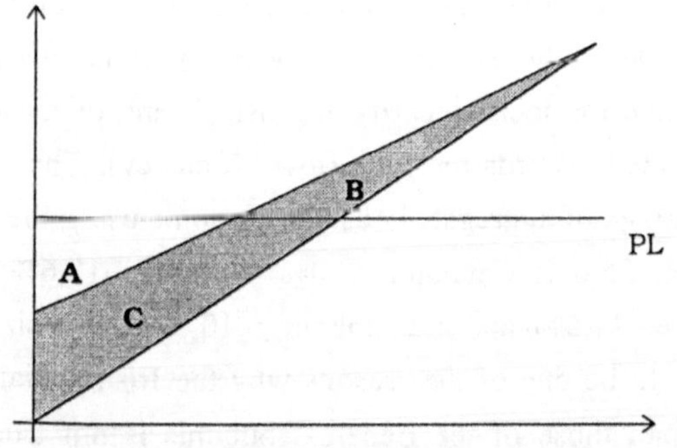

Figure 6.1: Illustration of Beckerman ratios

Table 6.4: "Effectiveness" of social security: percentage of pre-transfer aggregate poverty-gap eliminated by social transfers

		CSP-standard	SPL-standard	EC-standard	LEGAL-standard
B	1985	86.5	84.7	95.7	98.2
NL	1986	90.9	86.9	90.9	91.3
L	1986	88.1	89.9	92.6	96.7
LOR.	1986	73.3	77.3	88.3	94.0
IRL	1987	75.0	76.9	83.0	86.6
CAT.	1988	57.9	52.7	74.8	-
GR	1988	N.A.	N.A.	N.A.	-

* figures calculated on the basis of average amounts

From Table 6.4 it appears that social security is most effective in the Benelux-countries: using the EC-standard or the legal standard, more than 90% of the pre-transfer poverty gap is eliminated; using the subjective standards 85% or more is closed. In Lorraine and Ireland the effectiveness of social security is slightly less. In Catalonia social security seems relatively ineffective: using the EC-standard less than three-quarters of the poverty gap is eliminated, by the subjective standards barely half of the poverty gap is closed.

Generally speaking, there can be three reasons for low effectiveness: either the size of the problem (the pre-transfer poverty gap) is relatively large, or the resources available for social security are insufficient, or these resources are not sufficiently targeted towards the poor (low efficiency). The pre-transfer poverty gaps as a percentage of aggregate household income using the EC-standard are as follows: Ireland: 15,6%; Catalonia: 7,0%; Belgium: 12,6%; The Netherlands: 10,0%; Lorraine: 11,5% and Luxembourg: 10,8%. The size of the problem, therefore seems to be one of the reasons why the Irish social security system is less effective than those of the Benelux, but this is not true for Lorraine and certainly not for Catalonia.

Expressing the available means (total social security transfers) in the same way, as a proportion of aggregate household income, we get the following result:

Table 6.5: "Efficiency" of social security: percentage of aggregate social transfers that helps to close the poverty-gap

		CSP-standard	SPL-standard	EC-standard	LEGAL-standard
Belgium	1985	59.1	59.7	42.7	43.8
Netherlands	1986	49.8	51.8	42.3	46.7
Luxembourg	1986	47.9	44.0	39.3	33.7
Lorraine	1986	55.6	51.8	38.5	23.2
Ireland	1987	62.3	61.5	53.7	45.0
Catalonia	1988	57.0	61.1	41.4	-
Greece	1988	N.A.	N.A.	N.A.	-

* figures calculated on the basis of average amounts

Greece, 17.4%; Ireland, 24.1%; Catalonia, 12.7%; Belgium, 28.2%; Netherlands, 24.1%, Lorraine, 26.4%; Luxembourg, 25.3%[7]. Comparing these two series, it is clear that in the Benelux countries and Lorraine, the available resources of social security are much larger relative to the 'needs' (as indicated by the poverty gap before social transfers) than in the other countries. In Ireland and Catalonia, the ratio resources /needs is much more unfavorable, in Ireland mainly because of the higher level of need, in Catalonia because of the much smaller means.

Less than perfect effectiveness, in combination with resources that are at least in theory sufficient, implies inefficiency. From the point of view of eliminating poverty, all social security systems are indeed rather inefficient (Table 6.5): between 35% and 60% of aggregate social transfers goes to households that are not poor before social transfers, or to households in excess of what they strictly need to be above the poverty line. By all standards, the Irish system is one of the least inefficient: using the CSP-standard, 62% of total transfers serves to eliminate

7 These figures are not quite in agreement with official statistics on social security transfers as a proportion of G.D.P., especially as regards the position of The Netherlands. This is partly due to the well-known problems of household survey data, but also to definitional differences in both the numerators and the denominators of the ratios.

the poverty gap. Table 6.5 also shows that the relatively low effectiveness of social security in Catalonia is not related to lower efficiency: the efficiency of social security in Catalonia is not lower than in the Benelux-countries. Much of this inefficiency is accounted for by the amounts that pre-transfer poor households receive in excess of the poverty line, though this is less true for Ireland and Catalonia, than for the Benelux and Lorraine.

7 Summary of Findings

In this paper comparative results on poverty in seven countries and regions of the European Community (Belgium, The Netherlands, Luxembourg, Lorraine (region of France), Ireland, Catalonia (region of Spain) and Greece) have been presented. The data were obtained from comparable socio-economic surveys in each country. Subjective as well as relative and legal (official) poverty lines were used. Subjective poverty lines are based on judgments of the population about minimum income levels, as expressed in sample surveys. The use of several poverty lines enables us to draw more robust conclusions regarding the distribution of poverty between and within countries.

As has been reported in other studies, the extent of poverty is much greater in the 'peripheral' EC-countries Ireland, Greece and Catalonia, than in the 'central' ones Belgium, The Netherlands, Luxembourg and Lorraine. In the former countries the number of households below the relative EC-standard exceeds 15%, while the poverty rate is only 6 to 7% in the latter countries (except in Lorraine, where it is around 10%).

Looking at the characteristics of the poor, a number of factors are found to be associated with poverty in all countries. In general, households with no, or a weak attachment to the labor market (as indicated by the labor-market status of the head of household, and the number of earners in the household) are at a higher than average risk of poverty. In particular, households where the head is unemployed have a very high risk of being in poverty. Furthermore, non-traditional households are also relatively likely to be in poverty. If the head is divorced or separated, the risk of poverty is generally considerably higher than average. Single parents are also relatively likely to live in poverty.

However, there are also important differences in the characteristics of the poor across countries. Very young householders are at high risk of poverty in the northern countries, but not in the southern. In Greece, poverty is much more prevalent among households with one or even several persons at work than is the case in the other countries. In Ireland, poverty seems to be concentrated with two-parent families with many dependent children, while the elderly appear at a comparatively low risk of poverty.

An interesting finding is that a sizable minority among the poor in all countries consists of households where the head is working, even though the poverty incidence in this category of households is not particularly high. In most of these cases, the head is probably the sole breadwinner.

Panel results for five countries suggest that mobility into and out of poverty is high in virtually all social categories. It appears that, broadly speaking, longer-term poverty occurs most in countries and social categories, where the poverty rate at a single moment is also high.

The impact of social security transfers on poverty appears to be much smaller in the southern countries Greece and Catalonia, than in the Benelux, Lorraine and Ireland. The main reason seems to be that in the southern countries fewer resources are allocated to social security transfers. This might be among the causes of the higher incidence of poverty in these countries. In the Benelux countries social security transfers are in theory amply sufficient to fill the poverty gap completely, and they are indeed fairly effective in eliminating poverty. Some poverty remains, however, because the transfer system is not very efficient, from the point of view of minimum income provision. Many pre-transfer poor households receive social security transfers that are considerably in excess of what they strictly need to reach the poverty line. (The reason for this is, of course, that social security transfers have other functions besides poverty alleviation.) In Ireland, on the other hand, the pre-transfer poverty gap is relatively large, mainly because of high unemployment among main breadwinners, whilst social security resources are not proportionally larger. Therefore, rather many households are left in poverty, even though the transfer system is relatively efficient from the point of view of poverty alleviation.

Appendix: Survey Procedures and Sample Characteristics

Table A1: Survey Procedures

	Population of survey	Coverage of total population	Sampling unit	Who are respondents in the household	Realised sample size	Imputation of missing income information	Weighting of cases
B 1985	Private households in Belgium	98%	'Reference person' of household	Head of household	6471	Yes, for 417 cases (6%)	No
NL 1986	Private households in The Netherlands, except those without an address	90%	Address of home	All persons aged 16 or older	5165	Yes, for few cases	No
L 1986	Private households, except those with no link at all to the Luxembourg social security system	97%	Main breadwinner according to social security register	Head of household or spouse, income group head	1793	Yes, N of cases NA	Yes, to correct for bias due to choice of sampling unit and for selective nonrespons
LOR. 1986	Private households in Lorraine	98%	Individual	Head of household or spouse, income group head	2092	Yes, for 250 cases (12%)	Yes, to correct for bias due to choice of sampling unit
IRL 1987	Private households in Ireland	97%	Individual elector	All individuals aged 15 or over	3294	Yes, N of cases NA	Yes, to correct for bias due to choice of sampling unit. and to adjust to independent statistics from Labor Force Survey
CAT. 1988	Private households in Catalonia	99%	household (home)	Head of household	2997	No	No
GR 1988	Private households in Greece	N.A.	head of household	Head of household	2958	No	No

Source: Van den Bosch et al. (1993)

Table A2: Some Characteristics of the Samples

	B 1985	NL 1986	L 1986	LOR. 1986	IRL 1987	CAT. 1988	GR 1988
Average household size	2.83	2.70	2.73	2.88	3.58	3.45	3.08
Percentage of households with characteristic in sample:							
single persons	17.0	21.8	21.8	17.3	16.6	8.8	11.4
single nonaged adult + children	2.4	2.4	2.4	2.2	2.3	1.1	2.2
two nonaged adults + one or two children	28.7	28.6	22.1	30.5	19.0	19.2	21.7
two nonaged adults + three or more children	6.0	7.3	4.5	5.9	18.4	2.6	4.8
head of household aged	20.7	15.9	21.9	19.5	14.5	17.4	19.9
head of household female	16.1	19.3	23.3	17.2	18.6	15.4	16.6
head of household widowed	12.2	9.6	17.1	11.8	14.7	8.8	9.2
head of household divorced or separated	5.6	6.1	5.5	6.5	3.0	3.8	3.8
head of household at work	60.4	64.0	62.6	61.5	57.8	68.2	70.2
head of household retired	29.1	19.2	17.6	26.7	14.5	18.6	23.6
head of household unemployed	5.5	4.6	0.7	4.0	10.6	4.4	1.1
receiving social security transfers	81.6	73.3	77.9	70.2	86.1	45.8	47.5
receiving replacement incomes[3]	46.4	39.7	45.4	42.8	58.9	40.3	44.8
Average household income (monthly, in ECU)	1299	1319	1853	1331	1058	1619	1013
Income Inequality (Gini-coeff.)	0.277	0.292	0.284	0.319	0.379	0.339	0.409
Average social security transfer of receiving households (monthly, in ECU)	449	462	618	526	332	449	
Average replacement income of receiving households (monthly, in ECU)	632	744	925	705	463	449	372

Source: Van den Bosch et al. (1993)

References

Beckerman, W. (1979), Poverty and the Impact of Income Maintenance Programmes, Geneva: International Labor Organization.

Barr, N. (1992), Economic Theory dand the Welfare State: A Summary and Interpretation, Journal of Economic Literature, vol. 30, pp. 741-803.

Buhmann, B., L. Rainwater, G. Schmauss and T. Smeeding (1988), Equivalence scales, well-being, inequality and poverty: sensitivity estimates across ten countries using the Luxembourg income study (LIS) database, The Review of Income and Wealth, vol. 33 , no. 2, pp. 115-142.

Callan,T. B. Nolan, a.o. (1989), Poverty, income and welfare in Ireland, ESRI research paper no. 146, ESRI, Dublin.

Callan, T., B. Nolan: Concepts of Poverty and the Poverty Line (1991), Journal of Economic Surveys, vol. 5 no. 3, pp. 243-261.

Cantillon, B. (1991), Socio-demographic changes and social security, International Review of Social Security, 1991, Nr. 4, pp. 399-426.

DeLeeck, H. (1989), The adequacy of the Social Security System in Belgium, 1976-1985, Journal of Social Policy, vol. 18 nr. 1.

DeLeeck, H., J. Berghman, P. van Heddegem, L.Vereycken (1980), De Sociale Zekerheid tussen Droom en Daad, Theorie, Onderzoek, Beleid, Van Loghum Slaterus, Deventer and Antwerpen.

DeLeeck, H., K. van den Bosch, L. DeLathouwer (1992), Poverty and the adequacy of social security in the EC, A comparative analysis, Aldershot: Avebury .

DeLeeck, H., B. Cantillon, B. Meulemans and K. van den Bosch (1992), Some Longitudinal Results of the Belgian Socio-Economic Panel, Journal of Income Distribution, vol. 2, no. 2, pp. 211-231.

Duncan, G. (1984), Years of Poverty, Years of Plenty, Institute for Social Research, University of Michigan, Ann Arbor.

Duncan, G., B. Gustavsson, R. Hauser, G. Schmauss, H. Messinger, R. Muffels, B. Nolan and J.-C. Ray (1993), Poverty dynamics in eight countries, Journal of Population Economics, vol. 6, pp. 215-234.

Eurostat (1990), La Pauvreté en Chiffres l'Europe au début des années 8O, Office for Official Publications of the European Communities, Luxembourg.

Flik, R. and B. van Praag (1991), Subjective Poverty Line Definitions, De Economis*t*, 139, nr. 3, pp. 311-329.

Goedhart, T., V. Halberstadt, A. Kapteyn and B. van Praag (1977), The poverty line: Concept and measurement, The Journal of Human Resources, vol. 12 nr. 4, pp. 503-520.

Hagenaars, A. (1986), The Perception of Poverty, North-Holland, Amsterdam.

Kapteyn A., S. van DeGeer and H. van der Stadt (1985), The Impact of Changes in Income and Family Composition on Subjective Measures of Well-Being, in: David, M. and Smeeding, T. (eds): Horizontal Equity and the Distribution of the Tax Burden, NBER and Chicago University Press, Chicago.

Muffels, R., J. Bergham and H.-J. Dirven (1992), A Multi-method Approach to Monitor the Evolution of Poverty, Journal of European social Policy, vol. 2, no. 3, pp. 193-213.

Mitchell, D (1991), Income Transfers in Ten Welfare States, Aldershot etc.: Avebury.

O'Higgins, M. and S. Jenkins (1990), Poverty in Europe: estimates for the numbers in poverty in 1975, 1980, 1985, in R. Teekens and B. van Praag, Analysing Poverty in the European Community, Eurostat News Special Edition, Office for Official Publicatons of the European Communities, Luxembourg.

O.E.C.D. (1976), Public Expenditure on Income Maintenance Programmes. Studies in Resource Allocation nr. 3, OECD, Paris.

O.E.C.D. (1982), The OECD list of social indicators, OECD, Paris.

Rendtel, U. and G. Wagner eds (1991), Lebenslagen im Wandel: Zur Einkommensdynamik in Deutschland seit 1984, Campus Verlag, Frankfurt

Ringen, S. (1989), The Possibility of Politics. A Study in the Political Economy of the Welfare State, Oxford: Clarendon Press.

Sawhill, I. (1988), Poverty in the U.S.: Why Is It So Persistent?, Journal of Economic Literature, vol. 26, pp. 1073-1119.

Sen, A. (1976), Poverty: an ordinal approach to measurement, Econometrica, vol. 44, pp. 219-231.

Van den Bosch, T. Callan, J. Estivill, P. Hausman, B. Jeandidier, R. Muffels and J. Yfantopoulos (1993), A comparison of poverty in seven European countries and regions using subjective and relative measures, Journal of Population Economics, vol. 6, nr. 3.

Van Praag, B. (1991), Ordinal and Cardinal Utility: An Integration of the Two Dimensions of the Welfare Concept, The Journal of Econometrics, vol. 50, pp. 69-89.

Van Praag, B., A. Hagenaars and J. van Weeren (1982): Poverty in Europe, The Review of Income and Wealth, vol. 28 pp. 345-359

Old Age Poverty in Selected Countries of the European Union - Are Women Disproportionally Affected?

Heinz Stapf

1 Feminization of Poverty in Old Age

The countries of the European Community are going through a process of aging. Since in general woman enjoy longer life expectancy than men, the relative share of women has increased along with this. Due to interruptions in the working life of women as a result of family responsibilities, women cannot accumulate sufficient pension entitlements, at least in contributory pension schemes, to cover the expenses that await them in retirement. As a result, women tend to constitute a larger share of the elderly poor than men. The term "feminization of poverty" in old age is used to discuss the genesis and institutionalization of this problem (see Kommission der Europäischen Gemeinschaft 1993, p. 35; Reinhard 1992, p. 29).

The following consequences can be expected in countries which employ earnings based and/or contributory pensions:

- Disproportionate levels of poverty among the elderly will increase in comparison to younger people, and with rising life expectancy and resulting increases in the size of the elderly population, the situation will be exacerbated. Moreover, this trend is reflected among different age groups commonly referred to under the term elderly. "Aged elderly" tend to find themselves in a worse economic position than their younger compatriots. One reason for this phenomenon could be insufficient indexing of pensions; another, perhaps more important reason, could include lack of compensation for both interruptions in working life and compensation for family work. Another important consideration is that steps taken to change potential discrepancies can only inherently effect people entering retirement. This means that retired people who are already receiving their entitlements must accept the possible discrepancies of older retirement benefit plans.

- The poverty rate of elderly women is higher than the poverty rate of elderly men. In contrast to the expected results generated from pension schemes which only provide benefits as a substitution for earnings, pension schemes that seek to prevent poverty in general and, as a result, grant retirement entitlements based upon residence do not produce gender inequalities. In order to test these hypotheses, the paper goes through the following steps:
- First, the various forms of compensation available are presented, ones which allow for; a) workers to receive the same social retirement benefits they would have received had the interruption not occurred, and/or b) pension credit entitlements granted for work done in the family context.
- Second, the various forms of minimum pensions are outlined which aim to prevent old age poverty.
- Finally, the extent to which the above described provisions contribute to the prevention of poverty in old age are examined.

2 Compensation for Interruptions of Working Life and Family Work [1]

2.1 Netherlands

Basic Pension financed by contributions

In the Netherlands, a flat-rate basic pension beginning from the age of 65 guarantees a minimum income in old age. The pension is financed through contributions that are adjusted depending upon the level of earned income. For the beneficiaries, the actual amount of the contributions paid are of no importance. To receive the full basic pension, one must simply live in the Netherlands for 50 years. Two per cent of the full amount is subtracted for each year in which a

1 For this subject see: Hohnerlein (1992, pp. 1-27); Reinhard (1992, pp. 28-51); Zacher (1991).

recipient did not live in the Netherlands. With regard to the basic pension, gender discrimination does not exist.

Additional income derived from pension plans which companies provide also represent an important contribution to income during old age. Company dependent pension schemes, however, penalize interruptions in the working life of employees and, therefore, have a disproportionally negative effect on the receipt of pension benefits by women, who are more likely than men to interrupt their work to fulfil family obligations. The full amount of the basic pension coincides with the level of social assistance available. Therefore in the case that the pension amount is insufficient, old people may depend on social assistance.

Voluntary insurance

A voluntary insurance is possible to:

a) continue insurance, in the case of moving abroad;
b) qualify for a pension, if one began living in the Netherlands after the age of 15.

2.2 Italy

Child-rearing credits

During the first year of childhood, parents may take a six month child-rearing leave. Since in principle the claim to a child-rearing leave belongs to the mother, men can only receive it upon approval by the mother. The obligatory post-natal maternity vacation lasts three months. Periods of child-rearing and post-natal maternity leave are free of contributions but are, treated as if the person taking leave would have paid normal contributions.

Voluntary insurance

Since 1963, a voluntary insurance has been available for housewives. The response to this voluntary insurance has been limited since a non-contribution based social pension plan was introduced in 1969.

Social pension

This is a tax financed, non-contributory and means-tested basic pension which exists alongside social assistance. It attempts to provide coverage to people who would not be entitled to benefits under a contributory system of social insurance pensions or who otherwise could not fulfill the qualifying conditions. The income of the claimant is not allowed to exceed a certain limit, and parties who receive other income benefits from the social security system are not eligible. Each husband has an individual entitlement for this benefit.

Women are the overwhelmingly beneficiaries of the social pension. The amount of supplemental income is, however, below the level of the minimum pension in the contributory system.

Minimum pension

If the entitled pension, calculated from insurance periods and contributions, does not reach a minimum level, it is supplemented with tax revenues. There is a minimum insurance period of 15 years and the calculation of the benefit depends only on the income of the individual.

Earnings component

The earnings component used for the calculation of a pension is taken only from the last five years of working life.

2.3 France

Child-rearing credits

In the general system of social security, insured women receive a child-rearing credit which is worth two years for each child before the age of 16 that they have raised for at least 9 years. If one of the parents has exhausted the voluntary child-rearing leave (3 years maximum), the insurance period is extended by the effective duration of the leave. Women can only apply for such an extension if they do not apply for the above mentioned child-rearing credit.

Reduced contribution requirements

This is a special regulation which allows for early retirement with full pension benefits for; a) people who work in labor intensive fields, and b) mothers who have at least acquired a 30 year period of contributions who have raised at least 3 children and who have worked manually for at least 5 of the 15 years before the application for pension benefits. In practice, women who fall into the latter category need only to prove 24 years of contribution.

Increase in small pensions because of child-rearing

Retirement pension can be increased by up to 10% to account for the costs of raising three or more children.

Compulsory insurance during the time of rearing and caring for disabled persons

This regulation serves to protect persons with low income who have family duties, through a tax-financed compulsory insurance.

Non-contributory minimum pension for certain persons

Allowance for family mothers (allocation aux mères de famille) for wives of insured employees begins at the age of 65 for those who have raised at least 5 children for 9 years before the children reached the age of 16.

Voluntary insurance

A voluntary insurance is possible for women with family responsibilities.

Earnings component

For the earnings component of the calculation of a pension, only the ten years in which they earn the highest income on average is taken into account and not the whole insurance period.

Minimum pension

The maximum amount of the contributory minimum pension is achievable after 37,5 years of insurance. There exists a minimum level for people with low income.

Non-contributory Minimum Pension (social pension)

There are 5 forms (among them the allowance for family mothers) which account for the income situation of the applicant.

Supplementary allowance (allocation supplémentaire)

It is granted in addition to contributory and/or non-contributory old age benefits. This tax-financed and means-tested benefit has the additional attribute of reaching the old age minimum (minimum vieillesse).

2.4 Belgium

Periods of child-rearing and care

Six to 12 months of leave for personal or family reasons is granted 5 times during the working life of an employee. The employee is replaced by an unemployed person. The acceptance of these interruptions, by retirement insurance, as periods in which employees still receive claims depends upon the granting of a special allowance (allocation d'interruption).

Protection of divorced

Contributions of the divorced husband are taken into account in the calculation of the old age pension of divorced women. Sixty per cent of the pension expectancy of the former husband are awarded to the pension account of the woman without reducing the pension account of the former husband.

Minimum pension

The full amount of the contributory minimum pension is granted only after a complete insurance career (40 years for women and 45 years for men).

Guaranteed income for the elderly

This is a minimum income beginning at 60 years of age for women and 65 for men. Personal income is not allowed to exceed a very low preset amount. It is a relatively small minimum income, too low to cover living expenses. More than half of the recipients of the guaranteed income for elderly are unmarried women.

If widows are factored in, the proportion of women increases to 75%. Persons 75 years and older are more dependent upon guaranteed income for the elderly.

Family pensions

Husbands decide whether they want to receive 60% of each individual pension or 75% from the pension account of one individual pension as a family pension.

2.5 United Kingdom

Reduced preconditions for benefits and credits (category A pension)

Full pension benefits require contributions for 90% of the working life. The prerequisites for the amount of time for contributions are reduced to benefit people with family responsibilities. Parties who receive other benefit income from the social security system are not eligible. The years of child-rearing or care of severely handicapped adults are subtracted from the number of years of contributions that are necessary to receive the full pension amount. The years of contribution, however, may neither be less than half of the obligatory insurance period nor 20 years of contributions. If one receives the invalid care allowance for the care of another person, the contribution is credited.

The British basic pension is only equivalent to 1/3 of the mean earnings of male workers and does not reach the level of income support (social assistance). The British basic pension cannot be considered as a manner in which to provide a sufficient minimum income. The public supplementary pension that can be contracted out in the case of the existence of company pensions, disproportionally benefits the male employment pattern.

Protection of the divorced

Divorced women who are not remarried can use contributions from the former husband to improve their own contribution account. The contributions must have been paid during the marriage or - if it is more favorable for her -, between her 16th birthday and the date of separation.

Non-contributory pension

There is a category D pension for people 80 years old and older, if they do not receive the basic pension or only a reduced one.

Protected years

In the Public Supplementary Pension Scheme (SERPS), years without income, or with very low income, are not taken into consideration for the calculation of the benefit.

Replacing the personal pension account with the pension account of the husband

The category B pension is for married women without eligibility for an old age pension or with a low pension. The benefit consists of 60% of the basic pension. Consequently, it does not provide a sufficient minimum income.

2.6 Germany

Pension according to minimum income (Rente nach Mindesteinkommen)

Insurance periods with low contributions until 1991 weighted more heavily if one has 35 credited years of insurance. Low contributions are multiplied by 1.5 and may, at best, reach 75% of the value of the contributions for the average income of the insured person.

Child rearing credits

Periods of child-rearing are credited at the rate of 75% for the average earnings of all insured persons. Before 1992, the period was one year, and after 1992, 3 years. Usually, the mother receives the credit, however if both parents sign a declaration, the father may receive the credit. A partition of the credit is also possible.

Statutory pension equalization upon dissolution of marriage

In the case of divorce, the pension claims that have been accumulated during matrimony are divided. The acquired pension claims are compared. The parent with the higher level of pension claims must cede half of the difference. The person required to make the adjustment can later increase their pension rights with contributions.

Voluntary insurance

Voluntary insurance exists from the age of 16 years on. Prerequisite is a qualifying period of 5 years.

Social assistance

In 1987, 20.2% of the social assistance benefits were granted to people 60 years of age and older. The share of women among this group amounted to 77.5%. Because of insufficient vested pension rights, women in particular are frequently in need of social assistance.

In the empirical section of this paper I want to show how the described forms of compensation for interruptions in working life and for family work help to prevent poverty among elderly women in comparison to similarly situated men in the countries selected. Because of differing forms of minimum pensions to prevent poverty, I want to systematise these forms.

3 Minimum Provisions

It is supposed to be the case that in countries with old age pension systems which grant a sufficient minimum pension, poverty among elderly women is not so pronounced. In the following table, the existing forms of minimum provisions are presented systematically.

In this context sufficient minimum conditions mean:

a) The conditions are rather easy to fulfill;
b) The benefit provides a necessary subsistence level to meet living expenses.

The following minimum provisions are possible[2]:

- Residence oriented minimum provisions (basic pension).
- Minimum provisions depending on periods of insurance within the framework of the general pension scheme (contributory minimum pension).

---

2 See Döring (1992); Hauser (1993); Schulte (1993).

Table 1: Form of minimum provisions for elderly

	NL	IT	FR	BE	UK	GE
Residence based	time of residence: 50 years, flat-rate basic pension from 65 years on	-	-	-	-	-
Depending on period of insurance	-	15 years minimum insurance period	after 37,5 years of insurance	only after a complete insurance career	90% of working life	-
Means-tested (social pension)	-	social pen-sion	5 different forms to reach the "minimum vieillesse"	does not reach level of subsis-tence	for people 60 years and older	-
Outside of pension schemes (social assistance)	-	-	-	of no relevance for the elderly	"income support"	social assistance
Is level of subsistence granted?	yes	yes	yes	no	no	no

- Means-tested minimum provisions granted categorically for the elderly (social pension).
- Minimum provisions external to the old age pension schemes (social assistance).

Consequently, the goal of preventing poverty in old age, especially of elderly women, should be better achieved in the Netherlands, Italy and France, than in Belgium, the United Kingdom and Germany.

Of course, other influences exist, such as the performance of the economy and work incentives for women. These "other influences" that also effect the rates of poverty among elderly women are not taken into consideration in this work.

4 Old Age Poverty in Selected EC Countries - Empirical Results

4.1 The data set

The calculations have been made on the basis of data sets from the Luxembourg Income Study (LIS). The LIS-project collects cross-sectional micro data from different countries and prepares these data sets in a manner that allows for relatively easy conception and comparison.

Unfortunately, data sets from all EC-countries are not yet available in the LIS-project[3]. Currently, data sets are only available for Belgium, France, Germany, Ireland, Italy, Luxembourg, the Netherlands and the United Kingdom. The data sets from Luxembourg and Ireland represent an insufficient number of cases in the considered household types. As a result, in the following examination only six EC-countries could be studied:

- *France*: The French Survey of Income from Income Tax 1984
  (Revenues Fiscaux 1984)
- *Germany*: The German Socio-Economic Panel Study: Wave 1/Wave 2
  (Das sozio-ökonomische Panel Welle 1/Welle 2) (1984/1985)
- *Italy*: The Bank of Italy Income Survey
  (Indagine Campionaria sui Bilanci Delle Famiglie 1986)
- *Netherlands*: Additional Inquiry on the Use of (Public) Services 87
  (Aanvullend Voorzieningengebruik Onderzoek 1987)
- *United Kingdom*: The Family Expenditure Survey 1986

Unfortunately, the objectives of the surveys differ, making comparisons of the result difficult. In Italy, families are the primary collection unit; in other countries, however, the collection units are households. Another problem is that the reference person differs in the surveys under consideration. The most troubling flaw is the differing definition of household used in each survey.

Another problem is that the time period spans the years from 1984 to 1988. As a result, no common reference year exists. Conscious of these imperfections, I

---

3 For further information on the LIS-project see Smeeding, O'Higgins and Rainwater (1990).

Table 2: LIS-Surveys

	FR 84	GE 84	IT 86	NL 87	UK 86
Sponsorship	National Institute of Statistics and Economic Studies (INSEE-DG)	German Science Foundation (DFG)	Bank of Italy	Social and Cultural Planning Office (SCP)	Department of Employment
Primary Objective of the Survey	Measurement of household income distribution	Provide information on the dynamics of individual welfare	Provide information on the economic behaviour of families	Measurement of income, household composition, and the use of public services	Provide information on spending patterns for the United Kingdom Retail Prices Index
Reference Person	In a one-family-household: the male adult. In a household with more than one family: oldest working person. If no member works: the oldest person	A single person, usually the head of the household, responds to general questions regarding the household as a whole and the dwelling in particular	Head of household: usually the husband or father, but if abroad, (or in another region of Italy), the person who is economically responsible for the family	Head of household: identified by the respondent. If the respondent refuses: the rent payer, the home owner, the person with the highest income, or the oldest person	Head of household
Household Definition	The household was formed by combining the tax returns of all household member	All persons living single or together form a single household	Related persons living together in one housing unit	Persons living and eating together form a single household	A person living alone, or a group of people living at the same address and sharing meals prepared together, and with common housekeeping

Source: LIS-User package

have still endeavoured to interpret the data. Even accounting for problems inherent in such a comparison, the lack of better data makes the further study of this material worthwhile.

The persons in the household types that are taken into consideration represent only a small percentage of the total population (table 3). Because most elderly people either live together as married couples or as single persons, I have organised the categories of my data set to reflect this reality.

Table 3: Frequencies of persons in different household types

		NL 87	IT 86	FR 84	BE 88	UK 86	GE 84
total number of persons		13629	62717	53817	10760	18330	58970
in %		100	100	100	100	100	100
one person household							
- male	-64	4.3	0.6	2.4	1.3	2.4	3.7
	65-74	0.4	0.3	0.3	0.4	0.6	0.4
	75+	0.7	0.2	0.5	0.5	0.6	0.6
- female	-64	4.5	1.1	2.6	1.4	2.2	3.8
	65-74	1.5	1.2	1.5	1.0	1.8	2.4
	75+	1.7	0.9	2.1	1.4	1.9	2.6
married couple							
	-64	13.8	6.4	11.6	11.6	12.5	13.0
	65-74	4.5	3.6	3.5	4.8	5.4	5.1
	75+	2.1	1.9	2.3	2.3	2.2	2.6
other							
	-64	64.7	76.3	69.8	70.7	66.6	62.4
	65-74	1.3	5.5	2.1	3.7	2.5	1.7
	75+	0.4	2.0	1.1	0.8	1.2	1.7

4.2 Poverty rates

The following analysis is based on a relative concept of poverty that defines poverty as a inability to participate sufficiently in the wealth of a society. Half of the average equivalent income (arithmetical mean) is considered as not sufficient and, therefore, represents the usual poverty threshold in the EU context.[4]

Because economies are the result of the common running of a household (economies of scale) and differing needs of the household members, the various incomes inside a single family have not simply been divided by the number of household members in order to calculate the disposable income per person. For this reason, I used the OECD equivalency scale. This scale gives the head of the

4 See Atkinson (1987, pp. 749-764); Kommission der Europäischen Gemeinschaften (1993, p. 31); Hauser (1984, pp. 329-355).

Table 4: Poverty rates (under the 50 % poverty line)

		NL 87	IT 86	FR 84	BE 88	UK 86	GE 84
One person household							
- male	-64	14.7	8.8	16.0	8.6	9.0	9.5
	65-74	0.0	12.4	1.8	13.6	2.6	0.0
	75+	0.0	24.8	1.1	10.7	1.9	1.8
- female	-64	15.4	11.7	14.8	9.0	9.0	13.5
	65-74	0.0	14.8	3.1	8.4	6.9	8.8
	75+	0.0	22.2	1.2	8.6	5.2	15.9
Married couple							
	-64	2.8	8.6	11.0	4.2	9.2	3.9
	65-74	0.3	7.5	2.7	8.2	7.4	8.5
	75+	0.0	13.0	0.8	12.0	13.6	17.9
Other							
	-64	15.9	19.2	18.5	7.9	18.7	12.0
	65-74	19.9	25.2	17.8	9.7	17.2	8.2
	75+	(15.8)	26.1	10.7	16.3	6.0	26.0
Average		12.3	18.2	15.7	7.8	15.5	11.0

( ) insignificant numbers

household a weight of 1, to each other adult a weight of 0.7 and to each child a weight of 0.5 (see Eurostat 1990, pp. 7-8). The 50% poverty rate Table 4) indicates the proportion of the so defined poor persons relative to the total number of persons living in the respective household type.

In the following, persons under 65 are "young", persons from 65 to 74 "elderly" and persons 75 years and older "aged".

Germany: Comparing single women with single men, the share of women who fall under the poverty line in all age groups is larger than the share of men. Contrary to the assumption that poverty rises with age, among those entering retirement, there is a decrease in the poverty rates. The poverty rate of single women is higher than the poverty rate of persons living together as couples. Only aged couples (75+) have a higher poverty rate.

No clear pattern can be found in **Belgium**. Also worthy of note is that the poverty rate of persons in aged couples is higher than the poverty rate of aged women.

Despite the outlined minimum income provisions, the findings in **Italy** are in accordance with the pattern predicted in the main hypothesis. In all age groups, the poverty rate of single women is higher than among persons who live together or men who live alone. Only aged single men have a higher poverty rate than aged single women.

France does not correspond to the expected pattern as France's method of compensation for a) interruptions of the working life, b) compensation for work done in the family, and c) the minimum income provisions seem to function with equitable results. There are neither noticeable differences with regard to comparisons of single women with single men nor with regard to comparisons of single men with couples. For the three household types taken into consideration, it can be seen that with increasing age, the poverty rate decreases. Because the data are collected from tax file documents, it can be presumed that poor households are underrepresented.

In the **United Kingdom,** the poverty rate among elderly and aged single women is higher than the poverty rate among the same age groups of single men. However, the poverty rate of couples in all three age groups tend to be the highest.

At first glance, the problem of poverty among the elderly and aged in the **Netherlands** seems to be resolved and there seems to be no discrimination between the sexes - this conclusion, however, must be drawn with care. Co-workers of the LIS-project informed me that in the Dutch data it was assumed afterwards that each old person receives his basic pension. Whether this reflects reality remains unproved.

The 60% poverty ratios (Table 5) confirm the preceding findings. The hypothesis that poverty rises with age can only be confirmed if persons 75 and older are compared to persons between 65 and 74. It cannot be confirmed by comparing people between 65 and 74 with those in younger age groups. Upon reaching the age of retirement, a decrease in the poverty rate can be seen.

The hypothesis that the share of poor people among women is greater than among men can be, as a result, confirmed. However, often the elderly and aged couples represent a greater potential of risk than single women. The reason for this phenomenon could be that couples often must live from only one pension

Table 5: Poverty rates (under the 60 % poverty line)

		NL 87	IT 86	FR 84	BE 88	UK 86	GE 84
One person household							
- male	-64	18.3	9.8	19.7	11.4	14.3	17.3
	65-74	0.0	22.0	11.4	18.2	12.2	11.6
	75+	0.0	41.9	14.4	21.4	24.1	7.5
- female	-64	17.4	19.5	20.2	17.9	16.3	23.5
	65-74	0.0	32.5	12.2	15.0	23.0	13.4
	75+	0.0	44.1	15.6	18.5	27.0	25.6
Married couple							
	-64	2.8	8.6	11.0	4.2	9.2	3.9
	65-74	0.3	7.5	2.7	8.2	7.4	8.5
	75+	0.0	13.0	0.8	12.0	13.6	17.9
Other							
	-64	30.0	29.7	30.5	17.2	27.8	24.0
	65-74	26.3	34.9	28.6	21.4	22.4	10.9
	75+	(15.8)	36.1	26.5	31.4	18.4	30.0
Average		22.4	28.8	27.0	17.2	25.5	20.6

( ) insignificant numbers

whereas single women have at least small personal or derived pension claims. This result is, of course, also influenced by the choice of the equivalence scale.[5]

In the Netherlands, the poverty rate of elderly and aged couples is also higher than the poverty rate of single women and single men; the reason being that single persons receive 70% of the net minimum wage as a basic pension, whereas couples together receive only 100%.

In the international comparison of old age poverty prevention, especially among the elderly, Italy, Belgium and the United Kingdom provide the least protection for their elderly single men. Concerning single women, Germany is second in the group which provides the least protection. The poverty rates of couples for all countries is moving closer together. At the 50% poverty line, Germany has the worst record with the prevention of poverty among its elderly couples.

5 On the problem of the effects of using different equivalence scales, see Mercader (1993).

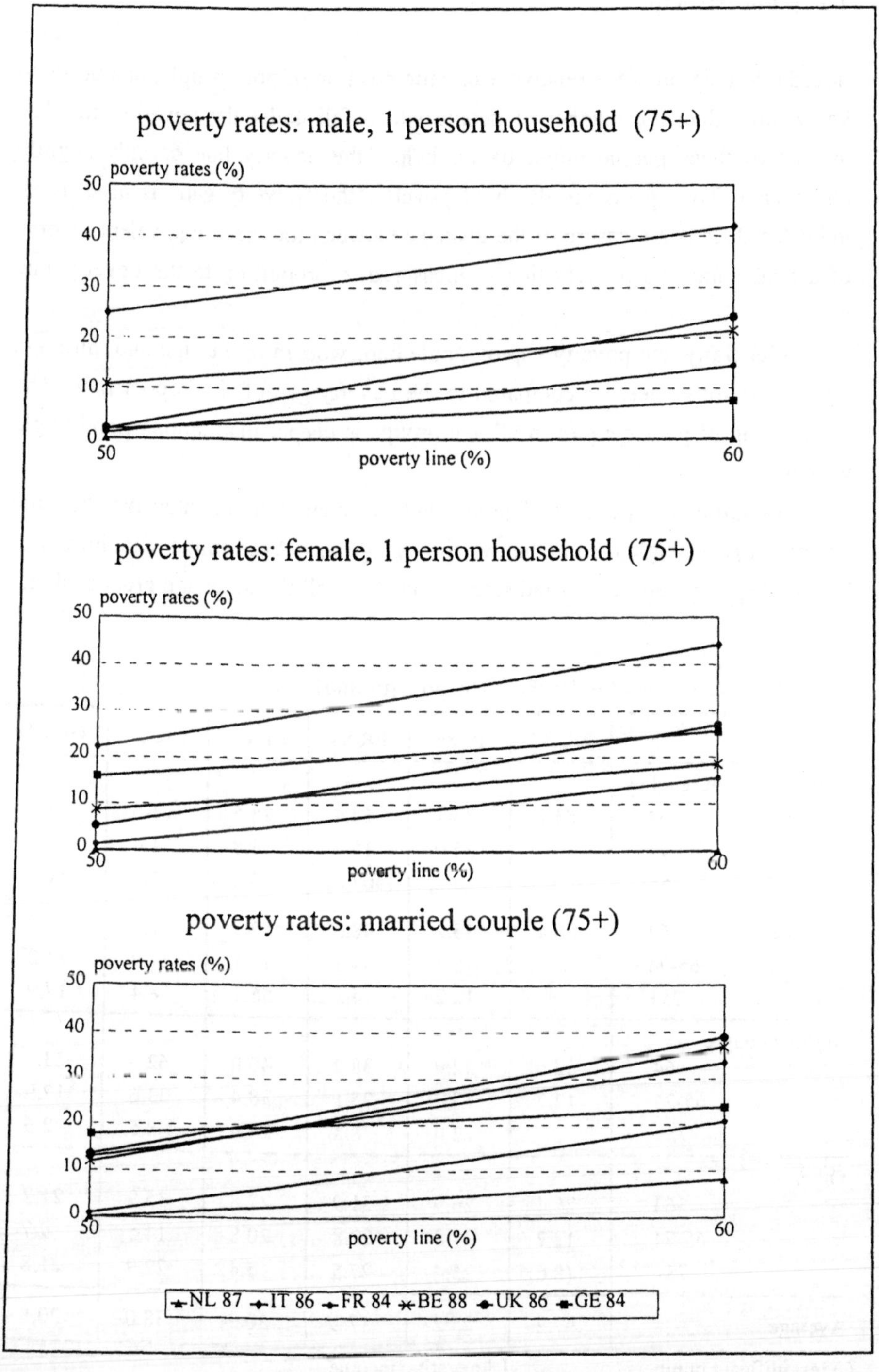
poverty rates: male, 1 person household (75+)
poverty rates (%)
50
40
30
20
10
0
50
poverty line (%)
60
poverty rates: female, 1 person household (75+)
poverty rates (%)
50
40
30
20
10
0
50
poverty line (%)
60
poverty rates: married couple (75+)
poverty rates (%)
50
40
30
20
10
0
50
poverty line (%)
60
NL 87
IT 86
FR 84
BE 88
UK 86
GE 84

4.3 Poverty gap

In order to determine the relative economic position of poor people, one needs to know more than the number of people which fall under the poverty line. The income of these people might be far below the poverty line or only slightly underneath. To express the depth of poverty, the "poverty gap" is used as an indicator. This is a measure of the distance between the mean equivalent income of the poor and the poverty line as measured in proportion to the poverty line itself.

In **Germany,** the poverty gap of single poor women in the first and third age groups are not so deep as compared to the poverty gap of single poor men. The poverty gap of poor couples in all age groups is deeper than among poor single women.

In **Belgium,** the poverty of poor single women is more intensive than the poverty of poor single men in the two first age groups. Aged single men, however, live in deeper poverty than aged single women. In all the three age groups, single

Table 6: Poverty gaps (under the 50 % poverty line)

		NL 87	IT 86	FR 84	BE 88	UK 86	GE 84
One person household							
- male	-64	84.2	33.1	68.4	28.5	61.6	23.5
	65-74		35.0	15.7	14.8	21.4	
	75+		13.6	[502.8]	66.3	5.5	51.8
- female	-64	88.4	15.2	48.6	52.9	52.1	21.5
	65-74		12.2	34.3	43.1	11.9	14.2
	75+		12.2	4.5	56.1	8.4	17.9
Married couple							
	-64	62.6	22.0	38.2	40.0	62.9	23.7
	65-74	17.7	18.7	25.1	38.4	33.6	17.9
	75+		22.0	8.3	24.0	8.5	22.5
Other							
	-64	26.4	26.9	31.9	22.8	35.9	21.2
	65-74	12.7	31.8	22.8	20.8	14.5	9.7
	75+	(8.6)	25.4	27.5	15.4	22.9	21.8
Average		47.2	25.2	37.2	30.2	38.0	20.8

( ) insignificant numbers [ ] negative income

Table 7: Poverty gaps (under the 60 % poverty line)

		NL 87	IT 86	FR 84	BE 88	UK 86	GE 84
One person household							
- male	-64	71.2	39.7	60.9	33.5	46.1	23.5
	65-74		28.7	9.6	22.6	15.4	9.7
	75+		19.8	37.1	39.6	9.5	24.2
- female	-64	80.5	21.6	44.1	32.1	35.6	23.6
	65-74		17.4	18.1	31.7	13.5	20.7
	75+		18.1	10.4	36.4	10.7	22.3
Married couple							
	-64	46.2	22.6	33.8	26.0	45.9	22.6
	65-74	11.6	17.5	11.0	21.5	17.4	22.0
	75+	9.7	17.1	7.7	16.6	13.5	28.4
Other							
	-64	23.5	27.5	29.8	19.7	33.6	21.1
	65-74	22.5	32.3	25.2	23.2	22.5	21.5
	75+	(23.9)	27.7	19.7	17.9	17.6	30.8
Average		35.9	25.7	30.3	22.8	29.9	22.3

( ) insignificant numbers

women are more affected by poverty than couples.

In **Italy,** poor single women are in a better position than poor single men and/or poor couples. This also applies to the **United Kingdom**.

In **France,** the poverty of poor single women is deeper than the poverty experienced of poor couples in both of the first age groups. Single young men that fall under the poverty line are on average poorer than young single women. With increasing age, this relation inverses itself. Note that the results for aged single men has not been interpreted because a negative average equivalent income makes a comparison with the other cases cited here (that all have a positive average income) impossible.

In the **Netherlands,** little can be said about the intensity of poverty during old age of single women and men because, according to the data set, poverty does not exist. Despite the existence of a system of social assistance in the Netherlands, the intensity of poverty among single young men and women is frightfully high. The preceding interpretation results for the 50% poverty gap are essentially confirmed by the analysis of the 60% poverty gaps.

The following conclusions can be drawn: In all countries there is a decrease in the intensity of poverty when people reach the age of retirement. Nevertheless, in some countries, namely Belgium, Italy, Germany and UK, the poverty gaps among the elderly and aged are very high. The old age security in this cases does not contribute satisfactorily to the prevention of poverty.

Here one can see a trend that the poverty of single women is not so deep as the poverty of single men or couples. A possible reason for this trend could be the frequent accumulation of personal and derived pensions in the case of widows.

4.4 Summary of results

When individuals reach retirement, the moment when the systems of old age security start to work, a decrease in poverty rates and poverty gaps can be observed. In general, poverty rates with regard to older people increase with age. However, this pattern cannot be found for the intensity of poverty (poverty gaps). The poverty rate of single women is higher than the poverty rate of single men. Poor single women, however, do not live in such deep poverty.

5 Further Research

Further research is necessary to see the influence of; a) different income sources on the prevention of poverty, and b) to better understand the influence of pensions on prevention of poverty among the elderly. Especially with regard to a comparison of males and females, it would be desirable to have a data set that separately identifies personal and derived pensions. Unfortunately, the LIS data set does not provide such information.

It would be ideal to have data which were collected using the same survey method within the EU. Of course, a common and up-to-date reference year would also be desirable.

References

Atkinson, Anthony B.: "On the Measurement of Poverty", in: Econometrica, 55, 4, 1987

Döring, Diether et. al.: Old-age Security of Women in Twelve EC-countries - To what extent are Beveridges Two Main Principles of Universality and Guaranteed Minimum Income Fulfilled, Luxembourg Income Study, Working Paper No. 81, Walferdange 1992

Eurostat: Armut in Zahlen: Europa zu Beginn der achtziger Jahre, Luxembourg 1990

Hauser, Richard: Mindestsicherung im Alter - ausgewählte ökonomische Aspekte unter Berücksichtigung von Wanderungen, in: Winfried Schmähl (ed.): Mindestsicherung im Alter, Erfahrungen, Herausforderungen, Strategien, Frankfurt am Main/New York 1993, pp. 75-99

Hauser, Richard: Some Problems in Defining a Poverty Line for Comparative Studies, in: G. Sarpellon, (ed.): Understanding Poverty, Milan 1984

Hohnerlein, Eva-Maria: Kompensatorische Regelungen der gesetzlichen Alterssicherungssysteme bei durchbrochenen Erwerbsbiographien - Ansätze zur Anerkennung unbezahlter Familienarbeit in den Ländern der Europäischen Gemeinschaft, in: Informationsdienst der Gesellschaft für Versicherungswissenschaft und -gestaltung, No. 231, 1992, pp. 1-27

Kommission der Europäischen Gemeinschaften: Ältere Menschen in Europa: Wirtschafts- und Sozialpolitik. Bericht 1993 der europäischen Beobachtergruppe, Brüssel

Mercader, Magda: The Low Income Population in Spain and a Comparison with France and the UK: Evidence from the Household Expenditure Surveys, Discussion Paper of the Suntory-Toyota International Centre for Economics and Related Disciplines # WSP/95, London, 1993

Reinhard, Hans-Joachim: Die Stellung der Frau in den Alterssicherungssystemen des Auslandes, Köln 1992

Schulte, Bernd: Praktizierte Formen der Mindestsicherung im Alter - ein rechtsvergleichender Überblick, in: Winfried Schmähl (ed.): Mindestsicherung im Alter - Erfahrungen, Herausforderungen, Strategien, Frankfurt am Main/New York 1993, pp. 27-74.

Smeeding, Timothy M., Michael O'Higgins and Lee Rainwater (eds.): Poverty, Inequality and Income Distribution in Comparative Perspective. The Luxembourg Income Study, New York et al. 1990

Zacher, Hans F. (ed.): Alterssicherungssysteme im Rechtsvergleich, Baden-Baden 1991

Changes in the Rate and Types of Poverty: The Czech and Slovak Republics 1990-1993[1]

Jiri Veçerník

The beginning of the economic transition in all post-communist countries has caused a number of social problems. First, price liberalization has led to a general decrease in the purchasing power of incomes and thus has made an increasing part of the population vulnerable to poverty. Second, the reduced state monopoly and the start of privatization of big enterprises has resulted in unemployment, which was mostly unknown until this time. In addition to the "old poverty", which especially endangered single headed or large families and the oldest pensioners, there is an emerging "new poverty" which stems from unemployment or the low adaptability of some households to the new conditions. Economically unstable households are those that are the least able to take advantage of the new possibilities and to mobilize alternative economic sources (e.g., transferring to the expansive segments of the labor market, utilizing secondary incomes, making use of old or newly acquired real estate, etc.).

Although the actual socio-economic situation is not so acute in the Czech Republic, the threat of future poverty to a part of the populace is worthy of attention by the economic and other social research communities. Greater problems are appearing in the Slovak Republic, mostly due to the much higher rate of unemployment. However, unlike Western countries, where the study of poverty has a long tradition and constitutes an important topic within economics

---

1 This research was supported by the ACE Grant No. ERB4012PL9 10135 "Poverty, Welfare Policy and Work Incentives in the Czech and Slovak Republics" of the European Community and Grant No. 828106 "Labor Market, Income Distribution and Social Policy during the Period of Transformation" of the Grant Agency of the Academy of Sciences, Czech Republic. Thanks are due to Stein Ringen, Oxford University, Vanessa Fry, University of Essex and especially to Thesia I. Garner, U.S. Department of Labor for valuable comments.

and the social sciences, such a tradition was broken in the former Czechoslovakia. Behind the macro-economic mainstream, the economics of inequality and social security are only slowly emerging and there is but little research activity on the relationship between economics and sociology.

In this paper, we aim to show the relevance of the poverty issue in the Czech and Slovak societies and use various indicators for its measurement. For this, we use data from statistical surveys, and especially original microdata from the regular sociological surveys "Economic Expectations and Attitudes" from 1991-1993. First we present the relevent historical background, followed by a description of poverty under emerging markets. Section three contains a description of the data and the various indicators of poverty. Section four discusses the particulars of the poverty populations, and section five provides conclusions. In the historical part, we refer to former Czechoslovakia and also to the Czech and Slovak Republics (still being covered by the Federation) separately. For development after the split of CSFR, we refer mostly to the Czech Republic only.

1 Poverty under "Real Socialism"

Discussions of poverty in "socialist" Czechoslovakia were taboo. Officially, there was no poverty. However, the very reason for the small incidence of relative poverty was low income inequality. The narrow range of income distribution created a situation in which the bottom sector of the population was not too far from the average. By impoverishing the population as a whole (in absolute terms), the communist regime succeeded in mitigating individual poverty (in relative terms). Individual poverty was, then, camouflaged by the poverty of the population as a whole.

In terms of starvation, primitive shelter, etc. there was little absolute poverty in former Czechoslovakia. Due to the continuing pre-war traditions, the high level of industrialization and the economy's relatively good performance, the Czechoslovak populace succeeded in maintaining a decent standard of living indeed, one of the among the former communist countries best (together with the former GDR). The social security system also functioned quite well and met at least the subsistence needs of an overwhelming majority of the population.

However, it does not mean that poverty in absolute terms was entirely eliminated or camouflaged. Extremely low pension benefits given to the members of the former "bourgeoisie" (including expropriated peasants) were used as weapons in the "class war" against them. Due to the absence of any valorization or indexing, the purchasing power of older people's pensions dropped below the average pension and the average pension dropped behind the average wage.[2] The material situation of single women with children was also very acute. In addition, the living conditions of Roms (Gypsies) concentrated in some East Slovak regions could be characterized as those of an underclass - with the absence of elementary facilities of civilization (e.g., running water, sewerage and heating).

Except for some unofficial calculations on relative poverty in the late 1960s, socio-economic research on poverty was officially prohibited. Neither existing income surveys (microcensuses) nor family expenditure surveys were used to depict the situation of low-income households. But we must mention Miroslav Hirçl, who worked in the Research Institute of Labor and Social Affairs. Hirçl used statistical microcensuses to compute changes in the number of households and individuals under the relative poverty line. He defined a "social minimum" as 56% and a "subsistence minimum" as 42% of the average equivalent household income. In calculating the equivalence units, the economic status (active or inactive head of household) and the ages of children were taken into account -no other economies of scale were considered in the calculations.

A compilation of Hirçl's calculations is presented in Table 1. Percentage changes of the population which fell below both the subsistence and social minimum lines resulted mostly from shifts in the distribution of household incomes. Because of the low and stable range of the distribution of market incomes (wages), these shifts were caused mainly by changes in the size and composition of households regarding economically active and dependent members.[3] The profile of the categories under the "threshold of social necessity"

---

2 Pension and other benefits were increased from time to time according to government decisions or new law. The increase used to be presented as a "gift" from the party/state.

3 As we have revealed, the per capita income distribution had a marked demographic character in the former Czechoslovakia (unlike other Central European countries), i.e. was mainly a function of the proportion of active and dependent members in households (Veçerník 1991a).

Table 1: Population below the subsistence and social minimum in 1958-1988 Former Czechoslovakia

	1958	1965	1970	1973	1976	1980	1985	1988
Subsistence minimum (42% of average equivalent household income)								
Thousands of:								
households	223	145	109	100	115	60	50	0
persons	725	363	315	287	289	141	142	0
children	244	108	116	100	96	49	59	0
Percent of:								
households	5.5	3.4	2.4	2.1	2.3	1.1	1.0	0.0
persons	5.5	2.6	2.2	2.0	2.0	0.9	0.9	0.0
children	5.7	2.5	2.8	2.4	2.2	1.1	1.3	0.0
Social minimum (56% of average equivalent household income)								
Thousands of:								
households	439	429	568	606	583	506	406	404
persons	1434	1259	1502	1539	1539	1233	1039	1141
children	499	445	487	466	500	423	386	456
Percent of:								
households	10.9	10.0	12.3	12.6	11.7	9.5	7.7	7.3
persons	10.9	9.1	10.6	10.7	10.1	8.2	6.8	7.4
children	11.7	10.3	12.0	11.0	11.4	9.3	8.3	10.0

Source: Calculations of M. Hirçl based on the Microcensus data.

was, an especially demographic and overwhelmingly transitory one.[4] The effect of narrowing the per capita income distribution induced a decrease in or even disappearance of the main categories of the poor.

Since the early 1980s, the "threshold of social necessity" served as an orientation base for local authorities to administer means-tested social benefits. This threshold was established through a compilation of individual and household benefits, with requirements for special diet and rent having been considered

4 The transitory character of poverty was proved in a retrospective quasi-panel study on Microcensus data 1980-1984 in which less than 10% of the low income households in 1980 remained in the same position in 1984 (analysis was made by M. Hirçl and J. Veçerník but was never published).

separately. No exact rationale was given by government authorities for the amounts of money to be given to households in need. No statistical information on the number of households and the proportion of the "officially poor" was ever published.[5] This differs from the situation in Poland, Hungary and the former Yugoslavia, where the officially established minimum is not connected to social benefits, but where statistical information on the percentage of the poor has been available for many years (Milanovic 1990).

2 Poverty under Emerging Markets

The new economic and social situation after the visible collapse of the communist regime in November 1989 has exposed the problem of poverty manifestly and urgently. In addition to the fact that social problems could be finally treated explicitly and barriers to research were removed, several important changes occurred in the economic life and material well-being of the Czechoslovak population. In part, these were changes that led to a considerable lowering of household incomes and their purchasing power.

1. In July 1990, the old system of price subsidies was partly removed and replaced by a flat-rate benefit given to everyone. Instead of heavily subsidized prices for foodstuffs, everybody received an equal amount of money calculated as an "average" subsidy. Due to the various economies of scale, pensioners and families with older children were therefore substantially discriminated against.[6] In 1992, these subsidies were partly removed and maintained exclusively for children and pensioners.
2. In January 1991, price liberalization commenced and the prices of almost all goods, except several food items (where ceilings on prices were established) increased rapidly. After the initial rise, price levels more or less stabilized with some prices even falling a little. On average, living costs increased by 54% in 1991 (by 45% for food, 72% for other commodities and 40% for services), a

5 Official statistics from the Ministry of Labour and Social Affairs inform us solely about the amount of money spent for this purpose; they do not give exact details on the number of recipients or the number of months that benefits were paid.

6 The actual function of the old and new systems was compared by using family expenditure data in Veçerník, 1991c.

real contrast to the outcome of the huge rise in energy prices (150-300%) that occurred in May, 1991. In 1992, the remaining price ceilings were removed but rents (heavily undervalued, very often ridiculously low) were allowed to increase by a mere 100%.

3. With the first steps of the economic reform, unemployment has emerged. The apparent overemployment and labor shortages under the communist regime transformed into increasing unemployment: 1.5% in January, 3.8% in June and 6.7% in December 1991. Since January 1992, the unemployment rate has once again declined and in early 1993, it fell below 3%. It should be stressed that the enactment of the so-called law on bankruptcy was postponed from one month to another and ever since its acceptance in early 1993, it has not yet actually been applied. The largest number of dismissals is probably yet to come.

On the other hand, however, personal and household incomes saw a significant increase as a result of a few relevant factors.

1. Most social benefits (pensions and family allowances) were valorized several times; low wages rose due to the establishment of a minimum wage; and within limits determined by the government, the average wage has risen considerably.
2. The slowly growing private sector started to bring profits to the new self-employed and capitalists (and even more to old speculators); and the low efficiency of the revenue institutions has allowed a large amount of tax and customs-duty dodging.
3. Many people started to work for foreign firms (for doubled or tripled earnings) or abroad (benefiting from a very advantageous exchange rate when returning home); and any official or unofficial possibilities to profit from open borders were used.

Main indicators of change for the Czech Republic are summarized in Table 2. According to the official figures, real incomes of the population fell by 25% in 1991 and rose again by 6% in 1992. The actual growth of incomes was, however, probably much higher, due to hidden incomes from the "informal economy" and abroad. At the same time, inequality in living conditions rose considerably and economic hardship affected many households. Income inequality rose by different degrees according to various indicators. Based on our calculations, between 1988 and early 1993, a Gini coefficient of earnings increased from 0.19 to 0.26,

Table 2: Main economic and social indicators of the Czech Republic 1990-1993

	1990	1991	1992	mid-1993
Indicators of growth (%):				
GDP (constant prices 1984)	-1.2	-14.2	-7.1	1.1
Consumer prices	9.7	56.6	11.1	21.8
Real income of population	-1.2	-24.8	5.9	3.2
Real wages	-5.7	-25.7	9.8	5.2
Unemployment rate (%)	0.8	2.6	3.1	2.7
Minimum wage (CRK* monthly)	2000	2200	2200	2200
Minimum wage in % of average wage	x	52.8	47.1	37.9
Minimum pension (CRK* monthly):				
for single person	1340	1800	1980	2060
for couple	2280	3060	3360	3500
Minimum pension for single person in % of average net wage	51.6	59.4	53.0	44.1

Source: Main economic and social indicators of the Czech Republic 1993.
* CRK = Czech Republic Crown, 100 CRK = about 3,5 USD

household incomes from 0.27 to 0.31, and incomes per capita from 0.18 to 0.27.[7] The difference between a small increase of inequality in household incomes and a bigger increase in per capita income is given by the fact that income position of pensioners' households was kept (by social benefits) relatively better than the income position of families with more children. One must stress that not only the top but also the bottom income level rose quicker than average because the increase in income inequality was considerably reduced by social transfers.

7 Here, we compare data from two methodologically different sources: for 1988, we use Microcensus 1989 effectuated on a huge sample with wages verified by employers. For 1993, we use the Economic Expectations and Attitudes Survey from January 1993. This comparison has only approximate informative value.

Figure 1a: Poverty will be considerable - Czech Republic

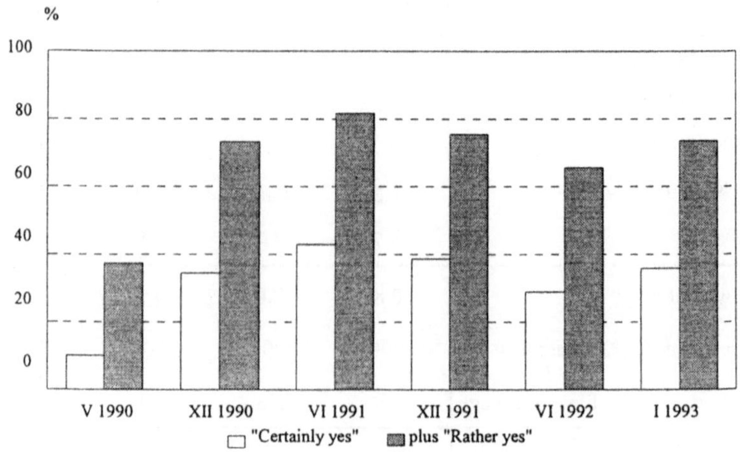

Figure 1b: Poverty will be considerable - Slovak Republic

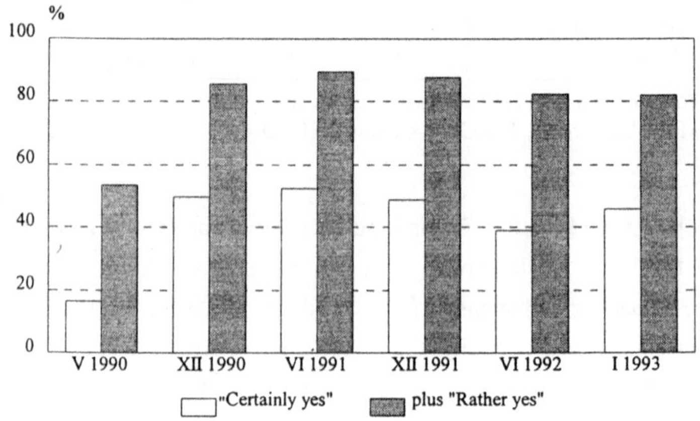

Ongoing real changes were perceived by the population as rapidly increasing threats. By using the data of "Economic Expectations and Attitudes" (Figures 1 and 2)[8] we see two slightly different stories. When regarding the fear of poverty, it

8 The exact wording of questions used in Figures 1 and 2 is: 1. "Do you think that problem of poverty will be in our society vital in the near future?" with answers "certainly yes", "rather yes", "rather no" "certainly no"; 2. "Can you make ends meet with the actual net income of your household?" with answers corresponding to the Deleeck question - see Appendix.

Figure 2a: Financial difficulties - Czech Republic

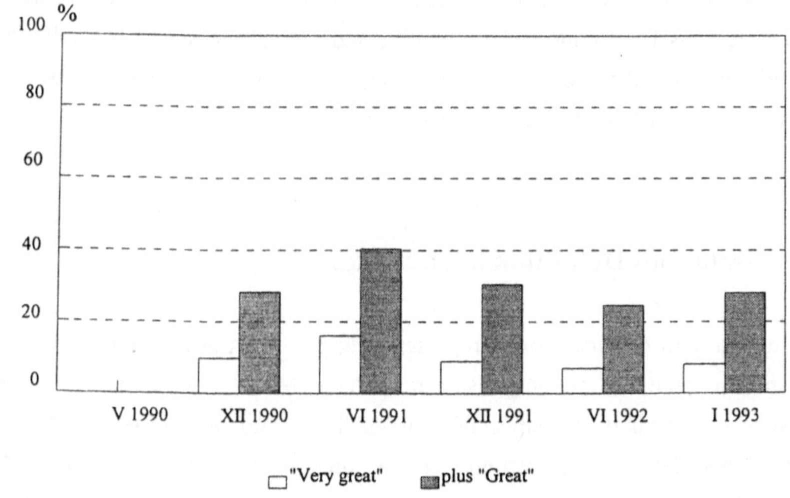

Figure 2b: Financial Difficulties - Slovak Republic

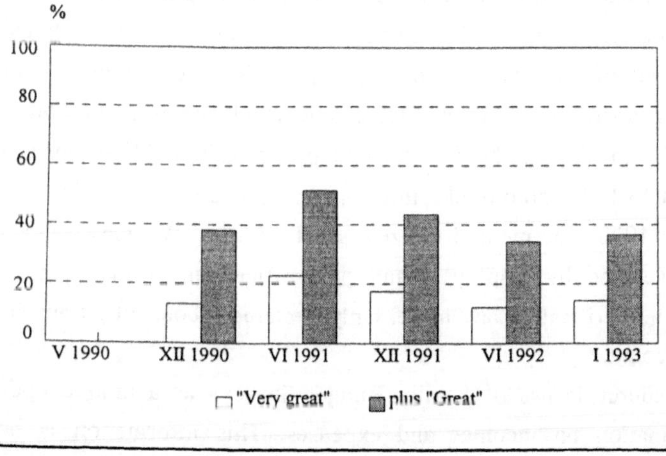

increased suddenly during second half of 1990 (when foodstuff price subsidies were removed) and first half of 1991 (when prices were liberalized), decreased in mid-1992 (when the population "adapted" itself on higher prices) and rose again in early 1993 in the Czech Republic (when a new tax and benefit system was introduced). However once established, its level remained considerable. When regarding actual financial troubles of households, they manifest more or less the same alteration over time, but unlike the fear of poverty, they remain on a much lower level. The highest percentage of households with serious financial difficulties was 16% in the Czech Republic and 23% in the Slovak Republic (both in mid-1991, i.e. the peak of the price rise). One can say that fear of poverty is still much greater than its reported occurrence.

3 Data and Definition of Indicators

It is not easy to provide current representative data on poverty when changes in the income composition and distribution have been very rapid. The official statistics on earnings, incomes, the cost-of-living and unemployment are very often incomplete. No governmental documentation is provided concerning households under the official poverty line which are receiving social benefits.

Nevertheless, there are three potential sources of information on poverty. The first and most reliable source is a large number of Microcensuses (income surveys) which describe household monetary and in-kind incomes, the housing, and the equipment of households with durable goods. The last pre-transition Microcensus was carried out in March 1989 and depicts incomes in 1988 on a 2% sample of Czechoslovak households. The first post-transition Microcensus was conducted in March 1993 and provides information on incomes on a 0.5% sample of households in 1992. The method utilized is not uniform. Whereas wages and pensions were verified by employers and post offices under the communist regime, there is no verification any more. Only declared incomes by households are taken into account.

The second source is use of Family Budget Surveys as a unique updated source of information on incomes and expenses. This information is being collected in the Czech Republic on a sample of about 3,150 households in 1993 and is being published quarterly for various types of households.[9] A particularity of Czechoslovak Family Budget Surveys is that they are not collected from a random sample, but gathered from a quasi-panel of volunteer households with a

---

9 The sample size of Family Expenditures was, for economic reasons, significantly reduced after 1990, from about 4000 to 3150 households.

limited representativeness. Beginning in 1991, a special sub-sample of low income households was added to this survey which serves as the calculation of the minimum income.

The two above mentioned statistical surveys indicate the objective situation only. A comparison of the objective and subjective indicators of poverty are missing. For this reason, we have included several questions on income and poverty in the periodical survey Economic Expectations and Attitudes questionnaire which encompasses a large area of the economic climate, as well as the material conditions and behavior of households and expected reactions to the new economic problems. Here, we use the question about feeling poor and the Minimum Income Question for the respondent's household.[10]

For simplicity's sake, poverty in this study is measured by four indicators, two of them being "objective" (POOR1 and POOR2), two "subjective" (POOR3 and POOR4), two "international" (POOR2 and POOR3), two "domestic" (POOR1 and POOR4), two rather "absolute" (POOR1 and POOR4) and two rather "relative" (POOR2 and POOR3).

- **POOR1. Official poverty.** Households below the "subsistence minimum" line (or "threshold of social necessity") which serves as a base for means-tested social benefits.
- **POOR2. The European Community Standard.** Households below 50% of the median of income per equivalent adult which is compute as 1.0 for the first adult, 0.7 for other adults and 0.5 for each child.
- **POOR3. Subjective poverty.** Households below the Subjective Poverty Line (SPL) as measured by the Minimum Income Question.
- **POOR4. Feeling of poverty.** Respondents' households who answered "definitely yes" to the question "Do you feel your household is poor?"

Through these indicators, we can compare not only various measurements of poverty in the Czech and Slovak Republics, but also compare the situation in our countries with EC countries or the USA. In such a way we can also identify different levels of poverty and various groups of the population affected by it.

---

10 For other uses, we also included in the questionnaire the Van Praag's "Income Evaluation Question" (in six levels) and the "Delleck Question" about making ends meet (in six categories) - see Appendix for exact wording of individual questions.

4 Results: Different Faces of Poverty

Poverty measurements have been discussed at great length from both the methodological and statistical points of view (Atkinson 1989, Atkinson 1990, Townsend 1970, Goedhart, Halberstadt, Kapteyn and Van Praag 1977). Therefore, in this paper we shall not go into detail concerning theories and methods. Using the data from the surveys noted earlier, we will give basic information and show the population characteristics of those falling below the four thresholds of poverty: official (POOR1) and EC standard (POOR2) which gives the lowest level, subjective poverty (POOR3) which gives the highest level and perceived poverty (POOR4) which is in the middle.

4.1 "Official" poverty

For social policy, poverty is conceived to be either an objective situation of means insufficiency, calculated either with reference to nutrition and other basic needs (an absolute approach) or as a distance from the average income in a society (a relative approach). The latter definition is the European Community poverty line in which the poverty line is calculated as half of an average equivalent household income (O'Higgins, Jenkins 1990) when the equivalence scale is computed as 1.0 for the first adult, 0.7 for other adults and 0.5 for children. A combination of the absolute and relative approaches was recommended by a Czechoslovak expert committee and applied by the Ministry of Labor and Social Affairs. This calculation is not only a theoretical exercise but a legal definition used for social measures aiming to support households whose incomes are below the poverty line (POOR1).

A new Law on Subsistence Minimum was accepted by the Czechoslovak Parliament in the Fall of 1991 in order to replace the former rather vague regulation of state aid for low income households. According to the new law, assistance is given to all citizens whose incomes do not reach a certain level and who are not considered able to increase their incomes due to their age, health situation or other serious reasons. Eligibility is reviewed by social security offices in districts following individuals' requests and the household's income and living situation is tested by them. Until now, this poverty line has not included the costs

Table 3: Changes in official subsistence thresholds 1989-1993
Former Czechoslovakia (1989 and 1991) and the Czech Republic (1993)

	Before 1990	November 1991	March 1993
In CSK (CRK) monthly:			
child under 6 years	600	900	1020
child 6 - 10 years	700	1000	1130
child 10 - 15 years	800	1200	1360
child 15 - 25 years	800	1300	1470
adult	800	1200	1360
plus for household composed of:			
one person	300	500	600
two persons	300	650	780
3-4 persons	500	800	960
more persons	500	950	1140
In equivalence units (one adult's household=1,00):			
child under 6 years	0.54	0.53	0.52
child 6 - 10 years	0.64	0.59	0.58
child 10 - 15 years	0.73	0.71	0.69
child 15 - 25 years	0.73	0.77	0.75
adult	0.73	0.71	0.69
plus for household composed of:			
one person	0.27	0.29	0.31
two persons	0.27	0.38	0.40
3-4 persons	0.45	0.47	0.49
more persons	0.45	0.56	0.58

Source: Social Legislation, Documents of the Ministry of Labor and Social Affairs.
The total benefit for a household is computed as a sum of individual benefits. E.g. the benefit for a 4-member household composed of a couple and two children in the age of 10-15 years is calculated as 2x1360 + 2x1360 + 960 = 6400 CRK.

of housing, for which a special benefit is being prepared and will be introduced by January 1994 in the Czech Republic.

Subsistence minimum income is composed of the amounts of money required to meet the basic needs of citizens and the amounts needed to meet the costs of households (Table 3). It was set at about half of the average household income.

The subsistence minimum is increased each time the rise in the cost of living of households below the official poverty line surpasses 10%. The ratio of newly established minimum amounts of money and the average incomes should be maintained by this procedure. Good evidence may be supplied by family budgets of households eligible for the state benefits who are surveyed separately by the Statistical Office.

According to the estimates of the Czech Ministry of Labor and Social Affairs, some 30,000 households (2-3%) and 50-60,000 people fell under the official minimum income in 1992. Because the minimum pension slightly exceeds the official minimum income, no pensioner households should be below the official poverty line. But no detailed information about the composition of the officially poor (how many single parents, how many families with unemployed members, how many households with three and more children, etc.) is available now. The problem is that regional social departments' statistics only indicate how much money is spent to support people living under the official minimum; they do not report how many recipients there are nor report how long recipients receive benefits.

Table 4: Percentages of poor according to various measurements in 1991-1993 Czech and Slovak Republics

	Households		All persons		Children	
Indicator	CR	SR	CR	SR	CR	SR
June 1991:						
POOR1 (official)	2.4	2.9	3.1	3.8	3.8	3.8
POOR2 (EC)	3.7	5.2	3.1	4.8	3.3	4.9
POOR3 (subj. income)	22.2	28.6	18.8	25.1	19.7	27.8
POOR4 (feel poor)	10.8	18.5	10.0	13.9	10.6	12.9
June 1992:						
POOR1 (official)	2.7	2.9	4.1	3.7	6.1	4.7
POOR2 (EC)	2.7	3.7	3.5	3.3	4.5	2.7
POOR3 (subj. income)	24.9	39.7	20.9	35.7	21.0	35.1
POOR4 (feel poor)	8.1	8.7	7.4	7.0	8.4	6.0
January 1993:						
POOR1 (official old)	2.0	3.3	2.6	4.8	4.1	7.3
POOR1 (official new)	3.8	4.5	6.8			
POOR2 (EC)	2.8	3.8	3.0	4.9	3.9	6.3
POOR3 (subj. income)	28.0	29.3	22.1	24.0	18.5	22.9
POOR4 (feel poor)	9.7	10.5	8.6	10.1	7.9	11.2

Source: Economic Expectations and Attitudes, 1991-1993.

Due to the rising costs of living in 1992, the calculation of the minimum income was updated at the beginning of March 1993 for the Czech Republic. Amounts for the needs of children and adults were increased by 13.4% and amounts for common needs of households were increased by 20%, leading to a 14-15% per capita increase on average, according to the type of household. Because minimum pensions were simultaneously increased and the tax burden for the low income population decreased with the introduction of new tax and benefits rules, it is estimated that the number of households below the poverty line will not increase dramatically in 1993 - the predicted rate is set at 70,000 households, i.e. to 4.2% of households. At the same time, the revised Law on Subsistence Minimum introduces stricter eligibility conditions, i.e. it excludes cases where people are reluctant to work, change their job without serious reasons, do not cooperate with their labor office and so on. Mutual responsibility between household members is an important part of means testing now.

Table 5: Percent poor in EC countries (1980s) and the Czech and Slovak Republics (1993)

Country	Year	POOR1 (official)	POOR2 (EC)	POOR3 (subjective)
Czech Republic	1993	2.0	1.4	28.0
Slovak Republic	1993	3.3	1.3	29.3
Belgium	1985	2.9	6.1	24.9
The Netherlands	1986	7.2	7.2	15.9
Luxembourg	1986	5.0	7.6	12.5
Lorraine	1986	4.0	10.8	26.5
Catalonia	1988	n.a.	15.1	37.3
Ireland	1987	8.1	17.2	31.6
Greece	1988	n.a.	19.9	42.0

Sources: Deleeck, Van den Bosch 1992, Economic Expectations and Attitudes, January 1993.

With respect to the percent of households or persons or children, the results from the Economic Expectations and Attitudes surveys are not far from official estimates (Table 4). Between June 1992 and January 1993, the number of households fell from 2.7% to 2.0% according to the 1991 official rate of poverty (POOR1), but rose to 3.8% according to the newly proposed 1993 rate, but actually acting from March 1993 (POOR1a). Because of the fact that below the official poverty line fall families with children only, the percentage of persons and especially the percentage of children who are poor is considerably higher than the percentage of poor households.

Compared with the EC countries, the Czech Republic appears as a country with the lowest portion of the population below the guaranteed subsistence line (POOR1). The figure is even lower than in Belgium where legal poverty is being reported as the lowest among the countries surveyed by Deleeck, Van den Bosch et al. in a comparative survey (Table 5).

4.2 EC poverty

By definition, the establishment of the official poverty line for the Czech and Slovak Republics actually differs only minimally from the European standard as mentioned above (POOR2). The percentages of poor households and persons are

Table 6: Percentage of poor (half average equivalent income - POOR2) in EC countries and former Czechoslovakia in the 1980s

	Households		Persons	
	1980	1985	1980	1985
Belgium	6.3	5.2	7.1	5.9
Denmark	8.0	8.0	7.9	8.0
Germany	10.3	9.2	10.5	9.9
Greece	20.5	17.4	21.5	18.4
Spain	20.3	17.8	20.9	18.9
France	18.0	14.8	19.1	15.7
Ireland	18.5	17.4	18.4	19.5
Italy	12.0	14.7	14.1	15.5
The Netherlands	6.9	7.9	9.6	11.4
Portugal	31.4	31.7	32.4	32.7
U.K.	14.1	18.9	14.6	18.2
Czechoslovakia	5.8	6.2[1]	2.1	3.2[1]

Sources: Eurostat 1990, Microcensuses 1981, 1989.
[1] 1988

only slightly higher than in the official poverty rate, given by a different calculation of equivalent units. In this calculation, the weight of children is higher and that of adults lower in the Czechoslovak calculation than in the one for the EC. The burden of "common household costs" is slightly higher in the Czechoslovak official poverty line.

The calculation of equivalent income using the same scale over different countries is very problematic due to various consumption baskets and various economies of scale. The advantage of it, however, is its easiness of comparison. In the 1980s, the percentage of poor was extremely low in the former Czechoslovakia and especially affected households of pensioners (Table 6). After 1989, this proportion decreased due to a state intervention policy which affected the bottom of the income distribution. As a result, the poverty population changed. Until 1989, there was a substantial percentage of pensioner households at the bottom of the income hierarchy, and due to this, the percentage of households was higher than the percentage of persons. After 1989, pensioners were mostly replaced by families with children at the bottom of the income distribution. These families were favoured by social policy much less than were pensioners.

4.3 Subjective poverty

According to Van Praag, Kapteyn, Goedhart, Rainwater and others, the objective definition of poverty manifests a paternalistic and statist approach. They posit that it is the citizens or families themselves who should decide about the adequacy of their means to meet needs (Goedhart et al. 1977, Kapteyn et al. 1985). Poverty is understood as "a feeling and not an objective situation" (Van Praag and Flik 1991). According to Rainwater, both poverty and the equivalence scale are social constructs and we should distinguish between *state* and *societal* poverty lines (Rainwater 1977, 1990).

There are several possible measures of "subjective poverty" that are based on respondents' declarations about the distance between an actual and needed income and their relative deprivation (see Appendix B for various questions). Diverse subjective indicators of poverty yield different figures concerning the poverty incidence, although in actual fact, they correlate very closely with each other. Here, we use the Subjective Poverty Line, i.e. the "basic needs amount" calculated as a national (not individual) income sufficiency threshold (POOR3).[11]

Using this measurement, there is a considerable proportion of households who declare their own minimum income as lower than the Subjective Poverty Line. There are two possible reasons why these percentages are high. First, the "basic needs amount" could be exaggerated and second, the current income could be underestimated. Underreporting of actual income is a likely result since people probably do not declare income from informal sources, single gains and gifts, etc. Taking both reasons together, the percentage of households below the Subjective Poverty Line can reach almost one third of the population in the Czech and Slovak Republics, but the figures are not very far from those for Belgium, Lorraine or Ireland (Table 5).

---

11 In the calculation, logarithm of Y_{min} (income estimated by the Minimum Income Question), Y (current income of the household) and fs (size of the household) are computed first. Then, the log-linear relationship is calculated

$$\ln Y_{min} = \beta_0 + \beta_1 \ln fs + \beta_2 \ln Y,$$

and poverty thresholds for each household size are calculated as:

$$Y_{min} = \exp[(\beta_0 + \beta_1 \ln fs)/(1-\beta_2)].$$

Table 7: The "get along" and "minimum income" amount in loglinear regressions in the former Czechoslovakia (1991) and the USA (1986)

	"Get along amount" for a family of four		"Minimum income" for the own household	
	CSFR 1992	USA 1986	CSFR 1992	USA 1986
Constant	8.202	8.282	6.334	6.686
ln household income	0.031	0.147	0.278	0.286
ln household size			0.290	0.186
Age of the head[1]			-0.011	-0.010
Adj R^2	0.003	0.085	0.246	0.322

Sources: Source: Economic Expectations and Attitudes, July 1992; Rainwater 1990.
[1] Absolute difference between 43 and respondent's age: in both the USA and former Czechoslovakia, the age around 43 means a culmination of the subjective need.

Some particular features of poverty "as a social construction" can be seen from a comparison with the USA using regression analysis (Table 7). The main difference between the two countries is in the proportion of household income and size in determining the "minimum income" amount. In the USA, the household income contributes more to "minimum income" while in the former Czechoslovakia there is a similar contribution of household income and size. In contrast to Rainwater's finding for the USA, using a Gallup Poll (Rainwater 1990), children in former Czechoslovakia do not seem to be as "cheap". Nevertheless, they are much cheaper according to subjective measures than in the construction of the official poverty line. This is due not only to the income level, but also to the expenditure structure. The size-dependent expenditures (food, clothing) still represent a much higher proportion of expenditure in the former Czechoslovakia than in Western countries.[12] The liberalization of rents and other housing services should push the consumption and prices of food down, relative

12 According to the Family Budget survey data, in the Czech Republic, expenditures on food has not changed greatly between 1989 and 1992 and represents about 27% of average household expenditures. This stability, however, camouflages significant changes in the behavior of households who should adjust to the withdrawal of subsidies and the full liberalization of food prices.

to other commodities, and change the expenditure structure in favor of the less size-dependent items.[13]

4.4 "Feeling of being poor"

Although Van Praag and others refer to subjective poverty as feeling poor (Van Praag and Flik 1990), it is not necessarily the case. In fact, the various measures of subjective poverty are academic constructs which presume that poverty is an income insufficiency and that the respondents' declarations about both actual and minimum required income are reliable. But results yielded by subjective measurement and by declarations of feeling poor tell slightly different stories concerning the number of poor households, the character of the equivalence scales, and the social structure of poverty.

Unlike official and subjective poverty (as defined in this study), feeling poor (POOR4) seems to be more stable over time, reaching a maximum of 11% households in the Czech Republic and 19% in Slovakia (Table 4). The deviation in the mid-1991 in Slovakia was caused by the impact of a sudden price increase on especially pensioners' households. Unlike both of the above-mentioned indicators, it manifests similar but much weaker patterns of demographic and social determination (excepting families with three and more children who frequently feel themselves poor). Unlike the Subjective Poverty Line the indicator of feeling poor is only very weakly predicted by income. Its variance is less explainable in terms of demographic and socio-economic characteristics. This poverty measurement seems to be somewhat of a special case. Its most significant explanatory variables are not income, but wealth and property. Unlike other poverty indicators, this measure is relatively closely correlated with the household's estimated wealth and with its equipment, i.e. cars and other durable goods. This is related to Townsend's (1979) broader notion of poverty which measures more indicators of a household's material well-being.

The difference between the Czech and Slovak populations is significant especially when comparing reported feelings of poverty (POOR4). Ceteris

---

13 So far, only the prices of energy have increased (by some 200%) and they will rise again. Rent increases in state apartments, which (unlike cooperative apartments) are heavily subsidized, should have occurred in Fall 1992 but was postponed until January 1993.

paribus, Slovak households report needing higher minimum income and more often feel themselves to be poor than do Czech households. In other words, either the utility of the same amount of money seems to be lower in Slovakia or the minimum level is considerably higher. It can be explained by the ampler social protection expectations of the Slovak society and its closer identification with a climate of "social guarantees", given by the fact that it profited more from the communist redistributional system.

4.5 Socio-economic and demographic identification

From our surveys, we can identify the demographic and social structure of the poor population, as measured by various indicators. We select only several basic characteristics of economic status of the head (employed, unemployed), his or her social position (level of education) and the demographic status of a household (single or couple pensioners, number of children, age). Those indicators are summarized in the Table 8.

By definition, official poverty (POOR1) is limited to the economically active age group only because the minimum pension benefit is on a slightly higher level than the poverty line. Also by definition (by committing the larger economies of scale), official poverty is foremost a poverty of families with three or more children or, as the case may be, larger families of all kinds. This is associated with lower levels of education and also smaller localities and the agricultural or service sector.

The poor as identified by the EC standard (POOR2) are very similar in their characteristics as the officially poor. The difference is that only some pensioners can be included and families with more children are slightly less affected because of their lower weight in the calculation. Due to this, also the age differential is not so striking as in the official measurement.

Table 8: The percentage distribution of households in poverty according to economic, social and demographic characteristics

	Czech Republic				Slovak Republic			
	Poor1	Poor2	Poor3	Poor4	Poor1	Poor2	Poor3	Poor4
all	**2.0**	**2.8**	**28.0**	**9.7**	**3.3**	**3.8**	**29.3**	**10.5**
Age of the head:								
20 - 29	3.4	2.5	20.7	5.4	4.0	2.3	25.1	12.0
30 - 39	3.2	1.4	19.3	6.9	2.8	1.7	22.0	5.6
40 - 49	2.0	0.8	12.9	9.0	6.3	2.3	16.7	9.8
50 - 59	0.7	0.7	15.8	11.2	2.5	1.6	21.3	12.3
60 - 75	0.7	1.1	56.7	14.8	0.6	0.0	59.4	13.3
1 pensioner	0.0	1.2	92.6	16.0	0.0	0.0	98.1	19.2
2 pensioners	0.0	0.0	61.0	13.6	0.0	0.0	62.2	10.8
Number of children:								
1	1.2	1.8	67.5	13.3	0.0	0.0	72.7	18.2
2	0.8	0.8	30.4	12.0	1.0	1.0	32.7	8.9
3 and more	2.9	1.4	13.8	7.3	4.9	2.1	19.1	9.6
Education of the head:								
Elementary	2.8	1.1	58.0	15.9	4.0	1.7	49.7	18.9
Vocational	2.8	2.0	25.7	10.2	3.2	1.8	27.9	9.5
Secondary	0.7	0.7	21.1	6.4	3.8	2.1	25.6	9.0
University	0.6	0.0	9.1	6.7	1.7	0.0	6.8	2.6
Size of locality:								
less than 5,000	2.5	1.4	26.8	6.3	4.0	1.6	31.5	10.4
5,000 - 100,000	2.1	1.3	29.5	11.6	3.2	1.8	30.0	10.3
100,000 and over	1.1	1.1	22.9	10.7	1.0	1.0	15.5	10.3

Source: Economic Expectations and Attitudes, January 1993.

Unlike those in the official poverty category, households who declare their minimum income as the Subjective Poverty Line (POOR3) are better located in the socio-economic and demographic structure. First, they tend to be families with younger and especially older household heads and, then, those with one child (young) or childless (old). The proportion of subjectively poor in single pensioner households is especially striking. Second, there is the marked relevance of educational hierarchy, the poor being concentrated in the lowest educational

Table 9: Expenditure shares for households below the official poverty threshold in the first quarters of 1991, 1992 and 1993 - *Czech Republic*

	Expenditures in %			In % of the average		
	I/91	I/92	I/93	I/91	I/92	I/93
Families with children						
Food	34.7	34.1	37.1	84.1	76.6	73.1
Beverages and tobacco	6.0	5.9	4.9	81.0	68.1	65.5
Clothing and footwear	11.1	7.7	7.9	78.2	58.8	54.3
Housing	14.8	16.6	18.4	67.7	75.5	67.6
Household maintenance	3.9	3.3	4.1	75.7	68.9	57.3
Personal needs, health	2.5	2.7	3.1	70.8	64.1	52.7
Transport	9.8	10.5	9.8	65.8	68.2	54.3
Culture and leisure	9.4	8.4	8.4	61.4	51.6	50.4
Total	100.0	100.0	100.0	75.7	68.9	62.5
Pensioners' households						
Food	48.1	40.6	41.3	91.0	91.6	92.7
Beverages and tobacco	5.4	5.0	4.3	59.7	71.4	69.0
Clothing and footwear	5.5	4.9	4.7	60.0	72.4	79.3
Housing	18.1	21.1	23.7	92.8	90.0	86.0
Household maintenance	3.2	2.7	4.0	63.4	70.8	84.5
Personal needs, health	2.5	3.1	4.1	51.5	77.3	79.0
Transport	2.0	2.0	2.2	34.6	34.6	34.8
Culture and leisure	6.2	6.8	5.9	59.9	70.9	66.3
Total	100.0	100.0	100.0	76.4	80.0	81.8

Source: Family Budgets of the Czech Republic 1991-1993.

groups. We should also notice that even on the same income level and size of family, better educated people are less demanding on individual minimum income.

The lowest differences in representation of various categories of the population are seen in the feelings of poverty (POOR4). This indicator partly reproduces the distribution of other poverty measurements. They indicate lower poverty for educated people, and a higher one for pensioners. But POOR4 is much lower for younger people. As we already said, its better predictor is the wealth status of the household.

For only one indicator of poverty (POOR1) we can provide information on the expenditures patterns of households considered poor. According to the Family Budgets from 1991-1993, the difference in the expenditures of the poor from the average was increasing over this time for families with children (Table 9). Households with low incomes reduced especially expenditures on clothing, transport and leisure, some of them very considerably. The less reducible are, obviously, expenses for food and housing.

5 Conclusion

In "socialist" Czechoslovakia, the impoverishment of the population as a whole had mostly hidden poverty of its parts. Nevertheless, the "old poverty" existed and affected the elderly, single-parent families, the disabled population and also de-favorized the "bourgeoisie". The economic transformation, started in 1990, opened the door for an emerging "new poverty" that stems from the rapidly increasing costs of living and appearing unemployment. Neither the "old" nor the "new" poverty is as considerable as in neighboring (Eastern as well as Western) countries, but this does not change the relevance of this study of poverty.

According to the new Czech government's social strategy, economic transformation should be associated with a shift away from the paternalistic state and general "social guarantees" toward an efficient and well targeted welfare policy. Social security is developing in three directions: social insurance, state social support, and social assistance. State social support includes targeted and differentiated aid for households whose incomes are over the poverty line but who are victim to certain situations of financial hardship. Social assistance is oriented towards households with incomes below the poverty line and is conceived at the maximum possible de-centralization of decision making about benefit entitlements. The regulations and administration of social assistance have to ensure better targeting and means testing; only those who are not considered able to solve their financial hardship themselves will be eligible. In order to make social assistance more flexible with regard to the problems of households in need, a new, more effective network of institutions providing social support will have to be established.

According to the empirical results based on Economic Attitudes and Expectations surveys, the poverty rate could be seen from three alternative perspectives and measured by various kinds of indicators. The first is the poverty measured with reference to the official poverty line, which also conforms very well with the EC measure. It shows a poverty rate for households of about 2-4% and, the main determining factor of poverty is the number of dependent children. The second indicator is the subjective poverty measure and ist rate is about 30%. It is much more affected by the number of adults in the household, and by some social characteristics. From this perspective, economies of scale are much higher than in both the official and EC definitions. The third is a simple declaration of poverty with a level of about 10% which is less affected by demographic and social characteristics and more by the wealth status of a household.

Generally, the incidence of poverty has a clear but statistically weak localization in the social and regional structure. Sensitivity to low material status seems to depend on the previous "welfare" character of the social group or territory. This is the case for less educated people or the Slovak population: Under the ceteris paribus condition, both are asking for a higher minimum income and, consequently, manifest more poverty in subjective terms. We should mention the difference between the official poverty and income insufficiency. The first constitutes, except for a very small group of population, a rather tenuous and transitory situation. The second would be better predicted by permanent income or wealth status and manifests itself as a long-term or even permanent situation.

In all indicators, poverty seems almost stabilized in its levels over the past three years, and we should only hope that relatively good performance of the Czech economy and a clever social policy will confine its future incidence to reasonable limits.

Appendix A: Statistical surveys

Microcensus 1981 and Microcensus 1989

Periodical income survey begun in 1958, incomes gathered for the whole years of 1980 and 1988 on 2% sample of households (N= about 100,000). Made by the Federal Statistical Office, Prague.

Family Expenditures
Permanent observation of incomes and expenses of selected households began in 1957. After reduction in the last years, the main sample is about 3,150 households of employees, farmers and private businessmen plus about 500 households with incomes below the official poverty line. Made by the Czech Statistical Office, Prague.

Sociological surveys "Economic Expectations and Attitudes"

Biannual survey organized by the team for socio-economics of the Institute of Sociology of Academy of Sciences headed by the author. Surveys are financed partly by grants from the Academy of Sciences and partly by the Ministry of Labor and Social Affairs of the Czech Republic. The sampling procedure is two-step quota sampling, where in the first step the region and size of the locality were defined and in the second step, gender, age and education. Made by The Center for Empirical Surveys STEM.

Time and samples:		Czech	Slovak
I.	May, 1990	1107	544
II.	December, 1990	1160	584
III.	June, 1991	1092	597
iV.	December, 1991	1126	583
V.	July, 1992	1104	980
VI.	January, 1993	1142	829

Appendix B:

Indicators of poverty

POOR1. Households with incomes below the line as established by the Law on Subsistence Minimum from November 1991.

POOR1a. Households with incomes below the line as established by the update beginning in March 1993.

POOR2. Households with incomes below 50% of the median of income per equivalent adult.

POOR3. Households with incomes below the "Subjective Poverty Line" (computed as in footnote 11).

POOR4. Respondents' households who answered "definitely yes" to the question "Do you feel your household is poor?"

Questions used for measuring subjective poverty:

1. Feeling Poor (POOR4):
   "Do you feel your household is poor?"
   certainly yes
   rather yes
   rather no
   certainly no.

2. Minimum Income Question (POOR3):
   "Which minimum income would require your household to meet basic needs?"

3. Income Evaluation Question:
   "Please try to indicate what you consider to be an appropriate amount for your household for each of the following cases:

very bad income	.... CSK
bad income	.... CSK
Insufficient income	.... CSK
sufficient income	.... CSK
good income	.... CSK
very good income	.... CSK."

4. The "Deleeck Question" (POOR3):
   "Can you make ends meet with the actual net income of your household:
   with great difficulty
   with difficulty
   with some difficulty
   rather easily
   very easily."

References

Atkinson, A.B. 1989. *Poverty and Social Security.* Hemel Hempstead, Harvester Wheatsheaf.

Atkinson, A.B. 1990. "Comparing poverty rates internationally: Lessons from recent studies in OECD countries". Discussion Papers of STICERD, London School of Economics.

Deleeck, H., K. Van den Bosch. 1992. "Poverty and adequacy of social security in Europe: A comparative analysis". Journal of European Social Policy, 2 (2) pp. 107-120.

Eurostat. 1990. Rapid reports. Population and social conditions No. 7.

Goedhart, Th., V. Halberstadt, A. Kapteyn and B.M.S. Van Praag. 1977. "The Poverty Line: Concept and Measurement". The Journal of Human Resources, vol. 12 (4), pp. 503-520.

O'Higgins, M., Jenkins, S. 1990. Poverty in the EC: Estimates for 1975, 1980 and 1985. In R. Teekens and B. Van Praag (eds.) *Analyzing Poverty in the European Community.* Eurostat, Luxembourg.

Kapteyn, A., S. Van de Geer, H. Van der Stadt. 1985. The impact of changes in income and family composition on subjective measures of well-being. In: M. David, T. Smeeding (eds.) *Horizontal Equity and the Distribution of Tax Burden.* Chicago, NBER and Chicago University Press.

Main economic and social indicators of the Czech Republic. 1993. Research Institute of Labor and Social Affaires, Prague.

Milanovic, B. 1990. Poverty in Poland, Hungary and Yugoslavia in the Years of Crisis. Working Papers. World Bank.

Rainwater, L. 1974. *What Money Buys.* Basic Books.

Rainwater, L. 1990. "Poverty and equivalence as social constructions." Prepared for Seminar on Families and Levels of Living: Observations and Analysis. Barcelona. 1990.

Townsend, P. 1970. *The Concept of Poverty.* Heinemann, London.

Van Praag, B.M.S., R.J. Flik. 1990. Subjective poverty. Rotterdam, Foundation for Economic Research.

Van Praag, B.M.S., R.J. Flik. 1991. "Poverty lines and equivalence scales. A theoretical and empirical evaluation." Paper for the conference Poverty Measurement for the Economies in Transition in Eastern European Countries. Warsaw, October 1991.

Veçerník, J. 1991a. The system of distribution in socialist Czechoslovakia: empirical data and hypotheses of explanation (in Czech). Sociologický çasopis, 27 (1), pp. 39-56.

Veçerník, J. 1991b. Earnings distribution in Czechoslovakia: Intertemporal change and international comparison. European Sociological Review, 7 (3), pp 237-252.

Veçerník J. 1991c. Income distribution in Czechoslovakia. Bulletin BIRG (Basic Income Research Group), (13), pp. 14-18.

Social Inequality and Poverty in Russia

Alexander Surinov and Igor Kolosnitsyn[1]

As the reform process in the Russian economy develops, the necessity to provide a comprehensive system of social indicators characterising the impact of transformation upon the social situation in Russia becomes all the more evident. Under the sharp changes in the social structure and the growth of inequality, only the application of quantitative methods to describe the differentiation of the society makes it possible to generate realistic estimates that are useful to decision-making bodies.

1 Analyses

In the first quarter of 1994, due to a deceleration of inflation in Russia, the real value of consumer income increased. However, the additional income was unevenly distributed between different layers of the population. Per capita real income in the highest 20 per cent group (quintile) of households grew at the highest speed - in June 1994 the increase in the real income reached 30 per cent versus June 1993. In the lowest quintile real income decreased by 3 to 5 per cent. In the other income groups, a growth of 10 to 20 per cent was registered.

Income inequality has continued to increase. By June 1994, the relation of income between the groups with the highest and lowest 10-per-cent of the income reached 11.8 times, while the corresponding proportion was only 9.0 a year ago. The gini index increased to 0.365 from 0.325 a year ago.

[1] The Research on which this paper is based was conducted under a grant from the Ford Foundation, and was presented at the Conference on East-West Scientific Cooperation on Regional Structural Change in International Perspective, held at CEPS/INSTEAD, Luxembourg, 11-16 November 1994.

During 1994, the structure of consumer expenditure of different groups of the population changed. However, that change has been unevenly distributed across the groups with different income levels. The groups with lower income can satisfy only their most basic needs - they spend 70 % of total expenditure to procure food and clothing. The nutritional value of the food items that they consume makes up only 80 % of the food basket typical for the groups with higher income. Besides, groups with higher income spend much more on services and durables. It is because of these problems that the traditional average estimates of consumption and consumer behaviour are quickly becoming misleading and non-informative.

To study the life-style and consumption patterns of households in the transitional period, one needs to apply a comprehensive system of economic indicators differentiated according to the layers of households and groups with different income levels.

Currently, the only realistic option is to use the existing network of households who report for "budget statistics". To study the process of growth of income inequality, one should base the investigation on a detailed social, economic and demographic portrait of each and every family in the sample. In other words, income, consumption and expenditure patterns should be regarded within the context of each single family, which might be similar to the other families or else different from them in terms of individual characteristics. The essence of the method which is suggested in this report is that it is based on the unprocessed data of household budget surveys. Starting at this point, a multidimensional typology of families is established based on different indicators characterising their relative position in the society. Such an approach is different from those practices used by the official statistical authorities of the Russian Federation.

The advantage of such an approach is two-fold: it is not only possible to provide a quantitative estimate of the speed and direction of a change in terms of social stratification in Russia, but also portraits of poor, middle class and effluent groups in the population can be drawn with a reasonable degree of accuracy.

The incidence of poverty in the Russian Federation is one of the problems that requires an adequate analysis and that is critically dependent upon the researcher's ability to provide an individual analysis of household behavior. Measuring poverty is not only of interest to scientists and statisticans; it has an immediate political importance for decision-makers, especially at the transition stage. Unless an adequate portrait of poverty is drawn it is impossible to estimate the possible costs of social protection for the vulnerable groups of the population and predict the consequences of policies to combat poverty applied by the state authorities.

A poverty line is commonly defined as a criterion by which a researcher can decide in an empirical way whether a certain household is poor or not. Various methods have been proposed to define a poverty line. The one which is applied in Russia and in most European countries is normally referred to the budget method: A basket of goods and serices deemed necessary is defined, and its total cost is equated with the poverty line. This is the minimum subsistence income.

This procedure is fully described in a document produced by the Russian Ministry of Labour in November 1992. A minimum basket is defined for each of 8 climatic zones inside Russia; consumption standards are adjusted for children and pensioners - special coefficients are used to account for differences in their relative consumption standards. Using this document a researcher can define a subsistance income for every given household depending on the composition of a family and its geographic area of habitation.

This method is quite straightforward (which might be considered an advantage), though at the same time the composition of the basket is arbitrary, and this is especially true as far as the items outside of the food packet are concerned. In fact, to arrive at the poverty line the Ministry suggests that the minimum cost of the food packet should be multiplied by 1,5 and there is no reason to believe that this multiplier is accurate enough.

Inspite of the posssible drawbacks of the method itself, the share of households cut off by the average poverty line is currently regarded in Russia as the single most important social indicator. Suffice it to say that when in June 1992 a decline in the number of poor households (down to 13.5% from 31% in January) had been officially reported, the result was widely attributed to the efficiency of the governmental policy. Unfortunately, such a drastic decline in the incidence of poverty does not actually take place - in fact, those statistics were the result of mistakes that were made during the process of calculations in the Russian statistical agency - GOSKOMSTAT.

In Table 1, we provide the data on the poverty profile from 1993 as presented by the GOSKOMSTAT. Since the estimates of GOSKOMSTAT for early 1994 have not been confirmed in the later statistical publications, we included just one figure for 1994. In this report, an alternative procedure will be used to determine the number of poor households in Russia; it is based, however, on the currently

Table 1: Poverty profile in 1993/1994

	Poverty line (R)	Percentage of population below the poverty line
1993 March	8069	35
June	16527	28
September	28183	33
December	42800	27
1994 January to July	-	23(est.)

Source: GOSKOMSTAT

available sets from the Ministry of Labour standards. In using this official procedure, it is indirectly implied that the same set of "average" prices is effective throughout Russia; although, as illustrated by Table 2, interregional differences in prices can in some cases create relative wage differentials between highest and lowest region of four, even five times the amount. In fact, a set of average prices does not permit an accurate description the economic conditions in any particular region of the Russian Federation; therefore, the results of calculations based on such an indicator are, at best, inconclusive.

As has already been mentioned, the credibility of existing survey data is low, and the survey instrument used by GOSKOMSTAT is a direct translation of the 1950's U.S. Bureau of Labour Statistics Income and Expenditure Survey.

However, at this stage in the analysis, we have to content ourselves with this data base, since alternative sources of data are not currently availabe. For the detailed analysis of the incidence of poverty in the regions of the Russian Federation, the records of household budgets for 25 thousand families for the year 1993 have been used.

Actual income was compared with the individual subsistence minimum, calculated on the basis of the composition of the given family. Based on the relationship between the individual income and subsistance income, families have been divided into seven groups, and the resulting distribution is described in the attached Tables. One should note here that according to Popkin et al. (1992) the poverty line set by the Russian Ministry of Labour, is 10-20 per cent higher than would have been the case if Western dietary guidelines had been adopted.

Table 2: Relative Cost of the Basic Food Basket (April 1994)

	Relative Cost for the Basket of 19 Basic Food Item	Relative Wage (per cent)
Russian Federation	100	100
Altaj	100	72
Amur	160	142
Archangel	122	132
Belgorod	67	81
Bryansk	92	60
Ivanovo	100	65
Kabarda	86	52
Kaliningrad	94	85
Kaluga	92	69
Kamchatka	193	223
Kemerovo	112	158
Kostroma	94	74
Kurgan	101	68
Kursk	76	65
Magadan	270	276
Moscow	110	126
Moscow reg.	96	91
Nizhegorod	92	86
Novosibirsk	125	87
Omsk	78	89
Oryol	64	60
Penza	85	53
Perm	105	96
Pskov	97	68
Baskiria R.	93	83
Buryatia R.	113	110
Dagestan R.	96	39
Kareliya R.	112	141
Komi R.	134	192
Mari-El R.	73	60
Mordova R.	83	54

Table 2 continued

	Relative Cost for the Basket of 19 Basic Food Item	Relative Wage (per cent)
Sakha R.	200	232
Severnaya Ocetiya R.	81	52
Tatarstan R.	67	83
Tuva R.	119	77
Khakassia R.	107	116
Rostov	71	72
Samara	100	105
Sakhalin	264	195
Sverdlovsk	105	102
Smolensk	87	68
Tyumen	117	264
Udmurt R.	91	73
Ulyanovsk	60	76
Chita	145	120
Chuvash	84	60
Yaroslavl	95	81

Source: Own calculations

The results are fully described in Table 3 (in the appendix). In the sample survey, 15% of the population was described as being below the poverty line, (which is on average 30% less than in the GOSKOMSTAT official report), and 8% had income comparable to subsistence minimum; for 17% of the total population surveyed, minimum income was exceeded by 3 or more times.

The average size of the family with an income below subsistence minimum is 4.2 persons. In such a famliy there are normally one or two working members and two or more dependents. 20% of the poorest families include pensioners, 40% of those poor families consist of five or more members. 10% of the poorest families are single-parent households.

In terms of income structure, the poorest families are more dependent on social transfers: wages and salaries account for 66% of total income. In the families with incomes exceeding the minimum by five or more times the share of wages and salaries make up 81% of total income.

Consumer expenditure by families below the poverty line make up 85% of the total family income. More than 50% of income is spent on food items, 38% is spent on non-food items, 8% is spent on services. Per capita consumer expenditure in the poorest families is 8 times less than in the families with income exceeding the minimum by five or more times.

There are substantial differences in the structure of consumption by the poorest groups and the groups with the higher incomes: poor families consume two times less meat, milk, eggs and sugar than the more effluent groups of the society; consumption of fish and fruits is four times less.

The survey reveals substantial differentiation in the share of the poorest population in the regions of Russia. As can be seen from Table 3, five regions are clearly the "leaders" in terms of incidence of poverty: in North Ocetiya and Dagestan more than half of the total population under survey live in families below the poverty line, while three territories of Eastern Siberia (Buryatia, Chita and Amur regions) also demonstrate high incidence of poverty affecting 44 to 66 per cent of the total population surveyed. In the North Caucasus republics, such a situation can be explained by a low level of absolute income, while in Siberian regions relatively high income does not make up for the relatively high cost of living.

Minimum subsistence income in the Russian Federation in the post-reform period has oscillated between 45 to 55 per cent of average income. Incidence of poverty in 1992-1994 (22,6%) has been roughly comparable to the level registered in 1989-1991 in Eastern European countries, such as Poland and Hungary (17-18%).

A comparison of results with the US data might be quite instructive. Since the poverty line in the USA is determined to be three times the cost of the food package and the Russian Labour Ministry food package is 10-20% higher than the U.S. package and consists of about 68% of the subsistance minimum, it might be interesting to use Table 3 to estimate the share of the population below the "1.5 times minimum subsistence income". For the Russian Federation as a whole, it consists of 41%, while this share exceeds 80% in the poorest regions. There are quite a few regions with substantial subsidies in which this share does not exceed 20-30%. The corresponding figure for the USA is 12-13%, so the conclusion might be made that half of the Rusian population lives in conditions comparable to those of 12% of the poorest Americans.

Regional analysis of the structure of consumption also reveals strong regional differences in the pattern of consumption by vulnerable groups within the population. Since the budget method of determining the minimum income does not take into account different policies of regional authorities toward consumer subsidies, but is merely based upon "biological" nutrition standards, the groups identified as the poorest in different regions are very dissimilar in terms of their consumption structure. In the Oryol region, with high subsidies, less than 40% of expenditure is spent on food items, while in the regions which have eliminated subsidies - Moscow, Magadan and some others - this share is roughly two third of all expenditure.

2 Outlook

To provide a better basis for international comparisons, statistical or relative methods that define the poverty level in relation to average or median available household income should be used regionally at the next stage of analysis. On one hand , this procedure allows the elimination of the inevitable "arbitrariness" of initial standards; on the other hand, the relative position of vulnerable groups of the population is more fully revealed.

In studying poverty issues, the major methodological complication is connected with the growing share of unreported income. There are several factors contributing to an underestimation of officially reported income: decreasing government sector and growing small business sector, especially in retail trade; non-registration by official statistics; an increase in the number of tax laws and an incentive to bypass them; and an increase in unemployment, creating an incentive to work in an informal sector. For instance, an estimate of household income based on banking statistics is about 20 per cent higher than the by GOSKOMSTAT reported average until 1992, and this difference reached 70 per cent in the middle of 1994. If hidden income would be included in a survey, income distributions would become more unequal, and since unreported income is unproportionally distributed in the higher-income class, poverty lines would increase, and an estimate of the incidence of poverty would increase accordingly.

Table 3 Distribution of the Population under Survey Depending on the Proportion of Personal Income and Subsistence Minimum in 1993 (as % of total)

	All surveyed families	Less than subsistence minimum	Compared to subsistence minimum	Families with income greater than subsistence minimum				
				Up to 1.5 times	1.5-2 times	2-3 times	3-5 times or more	5 or more times
Russian Federation	100.0	14.5	8.1	18.6	19.6	22.5	13.0	3.7
Altaj	100.0	18.4	10.8	18.6	19.8	18.1	11.3	3.0
Amur	100.0	33.0	11.9	17.9	12.4	15.1	8.3	1.4
Archangel	100.0	6.1	5.5	21.1	22.8	28.0	13.0	3.5
Belgorod	100.0	6.2	11.3	25.3	23.6	21.8	10.1	1.7
Bryansk	100.0	5.9	4.7	19.0	17.8	31.1	16.8	4.7
Ivanovo	100.0	9.7	12.0	23.4	22.7	20.6	10.3	1.3
Kabarda	100.0	18.3	8.7	31.8	14.3	19.0	7.9	.0.0
Kaliningrad	100.0	8.1	7.0	21.0	19.9	25.2	16.	2.7
Kaluga	100.0	8.8	9.9	15.5	21.0	26.5	14.4	3.9
Kamchatka	100.0	7.1	6.3	13.4	3.4	24.1	26.8	8.9
Kemerovo	100.0	5.0	3.2	11.9	22.4	30.3	22.7	4.5
Kostroma	100.0	8.7	13.4	25.6	22.1	21.5	8.1	0.6
Krgan	100.0	10.2	5.6	19.3	22.7	21.8	16.8	3.6
Kursk	100.0	12.9	10.5	25.8	23.7	19.4	6.0	1.7
Magadan	100.0	6.6	2.5	15.7	18.2	27.2	20.7	9.1

Table 3 continued

	All surveyed families	Less than subsistence minimum	Compared to subsistence minimum	Families with income greater than subsistence minimum				
				Up to 1.5 times	1.5-2 times	2-3 times	3-5 times or more	5 or more times
Moscow	100.0	5.2	6.3	21.0	22.4	28.1	14.5	2.5
Moscow reg.	100.0	11.2	9.0	24.1	23.5	21.5	8.9	1.8
Nizhegorod	100.0	11.4	6.3	17.5	20.4	25.7	14.9	3.8
Novesibirsk	100.0	25.8	10.7	19.6	14.9	17.0	9.5	2.5
Omsk	100.0	10.9	6.9	15.8	18.8	22.2	18.8	6.7
Oryol	100.0	5.3	5.4	22.0	23.	25.6	16.1	1.7
Penza	100.0	5.0	8.5	17.2	24.2	28.8	12.5	3.8
Perm	100.0	21.1	8.1	15.8	16.0	21.1	14.1	3.8
Pskov	100.0	21.2	12.7	25.1	19.8	14.9	5.7	0.6
Baskiria R.	100.0	14.4	6.7	14.8	18.6	24.0	14.8	6.7
Buryatia R.	100.0	57.6	10.8	11.9	8.9	6.7	3.4	0.7
Dagestan R.	100.0	65.9	10.4	13.7	6.7	3.1	0.2	0.0
Kareliya R.	100.0	9.0	7.7	22.4	24.4	25.6	9.6	1.3
Komi R.	100.0	3.0	34.	10.7	15.1	29.2	23.8	14.8
Mari-El R.	100.0	10.4	8.0	18.4	23.3	27.0	9.8	3.1
Mordova R.	100.0	9.9	9.9	25.3	19.2	22.1	11.3	2.3

Table 3 continued

	All surveyed families	Less than subsistence minimum	Compared to subsistence minimum	Families with income greater than subsistence minimum				
				Up to 1.5 times	1.5-2 times	2-3 times	3-5 times or more	5 or more times
Sakha R.	100.0	13.5	7.1	12.3	16.9	29.9	11.4	3.9
Severnaya Ocetiya R.	100.0	43.1	19.0	17.3	14.3	4.6	1.7	0.0
Tartarstan R.	100.0	6.3	8.2	20.6	24.2	24.8	11.9	4.0
Tuva R.	100.0	10.4	7.2	20.8	24.8	20.0	11.2	5.6
Khakassia R.	100.0	4.2	6.4	20.1	26.2	26.1	14.3	2.7
Rostov	100.0	14.7	9.8	20.8	20.9	21.9	10.5	2.3
Samara	100.0	14.7	8.0	18.9	19.6	22.0	13.1	3.7
Sakhalin	100.0	15.1	10.1	22.0	20.5	21.3	10.0	1.0
Sverdlovsk	100.0	5.9	6.4	15.6	25.	28.9	14.5	3.6
Smolensk	100.0	13.7	12.2	20.9	19.4	22.9	8.9	2.0
Tyumen	100.0	9.0	7.6	18.7	15.11	16.9	19.8	12.9
Udmurt R.	100.0	5.6	5.6	24.5	25.0	28.5	9.4	1.4
Ulyanovsk	100.0	6.1	4.6	16.6	15.0	26.7	22.6	8.4
Chita	100.0	55.7	11.5	11.9	9.1	8.0	3.1	0.7
Chuvash	100.0	14.3	8.5	23.0	22.4	22.9	8.3	0.6
Yaroslavl	100.0	5.1	6.8	17.6	20.5	31.5	16.7	1.8

Source: Own calculations

Poverty in Hungary - Some Results of the First Two Waves of the Hungarian Household Panel Study in 1992 and 1993

Rudolf Andorka and Zsolt Spéder

1 Household Income Surveys in Hungary, 1962-1987

Since 1962, the Hungarian Central Statistical Office conducted surveys at 5-year intervals for household incomes. The questionnaires inquired in great detail about total monetary income and the consumption from the household's small-scale agricultural production (the so-called household plots) for the year. The data given by the household on wage income and on monetary social benefits were confirmed at the place of payment (working place, pension office). The results are considered to be relatively reliable, and only part of the income, that originating from the second economy, are considered to be understated. The samples are very large: 0.5 per cent of the households, or 15-20 thousand households, which includes about 50 thousand persons. The results of these surveys are published in detail. In consequence, reliable and detailed data are available to study income differences by social strata, residence, age, etc. (Andorka, Kolosi, Vukovich, 1992).

2 Poverty before the Regime Transition

The existence of poverty was officially denied by the Communist regime until the mid-1980s (Andorka, 1992 a). The first calculation of a subsistence minimum by the Central Statistical Office in 1968 was kept strictly secret and the calculations not made again until 1983. Two minima were calculated in 1968: 1. a "minimum of existence" and; 2. a "socially acceptable minimum". According to the household income survey of 1967, 10 per cent of the population had a per capita income lower than the minimum of existence and another 15 per cent had a per capita income lower than the socially acceptable minimum, but higher than the minimum of existence. Thus 10 per cent might be considered "poor" and an other 15 per cent "nearly poor".

At the end of the 1960s, parallel to the first calculation of subsistence minima, a survey of poverty was conducted by the Central Statistical Office by re-interviewing the households that had the lowest income in the 1967 household income survey. The results of the survey were kept strictly secret at that time (Kemény, n. d.). The main results of this first analysis revealed that for the second half of the 1960s, poverty was concentrated in the elderly age groups, in the semi-skilled, unskilled, agricultural social strata and in the population of so called Gypsy (Roma) ethnicity.

Under the pressure of public opinion, including in 1981 the Conference of the Hungarian Sociological Association on "multiple deprivation" (Böhm, 1981), the government asked the Central Statistical Office to calculate subsistence minima, beginning in 1983. The minima were also calculated for the years up to and including 1982 and published in the following years.

The calculation of the subsistence minima had two expenditure components; food and all other. Food expenditures were calculated for a healthy and adequate diet consisting of the least expensive foodstuffs. All other expenditures were added as a percentage adopted from the empirical data on household statistics, which represent the other expenditures of households whose food expenditures were equivalent to the calculated minimum food requirement. Expenditures for obtaining (buying, building, etc.) a new dwelling were not included.

The first analysis of the extent of poverty based on the household income surveys were published in the main paper of the above mentioned Conference on multiple deprivation (Huszár, 1981). In the following years, the scientific analyses of poverty usually defined poverty as those with a per capita income below the national average of the subsistence minimum (Andorka, 1989). In 1982, 11 and in 1987, 9 per cent of thepopulation had a lower per capita income than the minimum of existence. The number for those living in poverty were also computed by using the more differentiated minima of existence calculated for different types of households (smaller and larger households, urban and rural households, household containing at least one active wage-earner and households without an active wage-earner), which produced a somewhat lower statistic than using the national average minimum of existence.

The main patterns of poverty found by these studies were: (1) the shift of poverty from the peasant stratum to the semi-skilled and unskilled stratum, and (2) the shift of poverty from the rural areas to the urban areas, and (3) the shift of poverty from the elderly to the children, mainly through poverty in families that had more than two children.

3 Economic Changes since the Transition and their Impact on Poverty

It was expected that the transition from the command economy to the market economy would cause a certain decline of the GDP for a short period, but the deep economic crisis was not foreseen by any Hungarian or foreign social scientist or by any politician. In addition to the transition to the market economy based on the private property of the majority of productive assets, the deep crisis was caused by two unforeseen events. First, the world economic depression and second, the collapse of the export markets in the former socialist countries, beginning in countries which were formerly part of the Soviet Union.

From 1989 to 1993 the GDP declined by about 18-20 per cent, and the real per capita personal income by about 10-12 per cent. It ought to be added that the amount of the decline is not exactly known, since official statistics do not measure the contribution of the grey or hidden economy to the GDP, and to personal income. Recently it was estimated that the real GDP, taking into account the hidden economy, might be 16 per cent higher than the official GDP (Árvay, Vértes, 1993). Although the hidden economy also existed in the socialist period, its contribution to the real GDP has increased since the regime transition. If these estimations are correct, the decline of the GDP and real personal income was somewhat less than the above mentioned official statistics

As a consequence of the economic crisis and of the complete freedom to discuss the existence and characteristics of poverty, the topic came into focus, not only in scientific research but also in the press and mass media. However, the opinions expressed in the different publications often contradict each other. These opinions reflected the interests of different social strata, e.g. pensioners, and political parties, therefore, reliable data on poverty is crucial.

A new reason for accurate data on poverty stems from the need to reform the policy for the social system. In the present circumstances of increasing poverty it has been proposed that the social benefits should be more targeted to reach the poorest part of the population (Kopits et al, 1990; Kessides et al, 1992, Andorka, Kondratas, Tóth, 1994). In order to design a more targeted social policy, the categories of society must be identified that are overrepresented by the poor.

4 Sources of Data on Poverty

Since 1992, the Central Statistical Office has calculated and published yearly the subsistence minima for each quarter in order to follow the increase of the price index. However, since 1991 only the minimum of existence has been calculated, and the socially acceptable minimum calculation was abandoned. In addition, the national average for the minimum of existence is no longer calculated, only the minimumof existence for different types of households. Instead, the per capita minimum of existence for two-adults-two-children urban households, which used to be very close to the national average, has been substituted with an approximation using the national average of the per capita minimum of existence.

After 1990, other institutions began to calculate and publish subsistence minima. The Family Helping Center of Ujpest (a district of Budapest) regularly published minima based on their experience in Ujpest. These minima were higher than the minima calculated by the Central Statistical Office. Similarly a foundation called the "Representation of Workers", linked to the Socialist Party, recently began to publish higher minima based on data from five towns.

Other experts have the opposite opinion, that the minima of existence calculated by the Central Statistical Office is unduly high, which they support with methodological concerns in the calculation of these statistics.

The main lesson emerging from the debate around these calculations for subsistence minima seems to be that a minimum, although representing in principle the absolute poverty line, is nevertheless a rather vague relative value. The minimum depend not only on the objective social conditions in which the given household lives, but on both the subjective judgement of the person who calculates the minimum and the public which accepts or rejects its validity. Although detailed data on the subsistence minima are available, it is far from obvious at which income level the poverty line should be fixed.

The Central Statistical Office performed a new survey of household income in the first quarter of 1992, that inquired into the incomes for 1991 (i.e. 4 years after the previous survey). It seemed necessary to have new data in view of the change in incomes caused by the regime transition. However, the data obtained by the interviews seem to be rather unreliable because of an increase in the understatement of income from the hidden economy. This might be explained by the growth of the private economy, where incomes cannot be controlled at the place of work, or by the introduction of the personal income tax in 1989, which has lead to widespread tax evasion and distrust of any questions about personal income. With these complications, it is likely that the results of the survey of 1992 will not be published. That means that the main source of data on income distribution and poverty is no longer available.

In order to provide data on changes of income and living conditions, the incidence of unemployment, the participation in the hidden economy and on several related attitudes and opinions, the Department of Sociology of the Budapest University of Economic Sciences and the Social Research Informatics Society (TÁRKI) initiated a panel survey of household income. It is similar to the household panel surveys in other countries, and in part resembles the German "Socio-Economic Panel" survey (GSOEP) (Wagner et al. 1993). Questions from the GSOEP eastern subsample questionnaire were included verbatim in the Hungarian questionnaire (Headey, Krause, Habich, 1993).

The first wave of the panel survey in Hungary was conducted in May 1992. A national sample of 2059 households was taken, consisting of 5770 persons lived in these households, 4542 who were aged 16 and more years. They were interviewed individually, and as a household.

In May 1993, the same households, or the households in which the persons interviewed in 1992 lived, were re-interviewed. In total, 1931 households were interviewed, 5415 persons lived in these households, among them 4308 persons aged 16 and older, who were also individually interviewed.

For the first analysis, the 1993 sample was corrected by a simple method of weighting, which adjusted proportionately the number of households belonging to different categories to the 1992 sample ratio. A more sophisticated and exact weighting will be performed in the following months.

In consequence of the weighting, the number of households in the 1993 survey is 4254, the number of persons is 5425, and the number of persons aged 16 and older is 4301. There are 1905 households, 5443 persons and 4266 persons aged 16 and older which we have complete questionnaires from, for both the 1992 and 1993 surveys, i. e., whose conditions can be compared in both years (Sik, Tóth, 1992, 1993).

Two preliminary remarks ought to be presented on the utilization of the data from the household panel surveys for the analysis of poverty. First, the samples are relatively small, therefore the reliability of the data used for a detailed analysis is not very high and the data must be used very cautiously. Second, not all incomes for the interviewed households were accurately registered. T. Kolosi estimated that the household incomes registered by the panel survey were about 20 per cent lower that the income estimations of the Central Statistical Office (based on macrostatistical data) and taking into account all the incomes unregistered in the household panel surveys (Kolosi, Szívós, Bedekovics, 1993). If we assume that the unregistered incomes are more or less of the same importance in proportion to income in both the lower and higher income categories, with some exceptions, the panel survey data can be used to analyze the composition and the changes of poverty at an individual level.

5 The Decline of Income and the Growth of Poverty

The main cause of the decline in real income of the population was inflation. The rate of inflation was 29 per cent in 1990, 35 per cent in 1991, 23 per cent in 1992 and 22.5 per cent in 1993. In the 12 months preceding the survey in May 1992, the rate of inflation was 24-25 per cent, and between the surveys in May 1992 and May 1993 the rate of inflation was 23 per cent.

The average real per capita income of the interviewed households remained almost unchanged from the spring of 1991 to May 1992, and declined from May 1992 to May 1993. To understand the Hungarian social and political situation after the transition, it is more important to realise that, 46 per cent between 1991 and 1992, and 53 per cent between 1992 and 1993households suffered a decline

Table 1: Decile distribution of household income, in per cent

Decile	1962	1967	1972	1977	1982	1987	1992	1993
1	3.9	4.0	4.0	4.5	4.9	4.5	3.9	4.1
2	5.6	6.0	5.9	6.3	6.4	6.0	5.6	5.7
3	6.5	7.1	7.0	7.3	7.3	6.9	6.5	6.6
4	7.6	8.0	7.9	8.1	8.1	7.7	7.2	7.3
5	8.6	8.9	8.8	8.9	8.8	8.5	8.0	8.0
6	9.7	9.9	9.8	9.8	9.6	9.4	8.8	8.9
7	11.0	10.9	10.8	10.8	10.7	10.5	9.8	9.9
8	12.3	12.2	12.1	12.0	11.9	11.8	11.6	11.4
9	14.6	14.0	14.0	13.7	13.7	13.8	14.3	14.1
10	20.2	18.9	19.7	18.6	18.6	20.9	24.3	24.0
Ratio of 10/1 decile	5.2	4.7	4.9	4.1	3.8	4.6	6.2	5.9

Source:
Household income surveys of the Central Statistical Office and Household Panel Survey 1992, 1993

of their per capita real income. A minority of about 20-30 per cent achieved an increase in real income and about a further 10 per cent a significant increase in income. (Kolosi, Sík, 1992; Kolosi, Szívós, Bedekovics, 1993.)

Income inequalities which were measured by the decile distributions increased during the transition, however, did not seem to have continued from 1992 to 1993 (Table 1). It might be said that in the socialist period the income inequalities were on the "Scandinavian" level, while after the transition they increased to the "standard Western European" level (French or German), but they were certainly far from the American inequalities.

As a result of the underregistration of income and of the doubts about the minima of existence, only very tentative estimations can be made for the number of persons living below the poverty line. If we guesstimate, in the 1980s 10 per cent, in 1992 20 per cent and in 1993 25 per cent of the population lived on a per capita income which was lower than the national average of the minimum of existence.

For the purpose analysing the composition of poverty which is presented in the following section, and based on the subjective indicators for the poor and the individual changes from non-poverty to poverty and vice versa between May 1992 and May 1993, poverty has been defined as belonging to the lowest quintile of households, i.e., to the 20 per cent of the households having the lowest per capita income. In 1992, 23.0 per cent and in 1993, 24.6 per cent of the total population lived in households belonging to the lowest quintile.

6 The Composition of Poverty

When comparing the percentage of the persons age 16 and older belonging to the "poor" by education, social strata of active earners and the social categories of inactive persons, and percentage of the "poor" in the total population by ethnicity and by age (Table 2), some familiar and some unexpected trends are visible (Andorka, 1992 b; Andorka, Spéder, 1993).

- Non-skilled workers and the persons employed in agriculture, including both the self-employed peasants and the agricultural workers, are overrepresented among the poor.
- The unemployed are overrepresented among the poor, which would be expected. However, it is remarkable that less than half of the unemployed persons lived in households having an income lower than the poverty line.
- Old-age pensioners are surprisingly strongly underrepresented, while the disabled pensioners are overrepresented, among the poor.
- Inactive housewives, mostly older women and Gypsy women are very clearly overrepresented among the poor. This supports the conclusion that single-earner households are in great danger of becoming poor.
- Mothers on child care allowance with children less than 3 years old are noticeably overrepresented among the poor, which supports the opinion that the discontinuation of family assistance targeted to this group would cause a serious increase in poverty.
- The population of Gypsy ethnicity, amounting to about 0.5 million population number, is severly affected by poverty.

Table 2: Persons belonging to the lowest per capita income quintile of households by education, by social strata of active earners and by selected categories of inactive persons, 1992 and 1993, in per cent

Education, social stratum, inactive categories	Persons belonging to the lowest income quintile	
	1992	1993
Education		
0-7 years primary	30.6	31.6
8 years primary	26.5	29.2
Skilled worker school	21.8	23.2
Secondary	12.1	11.1
Tertiary	8.3	4.0
Social strata of active earners		
Higher manager	6.0	2.7
Professional	7.1	6.6
Supervisor	7.3	7.4
Clerical	11.2	10.7
Self-employed artisan, merchant	18.2	13.6
Skilled worker	17.4	16.7
Non-skilled worker	22.4	25.6
Self-employed peasant and agricultural worker	21.3	37.7
Categories of inactive persons		
Unemployed	44.7	43.9
Pensioner	15.8	11.9
Disabled pensioner	26.7	34.3
Mother on child care allowance	35.8	38.5
Inactive housewife	59.6	54.7
Ethnicity		
Gypsy population	66.0	81.0
Age		
0-2	.	40.1
3-6	.	42.9
7-14	.	33.7
15-19	.	29.8
20-29	26.4	30.1
30-39	23.2	26.0
40-49	20.1	23.9
50-59	17.0	15.6
60-69	17.4	11.7
70+	18.8	16.2
Total population	23.0	24.6

- Children, especially young children, are much more affected by poverty than the elderly. This supports the fact that family allowances are an important element in alleviating poverty when effectively combined with other efforts.
- From 1992 to 1993 the disadvantaged categories, including persons having lower education, non-skilled workers, peasants, the Gypsy population and children became more disadvantaged. The dramatic increase of poverty among the Gypsy population is especially striking and highlights the fact that the Gypsies are among the main losers in the transition.

Although the Gypsy populatio is highly overrepresented among the poor, only 16 per cent of the total poor population consists of those with Gypsy ethnicity. Thus, to reduce the problem of poverty to th Gypsy population would be highly misleading.

When analysing the composition of the population belonging to the lowest quintile of the households instead of the risk of being poor (percentages of different categories being poor), in 1993 we find that 37 per cent were children aged 0-19, 5 per cent were mothers on child care allowance, 10 per cent were old age pensioners, 6 per cent were disabled pensioners, 13 per cent were housewives, 10 per cent were unemployed, 10 per cent were non-skilled workers and peasants, and 9 per cent belonged to other categories. Thus the bulk of poverty is child poverty.

7 Dissatisfaction, Psychological Stresses, Anomie and Alienation among the Poor

The New Democracies Barometer surveys in autumn 1992 proved that among all Eastern-Central European countries, the level of dissatisfaction with their personal or family economic situation and with the overall situation of the economy was the highest in Hungary (Rose, Haerpfer, 1993). Comparisons with the Western and Eastern German household panel survey data seem to suggest that not only dissatisfaction, but also symptoms of psychological stress, anomie and alienation are much more frequent in Hungary than in both parts of Germany (Andorka, 1993a).

Comparison of dissatisfaction levels for the total population with the lowest income quintile for households demonstrates that the poor are much more

Table 3: Percentage of dissatisfied persons[1] in the total population aged 16 and more years and in the lowest quintile of households, 1993, in per cent

Domains of life	Dissatisfied[2]	
	total population	lowest quintile
Overall life satisfaction of respondent	21.1	37.0
Level of living	36.5	54.3
Income[3]	49.0	68.7
Future perspectives	41.5	55.0
Work[3]	6.9	9.6
Housing	11.3	22.1
Housing environment	13.8	18.2
Family	3.9	6.1
Health of respondent	23.1	28.1
Relations with kin and friends	4.2	6.1
Relations with colleagues	3.9	4.5
Public safety	29.0	29.4
Natural environment	29.4	27.5
Economic situation of Hungary	74.0	77.0
Possibility of citizens to participate in political decisions	45.3	55.0

[1] Measured on an 11-point scale (from 0 to 10), 5.00 being the central value
[2] Scale points 0-3
[3] Only those having an income and work

dissatisfied with the material domains of their life, including the level of living, income, future perspectives, housing and the housing environment, all of which reflect their worse objective living conditions. The higher dissatisfaction with personal health is also understandable, as we know from other surveys that the health of the poorest part of the population is much worse than average, which in turn is rather bad compared to other European countries. However, the poor are not much more dissatisfied with the more "spiritual" domains of life, such as family, kin and friends, colleagues, public safety and natural environment, and rather surprisingly, their work. Their evaluation in the economic situation of Hungary is as pessimistic as that of the average population, but their opinion on the possibility of citizens to participate in political decisions i.e., the state of democracy, is more negative than the opinion of the more affluent part of the population.

Table 4: Physiological and metal symptoms of psychological problems, 1993, in per cent

Symptom	Mentioning of the given symptom per cent	
	Total population aged 16 +	Lowest quintile of households
Often exhausted	61.2	67.6
Often strong heart-throb	34.2	37.3
Continuously nervous	30.5	38.6
Often strong headache	30.0	36.2
Often trembling	21.1	26.1
Usually feeling of being unlucky	57.3	73.5
Often concerned with own health	40.8	44.7
Completely confused when having to do several things in short time	28.8	38.6
Unable to get rid of anxieties	19.8	27.6

Overall life satisfaction of the poor seems to be influenced most of all by the material considerations in life since the life contentment of the poor is much worse than the more affluent strata.

In the 1970s, sociologists suggested that the very high and continuously increasing rates of suicide and alcoholism might be explained by serious mental health problems of the population. Surveys in the second half of the 1980s confirmed a very high prevalence of symptoms of neurosis and depression (Kopp, Skrabsky, 1992).

The questions in the 1993 household panel survey confirmed that the symptoms of psychological problems and serious stresses are often more frequent among the poor than among the more affluent strata (Table 4). It might be hypothesized that the poor are less able to cope with stressful situations and problems caused earlier, by the socialist system and presently, by the transition.

Previously it was hypothesized that the roots of the mental health problems are to be found in a deep anomie and alienation crisis of Hungarian society (Andorka, 1993 b). This notion was investigated by posing several questions on the questionnaire for the 1993 panel survey relating to the different aspects of anomie and alienation. It seems that the "normlessness" and "loneliness" dimensions of

Table 5: Indicators of anomie and alienation, 1993, in per cent

Statement concerning anomie and alienation	Respondents completely agreeingwith the statement	
	Total population aged 16 +	Lowest quintile
Those who would like to achieve something in life must break some norms	38.9	41.7
Nowadays I am barely able to find my way in matters of everyday life	24.7	32.8
I am barely able to influence the turn of events in my life	16.7	28.4
I often feel lonely	11.8	12.7

anomie are not more frequent among the poor than the average population, but "powerlessness" and "disorientation" or "estrangement from the surrounding society" are much more prevalent among the poor (Table 5).

At this point it is only possible to speculate about the possible consequences of the dissatisfaction, the psychological problems and the anomie and alienation which seem to be widespread among the poor in Hungary. From other surveys it seems that these present phenomena among the poor result in a higher rate of non-participation in national and local elections and overall political apathy. The danger that this passivity will at some point turn into active hostility, towards the economic and political system which the present transition processes are shaping, can not be ruled out.

Therefore, it is very important to know how long the experience of poverty is for both households and individuals, and whether poverty is of a short duration or not, to know whether a permanent, disadvantaged "underclass" is emerging in Hungary.

8 The Duration of Poverty

Comparing the situation of households and individuals in May 1992 with May 1993 provides some information on the transience of poverty. "Poverty" was also defined here as belonging to the lowest quintile of households. Forty-seven per

Table 6: Distribution of poor and non-poor households in 1992 by their position in 1993 and of the poor and non-poor households in 1993 by their position in 1992, in per cent

In 1992	In 1993			
	Poor	Non-poor	Total	n
Poor	53.0	47.0	100.0	388
Non-poor	11.2	88.8	100.0	1517
Total	19.7	80.3	100.0	1905
Poor	54.8	11.9	20.4	
Non-poor	45.2	88.1	79.6	
Total	100.0	100.0	100.0	
n	376	1529	1905	

Table 7: Distribution of poor and non-poor persons in 1992 by their position in 1993 and of the poor and non-poor person in 1993 by their position in 1992, in per cent

In 1992	In 1993			
	Poor	Non-poor	Total	n
Poor	58.8	41.2	100.0	1297
Non-poor	13.7	86.3	100.0	4146
Total	24.4	75.6	100.0	5443
Poor	57.4	13.0	23.8	
Non-poor	42.6	87.0	76.2	
Total	100.0	100.0	100.0	
n	1329	4114	5443	

cent of households and 41.2 per cent of persons who were poor in 1992 were no longer poor in 1993 (Table 6 and 7). In contrast, 45.2 per cent of poor households and 42.6 per cent of poor persons in 1993 were not poor in 1992 i.e., were "new poor". These data seem to suggest that at least an important part of the poor household and persons are oscillating between "poverty" and "non-poverty", or at least "near-poverty".

Table 8: Poverty and non-poverty of persons in 1992 and 1993 by education, in per cent

Education	Poor in 1992 poor in 1993	Poor in 1992 not poor in 1993	Not poor in 1992 poor in 1993	Not poor in 1992 not poor in 1993	Total	n
0-7 years primary	21.0	11.4	9.9	57.7	100.0	614
8 years primary	16.8	11.7	12.2	59.4	100.0	1193
Skilled worker school	11.7	8.5	11.5	68.3	100.0	1090
Secondary school	4.5	7.7	7.0	80.0	100.0	943
Tertiary education diploma	1.2	5.4	2.8	90.6	100.0	426
Total	11.8	9.3	9.6	69.3	100.0	4266

Comparing the "durably poor" (poor in both 1992 and 1993), the "outflow" (poor in 1992, not poor in 1993), the "inflow" (not poor in 1992, poor in 1993), with the percentages of poor based on both education (Table 8) and age (Table 9), it suggests that the inflow was higher than the outflow in the groups already disadvantaged in 1992, i.e., persons having lower education and among children. In contrast, the outflow was higher among those who had higher education and surprisingly, among the elderly.

The chance of "climbing out" of poverty was much lower among persons having a lower level of education and among children. The "falling back" into poverty was also rather high among the children aged 3-14 and among the adults aged 20-34, presumably from the birth of a new child into the family. However, it seems that the families finally having children after several years of being together are mostly able to attain the income level of "non-poverty". This likely occurs when the income of the parents has increased in parallel with the advancement in their occupational career. This is strongly hindered if the number of the children in the family is more than two.

Unemployment and the change in the size of the household could be two factors that might cause a relapse back into poverty, which could be investigated using the data from the two panel surveys. Surprisingly, becoming unemployed in

Table 9: Poverty and non-poverty of persons in 1992 and 1993 by age in 1993, in per cent

Age	Poor in 1992 poor in 1993	Poor in 1992 not poor in 1993	Not poor in 1992 poor in 1993	Not poor in 1992 not poor in 1993	Total	n
0-2	22.1	15.3	16.0	46.6	100.0	131
3-6	25.0	12.3	17.2	45.5	100.0	268
7-14	21.8	8.7	11.7	57.8	100.0	597
15-19	18.4	10.8	11.0	69.8	100.0	445
20-24	16.1	9.7	13.7	60.6	100.0	373
25-29	15.2	11.3	14.0	59.4	100.0	335
30-34	15.6	8.4	12.1	64.4	100.0	347
35-39	15.1	11.6	9.3	64.0	100.0	431
40-44	13.6	5.1	12.4	68.9	100.0	354
45-49	10.1	7.8	10.7	71.3	100.0	335
50-54	10.3	7.2	9.7	72.8	100.0	290
55-59	4.7	8.5	6.6	80.2	100.0	318
60-69	6.6	9.6	4.9	78.8	100.0	647
70 +	8.9	10.9	7.3	72.8	100.0	504
Total	14.0	9.6	10.5	65.9	100.0	5375

1993 caused a relapse into poverty in only in a minority of cases, and becoming employed in 1993 resulted in relatively few cases of climbing out of poverty (Table 10). The relation of poverty and unemployment needs further careful analysis.

On the other hand, the increase of the number of persons living in the household, in most cases through the birth of a new child, tended to increase the risk of poverty, while decreasing the number of members tended to help them "climb out" of poverty (Table 11). The link between demographic events and poverty also needs further study.

Table 10: Poverty and non-poverty of persons in 1992 and 1993 by unemployment in May 1992 and May 1993, in per cent

Unemployed	Poor in 1992 poor in 1993	Poor in 1992 not poor in 1993	Not poor in 1992 poor in 1993	Not poor in 1992 not poor in 1993	Total	n
Both in 1992 and in 1993	28.9	7.3	23.9	39.9	100.0	218
Only in 1992	29.4	11.8	13.7	45.1	100.0	102
Only in 1993	18.5	10.6	14.8	56.0	100.0	216
Neither in 1992, nor in 1993	12.8	9.8	9.5	67.8	100.0	4907
Total	14.0	9.8	10.4	65.8	100.0	5443

Table 11: Poverty and non-poverty of households in 1992 and 1993 by the change of the size of the household (number of household members) from 1992 to 1993, in per cent

From 1992 to 1993 the number of members of the households	Poor in 1992 poor in 1993	Poor in 1992 not poor in 1993	Not poor in 1992 poor in 1993	Not poor in 1992 not poor in 1993	Total	n
Unchanged	10.1	8.6	8.9	72.4	100.0	1637
Diminished	14.8	18.8	8.7	57.7	100.0	149
Increased	15.4	7.7	11.0	65.9	100.0	91
Total	10.8	9.3	9.0	71.0	100.0	1877

9 Implications for Social Policy

The resurgence of economic growth would be the most efficient solution for the problems of poverty in Hungary. Nevertheless, the potential of social policy to alleviate the gravest of problems should not be overlooked. Unfortunately, the social political system that was inherited from the socialist period is far from suited for that purpose. The old system is not sustainable because it spends more resources than the Hungarian economy and state budget can presently afford. In addition, an important part of the social expenditures are distributed among the more affluent strata of society instead of being targeted to the poor.

Earlier studies based on the income and household expenditures surveys of the 1980s (Atkinson, Micklewright, 1992; Van de Walle, Ravallion, Gautam, 1994) proved that cash benefits were not strongly targeted to the poorest strata. However some benefits were flowing predominantly toward the poorer part of the society, especially family allowances because families with children tended to belong to the lower per capita income categories. A first analysis of the data from the 1993 panel survey also confirms the benefit of targeted family and child care allowances because the data shows many in the lowest quintile would receive this money. Unemployment benefits, introduced since 1989, and means-tested social assistance, which had a relatively minor role before 1990, are also targeted to the poor, howeverhouseholds in the higher income quintiles sometimes receive not only unemployment benefits, but social assistance payments (Förster, Tóth, 1993). Further analyses of the incidence of cash benefits are in progress and will help clarify the extent of the situation.

In spite of the preliminary nature of the analyses and based on the data from only two waves of the household panel surveys, the demand for information on social policies is so urgent that some tentative conclusions may be formulated:

- it is desirable to maintain the present system of family allowances, as it tends to help many poor families and protects even more families from falling below the poverty line;
- there is a need of better targeting of unemployment benefits and of social assistance;
- contrary to many who proclaim that the pensioners are the social stratum needing and deserving most the help of social policy, only a minority of the pensioners are really poor.

References

Andorka, R., 1989, Szegénység Magyarországon. Társadalmi Szemle. vol. 44. no. 12. 30-40. p.

Andorka, R., 1992 a, Evolution of the debate over poverty in Hungary since the 1960's. Paper pressented at the Conference on "Extending the Public Policy Debate in Emerging Democracies", Bellagio, 35p.

Andorka, R., 1992 b, Szegénység. In Sík, Tóth, op. cit. 48-60. p.

Andorka, R., 1993 a, Elégedetlenség, elidegenedés, anómia. In Sík, Tóth, op. cit. 97-112. p.

Andorka, R., 1993 b, Ursachen, Probleme und Lösungsstrategien in der Revolution. In Schäfers, B., ed., Lebensverhältnisse und soziale Konflikte im neuen Europa. Frankfurt. Campus. 45-54. p.

Andorka, R., Kolosi, T., Vukovich, Gy., eds., 1992, Social report. Budapest. TÁRKI. 445 p.

Andorka, R., Kondratas, A., Tóth, I. Gy., 1994, Hungary's welfare state in transition: structure, initial reforms and recommendations. The Joint Hungarian International Blue Ribbon Commission, Policy Study no. 3.

Andorka, R., Spéder, Zs., 1993. Szegénység. In Sík. Tóth, op. cit. 47-58. p.

Atkinson, A. B., Micklewright, J., 1992, Economic transformation in Eastern Europe and the distribution of income. Cambridge. Cambridge University Press. 442. p.

Árvay, J., Vértes, A., 1993, A magánszektor és a rejtett gazdaság súlya Magyarországon (1980-1992). Budapest. Gazdaságkutató Rt. 36 p.

Böhm, A.,1981, A Magyar Szociológiai Társaság tudományos ülésszaka "A többszörösen hátrányos helyzet_ rétegek vizsgálatáról". Szociológia. vol. 10. no. 3-4. 279-332. p.

Förster, M., Tóth, I. Gy., 1993, A háztartások jövedelmi szerkezete és a szociális újraelosztás. In Sík, Tóth, op. cit. 83-96. p.

Headey, B., Krause, P., Habich, R., 1993, East Germany: rising incomes, unchanged inequality and the impact of redistributive government 1990-1992. Deutsches Institut für Wirtschaftsforschung, Berlin, Diskussionspapiere. no. 72. 30 p.

Huszár, I., 1981, A hátrányos helyzet_ek Magyarországon. Társadalmi Szemle, vol. 36. no. 6. 89-100. p.-

Kemény, I., no. date, Az alacsonyjövedelm_ lakosság életkörülményei az 1969. októberi felmérés alapján. Manuscript.

Kessides, Ch., Davey, K., Holzmann, R., Micklewright, J., Smith, A., Hinayon, C., 1992, Hungary. Reform of social policy and expenditures. Washington. World Bank. 193 p.

Kolosi, T., Sík, E., 1992, Munkaer_piac és jövedelmek. In Sík, Tóth, op. cit. 8-24. p.

Kolosi, T., Szívós, P., Bedekovics, I., 1993, Munkaer_piac és jövedelmek. In Sík, Tóth, op. cit. 13-26. p.

Kopits, G., Holzmann, R., Schieber, G., Sidgwick, E., 1990, Social security reform in Hungary. Washington. IMF. 187 p.

Kopp. M.,Skrabski, Á., 1992, Magyar lelkiállapot. Budapest. Végeken. 301. p.

Krupp, H.J., Schupp, J., eds., 1988, Lebenslagen im Wandel: Daten 1987. Frankfurt. Campus. 319 p.

Rose, R.,Haerpfer, Ch., 1993, Adapting to transformation in Eastern Europe: New Democracies Barometer -II. University of Strathclyde, Centre for the Study of Public Policy, Studies in Public Policy. no. 212. 122 p.

Sík, E.,Tóth, I. Gy., eds., 1992, Jelentés a Magyar háztartás Panel I. hullámának eredményeir_l. Budapest. Budapesti Közgazdaságtudományi Egyetem Szociológia Tanszék, TÁRKI. Magyar Háztartás Panel M_helytanulmányok no. 1. 117 p.

Sík, E.,Tóth I. Gy., eds., 1993, Egy év után Jelentés a Magyar Háztartás Panel II. hullámának eredményeir_l. Budapest. Budapesti Közgazdaságtudományi Egyetem Szociológia Tanszék, TÁRKI. 156 p.

Van de Walle, D., Ravallion, M., Gautman, M., 1994, How well does the social safety net work? The incidence of cash benefits in Hungary, 1987-89. Washington, The World Bank, LSMS Working Paper no. 102. 82 p.

Wagner, Gert, Burkhauser, R. V. and Behringer, F. 1993, The English Language Public User File of the German Socio-Economic Panel Study. In: The Journal of Human Resources. no. 2. 429-433. p.

Income Inequality and Poverty Dynamics in Poland and East-Germany Before and Under Transition

Joachim Frick
Irena Topinska
Gert G. Wagner
Klaus Mueller

One goal of the economic transition of Eastern Europe is a longterm increase in its national income. In order to realize this aim it is necessary to insure the economic freedoms which are complimentary to political freedom in modern democratic societies.

Restructuring Eastern Europe economies is likely to increase the inequality of earnings and income. Many people believe that this is a necessary incentive to stimulate profit oriented market behavior. But such inequality should not be allowed to increase too much, as the aim of social justice will be missed. While the optimal amount of inequality in these countries may not be agreed on, there is a broad consensus that poverty should be avoided.

The first aim of this paper is to compare the extent and structure of income inequality and poverty in two very different 'socialist societies': Poland (up to 1989) and the German Democratic Republic (up to 1990).

The second aim is to have a first glance at the development of inequality and poverty during the transition process of both societies. For this purpose we provide a cross-sectional as well as a longitudinal analysis.

The very difficult question of absolute growth of income is in fact not investigated. Instead, we compare changes in relative income position of households in each country discussed.

We start (Section 1) with some theoretical and methodological remarks concerning the comparative analysis of incomes. Section 2 discusses the data bases. Section 3 presents cross-sectional results on income distribution and poverty rates. Section 4 provides a first view of poverty dynamics from a longitudinal perspective.

1 Theoretical and Methodological Problems in Measuring Income Across Market Transitions

Comparing income levels and the distribution of income between countries with many differences in their political, economic and social security systems, and in the level of their economic development is fraught with difficulties. One large problem is how suitable money income is as a measure of living standards. Another one is the extent to which differences across nations are caused by the different systems, as compared to how they are influenced by initial conditions and by the behavior of individuals. These problems arise when making either cross-sectional or intertemporal comparison of household incomes for the economies under transition.

Some of the major differences between the systems to keep in mind in this case are:

1. differences in the price and market system, in the availability of goods and the time necessary to purchase them;
2. differences in the availability and security of jobs as well as social security provided by employers;
3. differences in type and quantity of goods and services which are provided by the government for free or below cost, as well as differences in eligibility to receive these goods;
4. differences in type and quantity of social security (based on contributions).

It is impossible to take all these differences in the empirical analysis. Take for example, the existence of groups enjoying special privileges in the former communist countries. These groups consisted of members of the "nomenclature" but also army or police officers, and workers in some industries (such as mining industry in Poland). They had access - mostly through administrative rationing or informal connections - to goods and services that were generally not available to the public. Privileges of this type quickly disappeared in the transformation process, but cannot be captured with the available data sets.

We assume that these privileges increased inequality, because they were most likely to prevail in the higher income ranges. This would mean that some of the differences in the distributions of income between formerly socialist countries and market economies are smaller at the upper end of the distribution than they appeared to be.[1]

All these shortcomings seem to be particularly important for the analysis of the overall income distribution problems In order to minimize these difficulties as far as possible, comparisons which follow are based on relative positions, relative to the average in the former socialiscountries.They are of minor influence on the poverty rate, especially if we assume that subsidies and social benefits affected low income households uniformly, and that the position of privileged groups (the 'socialist elite') had no impact on the life of the 'ordinary population'.

2 Databases and Methods

2.1 Data

We use longitudinal data from the late eighties and early ninethies for both East-Germany and Poland. Both panels start in the pre-transition period and cover the first years of the transition.

For East Germany, the Socio-Economic Panel Study (GSOEP) is used, which is a carefully designed longitudinal study, funded by the National Science Foundation of Germany (cf. Wagner et al. 1993). The following results are based on data from 1990 to 1992.

The Polish Household Panel is an artificial longitudinal data set based on the 'Household Budget Surveys', which have been conducted by the Polish Central Statistical Office for many years (cf. Górecki and Peczkowski 1992). The Household Budget Surveys are sampled by means of a partial rotation method on a quarterly basis (cf. Kordos 1982). A 'master sample' is selected for four years. In each quarter of a year different households are surveyed, and these same households will continue to be observed in that same quarter for four consecutive

1 Another example is the 'second economy' incomes in communist countries and their influence on the overall income distributions. The result would possibly be very similar to the one presented above (see M.Bednarski 1992 and M.Wisniewski 1989 for further comments on the Polish case).

years. Thus, it is possible to create an artificial but truly longitudinal data base with four measurement points. To date only a panel for the years 1987 to 1990 has been constructed.[2]

The size of the 'master sample' is approximately 30.000 households or about 0.3 % of all households in Poland. The panel data set used in the following analyses contains 3707 households. They are stratified by the sampling procedure into four socio-economic groups according to the household's main source of income. These groups are: workers, farmers[3], mixed households (household receiving income from farm and employment), and pensioners.

Due to the common standards of household surveys in Eastern Europe under communist regimes, the Polish household budget survey has some shortcomings. First, the master sample does not contain households with self-employed heads nor households with heads employed in the private non-agricultural sector or in military or police institutions. The excluded groups add up to approximately 12 % of all households in 1990, and thus the sample represents less than 90 percent of the population.

A second shortcoming is the sampling procedure itself. The sample unit is not a private household but a dwelling. In contrast to the follow-up rules of real panel studies, individuals who move to another address are not followed. But because of the extreme shortage on the Polish housing market, residential moves of entire households are very rare: only less than one percent of all households move per year.[4]

Furthermore, the Polish longitudinal data file follows a balanced-panel-design, not including any households which dropped out after the initial interview (Wave 1). Thus, we are not able to carry out any attrition analysis on our own.

---

2 The construction of the artificial panel is not done by the Central Statistical Office of Poland, but by a group headed by prof. Brunon Górecki at the Department of Economics of Warsaw University (cf. Górecki and Peczkowski 1992, Topinska and Górecki 1993). The panel construction has not been fully completed yet and contains only limited information.

3 Even under communist rule, almost all farms in Poland were private. They were only collectivized for a short period in the first half of the 1950s.

4 Residential mobility has been declining since the late seventies (except 1988). In 1991, for instance, only 13 out of 1000 inhabitants changed their place of residence (cf. Raport Komisji Ludnosciowej 1992).

Furthermore, we must make the assumption that the drop-outs follow a random process.

2.2 Methods

Income concept

We use a measure of net monthly income for East Germany and net quarterly income for Poland instead of the more common annual household income. In the transition process annual income makes less sense than "snapshots" by means of monthly data, which provide a clearer picture of the fast changing economic conditions underlying most household decisions.

Our use of a quarterly income concept for Poland requires some explaination. Since the master sample is on a quarterly basis, we have four independent subsamples of about 1,000 households per quarter. To avoid large standard errors we have pooled the four subsamples and made the income information comparable by deflation factors [5]

If the income of a household varies much in the course of a year its real income cannot be calculated correctly. But we are interested in the distribution of incomes only. Thus we calculate the relative income position for each household per quarter and pool this information per year. The distribution of income across different types of households can be affected differently by inflation. But for Poland inflation rates and thus the corresponding deflation factors were quite similar across groups through 1990. Hence we used one common deflator per year.

Equivalence scales

In analysing income distributions it is a common procedure to weight households by the number of their members. One should keep in mind that household

[5] These deflation factors have the major shortcoming that they are calculated on an annual basis.

Table 1: Household structure in East Germany and Poland 1990

Persons in Household	East Germany 1990	Poland 1990
1	25.2	13.3
2	30.5	27.7
3	23.1	17.5
4	17.3	20.5
5 and more	3.9	21.0
Total	100.0	100.0

Sources: GSOEP 1990; Polish Household Panel 1990.

structures in this respect have been very different in the two countries under investigation. In Poland, households of 4 or more persons accounted for over 40 percent of the total, whereas in the former German Democratic Republic (GDR) their share was slightly above 21 percent (see table 1). In other words, Polish households have been - on the average - considerably larger than German ones.

Using "equivalence adult income" would be the best solution to account for possible differences in living standards resulting from household size and composition. Unfortunately, due to limited information on individuals in the Polish panel we were not able to calculate equivalence scales reflecting detailed personal characteristics, i.e., age, sex or education of every household member.

From the variety of different equivalence scales available, we adapted the "LIS-scale"[6]. It has two advantages: Most of our results are comparable with the bulk of LIS-scale based analyses and we do not need more information than household size to calculate the equivalence weight for each household.[7] The LIS equivalence scale gives weights of 1.0 to the head of the household, 0.7 to other adults and 0.5 to children. Because we do not know the exact number of children per household, we used a slightly different version: 1.0 for the head, 0.7 for the second person and 0.5 for all other household members.

---

6 LIS: Luxembourg Income Study.

7 An alternative equivalence scale based on the German social welfare system needs information on the age of each household member.

Of course, there is a problem in using the same equivalence scale for both countries. We cannot safely assume that the savings for a couple that manages a household together and the differences in age-dependent needs were the same in both countries. If housing and other goods consumed particularly by children are subsidized to a greater degree in one country than in the other, a single set of equivalences will not capture this. But there is not that much one can do to solve this problem without a deeper investigation.

Poverty line definition

Following several international comparisons of poverty, we have defined 50 percent of the mean equivalence income as a relative poverty line for each country/region and year in the period under investigation (for a discussion of conceptual problems cf. Hauser in this volume). Additionally, we look at the poverty rates using to 40 and 60 percent of the median equivalence income. Using these alternative definitions shows the sensitivity of the results.

Re-weighing of Polish data

By the design of the sampling procedure, the Polish master sample is in principal a self-weighing random sample. But in 1988 farmers and mixed-type households were oversampled for some technical reasons. We used information from the 1988 census (and forecasts) to reweigh the sample for all four points of measurement.

3 Cross-Sectional Results

Pre-transition period

Table 2 provides overall income distribution and poverty rates figures in Poland and East Germany before the transition. Results are depicted for two

Table 2: Inequality and Poverty in Poland and East Germany just before their transition to market economies

	Poland		East Germany
	1987	1988	1990
Gini-Coefficient	.2303	.2333	.1913
Quintile			
lowest	10.58	10.52	11.35
next lowest	14.83	14.82	15.83
middle	18.33	18.19	19.45
next highest	22.64	22.57	23.04
highest	33.62	33.90	30.33
Total	100.0	100.0	100.0
Poverty rates: Poverty line as percent of mean equivalence income			
40 %	2.3	2.2	1.0
50 %	6.3	6.7	3.7
60 %	14.0	14.6	11.8

Sources: GSOEP 1990; Polish Household Panel 1987-1988.

pre-transition years in Poland and for one pre-transition year, 1990, in the GDR.[8] Under communist regimes, incomes were distributed rather uniformly in both countries as can be seen by relatively low Gini coefficients compared to market economies[9]. But East Germany differed considerably from Poland both in terms of inequality and poverty rates.

Inequality as well as poverty rates were much higher in Poland than in the GDR. Poverty rates (at the 50 percent level) were about twice as high in Poland,

---

8 By means of retrospective questions on individual income in May 1989 a second point of time is surveyed for the GDR, too. Principally, the aggregation of those individual incomes to household incomes is possible. But those aggregations are meaningful only for households who did not change their structure between May 1989 and the survey date in June 1990. Additionally only gross income is known as of 1989. Because the income structure in the GDR was quite stable between May 1989 and June 1990 we did not make an attempt to estimate household incomes for 1989.

9 For Poland, Milanovic (1993, pp.16) as well as Atkinson and Micklewright (1992, p. 137) report larger Gini-Cefficients. This is not surprising since they did not have access to data on individual households, and used "per capita" instead of "equivalence income".

Figure 1: Distribution of Equivalence Income in Poland and East Germany just before their transitions to market economies

Lorenz Curve

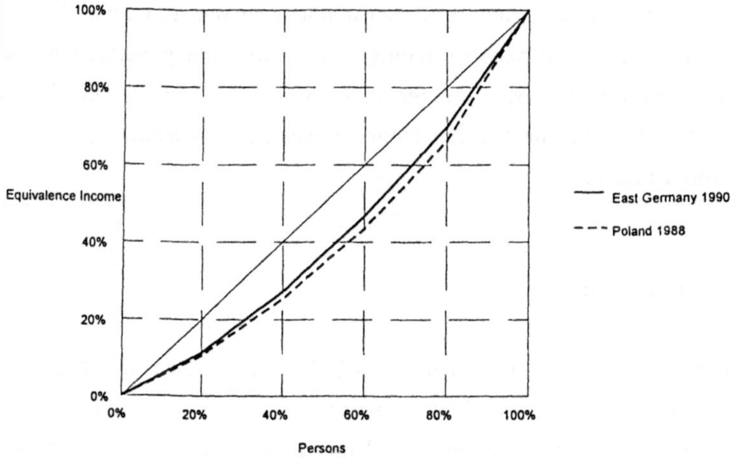

Source: GSOEP 1990; Polish Household Panel 1988.

while the population share living "at the edge of poverty" (between 50 and 60 percent of the mean equivalent income) was about the same size, i.e. 8 percent in each case.[10]

The large difference in income inequalities in pre-transition years between Poland and the GDR is also seen in the Lorenz curves on Figure 1.

Table 3 (see appendix) gives insight into the underlying determinants of the differences between these two "socialist societies". It shows the share of persons in a given socio-economic or demographic group by quintiles of the total population.

In Poland, in the rural sector - the one most influenced at that time by market rules - income inequality increased greatly. Mixed-type households with two major sources of income were in the best position (only 11.0% in the lowest income quintile). This could have been the result of the second job taking by farmers. Second jobs were rare in East Germany with only four percent of people between age 16 and 65 holding one (cf. Wagner et al. 1991, table 1106).

---

10 Again Milanovic (1993, pp.6) as well as Atkinson and Micklewright (1992, pp. 229) report higher poverty rates. This is due to a very different approach of defining poverty by a "basket of social minimum".

Incomes of pensioners were the most equally distributed in both countries. Pensioners were also the group most affected by poverty - regardless of the country considered.

The difference in the structure of household size between Poland and East Germany had also an impact on income distribution and poverty. One-person households were clearly disadvantaged in both societies; in Poland, they were mostly headed by pensioners living alone. Persons in households with children were in similar positions.

The period of transition

Table 4 looks at the period of transition in Poland and East Germany. For both countries there are two points of time observed.

Inequality and poverty rates increased during the transition process in East Germany as well as in Poland (see also Fig.2).[11] This is not surprising because one aim of transition is to introduce market forces in both countries. But the paths were very different: While there are remarkable changes in Poland, East Germany did not change very much (cf. Tables 5aI and 5aII in the appendix).

At first glance, the difference in inequality, which is estimated by the Gini-Coefficient, reveals only a slightly higher degree of inequality for East Germany. However, this difference is statistically significant, and significant in a substantial sense, too, when one takes into account the extreme stability of Gini-Coefficients for Western economies across time (in cross-section analysis).

In East Germany the development is mainly caused by unemployment, which is a result of the fast transition of the whole economic framework and (mainly the introduction of common currency). But German unemployment insurance does a good job of replacing lost earnings. It is financed mainly by transfers from West Germany, and not by a pay-as-you-go scheme within East Germany. The result is that in East Germany income inequality has not increased very much, although the official unemployment rate was about 15 percent in 1992. Additionally, 10

---

11 In Poland the poverty rate reached a higher level than in most Western Europe countries (cf. Duncan et al. 1992). But this rate is still lower than for the USA and Canada (and than the rate for foreigners in West Germany).

Table 4: Inequality and Poverty in Poland and East Germany during their transition to market economies

	Poland		East Germany	
	1989	1990	1991	1992
Gini-Coefficient	.2607	.2422	.2022	.2029
Quintile				
lowest	9.26	9.98	11.29	11.13
next lowest	14.15	14.51	15.82	15.84
middle	18.16	18.35	18.64	18.87
next highest	23.07	23.15	22.44	22.60
highest	35.36	34.01	31.81	31.56
Total	100.0	100.0	100.0	100.0
Poverty rates: Poverty line as percent of mean equivalence income				
40 %	5.1	2.8	2.3	2.3
50 %	10.6	9.0	4.2	6.1
60 %	19.8	17.4	11.2	10.4

Sources: GSOEP 1991, 1992; Polish Household Panel 1989, 1990.

percent of the labor force is on pre-retirement schemes or on job-creation programs (cf. Mueller et al. 1993).

A second reason is that in the old firms who still belong to the Treuhand-Trust as well as in privatized firms the distribution of earnings has changed only slowly (cf. Bird et al. 1993). Only in newly founded firms which employed no more than 4 percent of all workers in Spring 1992 are earnings distributed like they are in firms within West Germany.

The Polish case looks different. In Poland, transition to the market economy started in 1989.[12] At the beginning of the year, while still under the communist government, steps were taken in order to reform the economic system:

12 The starting point of the Polish transformation is not that clear. Quite often, January 1, 1990 is pointed out. But growing market forces, affecting household living conditions, were clearly visible already in 1989 (cf. Kochanowicz 1994 and Slay 1993).

Figure 2: Poverty Rates in Poland and East Germany during their transitions to market economies - All Persons -

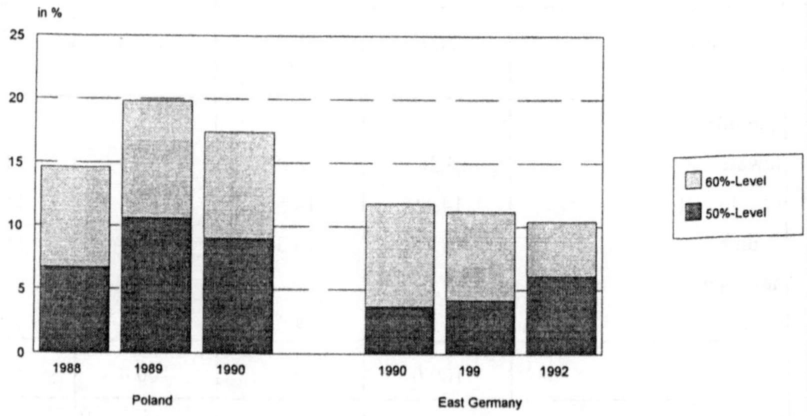

Sources: GSOEP; Polish Household Panel.

abolishing many subsidies and allowing for the growth of the private sector (wholesale sector, the foreign currency exchange). So called marketization of the food sector in August (mainly - price liberalization accompanied by termination of meat rationing) resulted in an increase in the inflation rate. In the last quarter of 1989, the first non-communist government simply followed the steps already taken. Growing inequality and poverty could have been the result of these already pronounced market forces.

At the beginning of 1990, the government proposed a "shock therapy" to fight inflation. As a part of the stabilization program, wages were not allowed to keep face with inflation rate. Pensions, on the other hand, were better protected. The principle of full employment was abolished, and the unemployment rate grew from 0.2 percent in January to 6.1 percent in December. Unemployment benefits, although relatively high, could not offset such income losses.

All in all, inequality and poverty in Poland increased in the first year of transition, but fell in the second year.[13] In contrast, East Germany experienced a

13 Findings concerning inequality change are supported by other authors (cf. Warunki zycia ludnosci w latach 1991, p.28), although they are sometimes questioned on the

further increase in poverty even though transfers continued to be paid by West Germany.

The decline of inequality in Poland in 1990 might have been caused by many factors. Firstly, it could have been the result of the measures undertaken in order to limit wage increases. This was a useful instrument in fighting inflation, unfortunately it also deadened market forces. Second, the opportunities of second job taking (in enterprises) for farmers shrank dramatically at that time. Third, farmers suddenly lost easy access to the market. With the growing import of food (due to the stable exchange rate of the zloty), selling domesticly became more difficult. The formerly rich farmers became losers of transition (in the appendix Tables 5b I and 5b II show that the share of farmers in the highest income quintile fell from 33 percent to 24 percent in 1990). These tables contain more information on the consequences of transformation for demographic groups in the first and the second year of the transition period respectively.[14] In both countries the pictures are surprisingly similar.

At the time, the income positions of the elderly, i.e., persons in households where the head of the family is over 60 or a pensioner, and the income positions of one-person-households (again mainly elderly people), improved: In Poland in the second year of transition, in East Germany immediately. In both countries pensioners became the beneficiaries of advantageous schemes for setting the pension level, and pensioners can not be affected by unemployment. Moreover, pensions were better protected against inflation than were wages.[15]

Families with children were also losers of transition. In Poland, the latter group had a doubled poverty rate. No specific protection for families with children were given in Poland or in East Germany. This is a major shortcoming of

---

basis of the non-representativeness of household budget surveys. On the other hand, poverty rates are found to be declining in 1989 compared to 1988, and then continuously growing (cf. Warunki zycia ludnosci w latach 1991, p.30). But these results are based on a quite different methodology: the money value of a 'minimum basket' as the poverty line, and incomes measured in per capita terms.

14 We subdivide the population by demographic variables only because we do not have information on unemployment in the Polish data base.

15 It should be mentioned that the position of Polish pensioners worsened quickly after 1990. Pension protection against inflation was too costly for the state budget, and so the government has created less generous pension indexation rules.

Figure 3: Poverty Dynamics in Poland and East Germany during their transitions to market economies - All Persons -

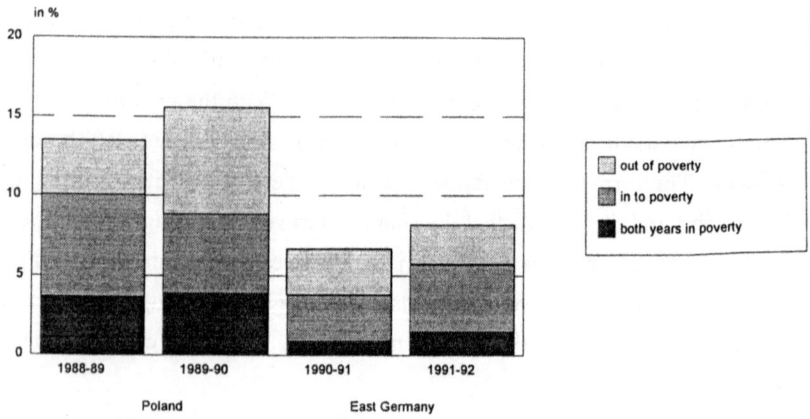

Sources: GSOEP; Polish Household Panel.

social policy under transition, because families with dependent children are less flexible when facing new labor market obstacles.

4 Longitudinal Results

The German as well as the Polish data permit analysis of income mobility and poverty dynamics which are comparable with those conducted by Duncan et al. (1992). We calculate very simple transition matrices for both countries (see table 6 in the appendix). The results are again very similar.

Overall income mobility was slightly higher in East Germany than in Poland. For instance in 1990 in the GDR, 53 percent of people from the lowest quintile were still in the same quintile the next year. However, in Poland in 1988, 60 percent of those in the lowest quintile were still in the same quintile the next year. The lower mobility in Poland seems plausible because the 'shock therapy' and growing unemployment had not yet started. On the other hand, the smaller mobility in Poland has the implication that duration in poverty was lengthening. Tables 7 and 8 and figure 3 show the poverty dynamics within the period of the transition of both economies. In Poland (1988-89), it was higher than in East Germany (1990-91) mostly because relatively more people entered into poverty: about 7 percent in Poland compared to 3 percent in East Germany. The percentage of those leaving poverty was rather similar in both countries (about 3 percent in each case).

The next year, poverty dynamics in Poland were still higher than in Germany, but this time the main difference involved those leaving poverty: The share of people leaving poverty reached over 6.5 percent of the total in Poland compared to less than 3 percent, in East Germany. In general, the 'Polish' pattern consisted of a rather considerable movement into poverty during the first year of the transition, and then a similar movement out of poverty the next year.

Underlying this pattern was the situation of pensioners which was rather exceptional in Poland. The relative number of the new-poor was extremely high in 1989 (over 18 percent), but in 1990, as much as 21 percent of Polish pensioners escaped from poverty. On the other hand, the percentage of the poor in all years was also relatively high (over 10 percent). In 1989, on the very eve of the transition period, pension protection was much more inadequate in Poland. The change came in 1990 - although not for long, as we now know.

5 Conclusion

On the eve of transition income inequality and poverty were very different in Poland and the German Democratic Republic (GDR). It shows that, clearly, the economic systems under communist regime were not the same in these countries.

Poland was, in a sense, much closer to Western societies, with higher inequality and poverty rate. It was, in part, a result of looser wage controls, but also inequalities among farmers. And state social protection was less developed in Poland than in East Germany. The income position of pensioners was especially low (but even in the GDR the pensioners were far below the mean).

Starting from different points, the overall pictures of the transition process reveal some similarities, an increase in inequality and poverty. But inequality is growing faster in Poland than in East Germany. It seems that from the very beginning Germany was better at adapting social policy measures to solve problems arising from the economic transformation - such as the unemployment explosion. In East Germany, the shock of a common currency came with more adequate social policy rules, which offset the income consequences of the market forces.

But the transition of East Germany is an unique economic event within Eastern Europe. It is a "transition with insurance" (cf. Schrettel 1992). This simply means that West Germany is paying most of the transition measures for the former GDR, subsidizing old industries, partially financing unemployment benefits, creating job-programs, and financing a good deal of the old age benefits. In 1992 two thirds of the "national" income of East Germany was transferred from West Germany. All in all, the transition with respect to income inequality and poverty rates is much smoother in East Germany. But the insurance provided by the West has a price: most of the privatized firms in East Germany are now owned by Western companies (cf. Bruecker 1995). Such insurance could be possible in Poland, but would mean the loss of economic independence, which no one is ready to accept.

References

Atkinson, Anthony B. and John Micklewright (1992): Economic transformation in Eastern Europe and the distribution of income, Cambridge University Press.

Bednarski, Marek (1992): Drugi obieg gospodarczy. Przeseanki, mechanizmy i skutki w Polsce lat osiemdziesiatych [Second economy. Formation process and effects in Poland in the 1980s], Wydawnictwa Uniwersytetu Warszawskiego, Warsaw.

Bird, Edward, Johannes Schwarze and Gert G. Wagner (1994): Wage Effects of the Move Towards Free Markets in East Germany, Industrial and Labor Relations Review 47(3), 390-400.

Bruecker, Herbert 1995: Selling Eastern Germany, in: Moct/Most, 5(4), 55-77.

Duncan, Greg J. et al. (1992): No Pain, no Gain? Inequality and economic mobility in the United States, Canada and Europe, Paper prepared for the workshop on the Polish Household Panel, Warsaw, November 20 to 21, 1992, Ann Arbour.

Górecki, Brunon and Marek Peczkowki (1992): Polish Household Panel - Preliminary Information, paper prepared for the workshop on the Polish Household Panel, Warsaw, November 20 to 21, 1992, Warsaw.

Headey, Bruce, Peter Krause and Roland Habich (1993): East Germany - Income, Inequality and the Impact of Redistributive Government 1990-1991, WZB Discussion Paper P 91-106, Berlin,

Kochanowicz, Jacek (1994): Transition to Market and Democratization in Poland in the 1980s and 1990s, in: Joan Nelson (ed.), A Precarious Balance: Democracy and Economic Reform in Eastern Europe, San Francisco, International Center for Economic Growth (forthcoming).

Kordos, Jan (1982): Metoda rotacyjna w badaniach budzetów rodzinnych w Polsce [Rotation Method of Surveying Household Budgets in Poland], Wiadomosci Statystyczne, no 9.

Milanovic, Branko (1993): Social Costs of Transition to Capitalism - Poland 1990-91, World Bank Research Project "Income Distribution During the Transition" Paper No. 2, Washington, D. C.

Mueller, Klaus et al. (1993): How Unemployment and Income Inequality Changed in East and West Germany Following Reunification, in: Vierteljahrshefte zur Wirtschaftsforschung, (3-4) (forthcoming).

Raport Rzadowej Komisji Ludnosciowej (1992): [Demographic Trends in Poland - Report of the Governmental Demographic Committee], Warsaw (mimeo).

Schrettel, Wolfgang (1992): Transition with Insurance: German Unification Reconsidered, in: Oxford Review of Economic Policy, 8 (1), 1-12.

Sinn, Gerlinde and Hans-Werner Sinn (1993): Jumpstart - The Economic Unification of Germany, Cambridge, Mass.

Slay, Ben (1993): The Dilemmas of Economic Liberalism in Poland, in: Europe-Asia Studies, 45(2), 237-257.

Topinska, Irena and Brunon Górecki (1993): Household Panel Study of Well Being Effects of Demographic Factors in Poland 1987-1990, Paper prepared for the Final Conference of the Scientific Network "Household Panel Studies" of the European Science Foundation, June 1 and 2, 1993, Luxembourg.

Wagner, Gert, Bernhard von Rosenbladt und Dieter Blaschke, eds. (1990): An der Schwelle zur sozialen Marktwirtschaft - Ergebnisse aus der Basiserhebung des Sozio-oekonomischen Panels in der DDR im Juni 1990, Beiträge zur Arbeitsmarkt- und Berufsforschung 143, Nürnberg.

Wagner, Gert G., Richard Burkhauser and Friederike Behringer (1993): The English Language Public Use File of the German Socio-economic Panel, in: The Journal of Human Resources, 28(2), 429-433.

Warunki zycia ludnosci w latach 1986-1990 (1991): [Living Conditions of the Population in 1986-1990], Glówny Urzad Statystyczny [Central Statistical Office], Warsaw.

Wisniewski, Marian (1989): Zróznicowanie dochodów w okresie radykalnych zmian warunków bytu - metodologiczne problemy badan empirycznych [Income Differentials in the Period of Complete Changes of Population Living Conditions - Methodological Problems of Empirical Investigation], Ekonomia no 46.

Appendix

Table 3a: Income distribution and Poverty rates in Poland 1988 by socio-economic characteristics

	Occupation of Head				Age of household head		one person households	other households without children	households with children	Population
	Workers	Farmers	Mixed	Pensioners	less than 60 years	aged over 60 years				
Quintile										
lowest	14.7	22.1	11.0	48.1	15.7	43.4	48.9	16.7	22.3	20
next lowest	22.2	14.2	13.6	23.8	19.7	23.2	15.9	15.6	27.5	20
middle	22.7	12.6	19.2	16.7	20.6	15.9	11.6	18.9	22.6	20
next highest	22.4	18.2	23.9	8.2	21.6	8.8	11.1	22.4	17.2	20
highest	18.0	32.9	32.3	3.3	2[illegible].6	8.7	12.5	26.4	10.4	20
Total	100.0	100.0	100.0	100.0	100.0	100.0	100.0	100.0	100.0	100
Poverty rates: Poverty lines as percent of mean equivalence income										
40 %	0.7	4.1	1.0	7.6	1.8	5.3	4.6	2.4	1.6	1.0
50 %	4.0	9.3	2.2	19.7	5.4	15.8	19.1	6.2	6.2	6.7
60 %	10.2	19.0	5.2	38.6	11.9	34.2	38.3	12.4	15.9	14.9

Source: Polish Household Panel 1988.

Table 3b: Income distribution and Poverty rates in East Germany 1990 by socio-economic characteristics

	Non-pensioners	Pensioners	Age of household head		one person households	other households	households with children	Population
			less than 60 years	aged over 60 years		without children		
Quintile								
lowest	14.4	52.8	14.8	46.1	57.5	10.7	19.8	20
next lowest	19.1	27.4	19.1	26.2	10.3	17.4	24.6	20
middle	20.2	11.4	20.0	13.0	6.5	15.5	23.7	20
next highest	23.1	3.7	23.2	6.3	15.6	21.2	20.3	20
highest	23.3	4.7	22.9	8.4	10.1	35.2	11.6	20
Total	100.0	100.0	100.0	100.0	100.0	100.0	100.0	100
Poverty rates:								
Poverty lines as percent of mean equivalence income								
40 %	0.9	1.5	0.9	1.3	1.9	0.7	1.0	1.0
50 %	2.8	8.5	2.9	7.3	11.2	1.1	4.0	3.7
60 %	7.7	34.7	7.9	30.0	42.5	4.9	10.5	11.8

Source: GSOEP 1990.

Table 5aI: Income distribution and Poverty rates in East Germany 1991 by socio-economic characteristics (1 year after transition began)

	Non-pensioners	Pensioners	Age of household head		one person households	other households without children	households with children	Population
			less than 60 years	aged over 60 years				
Quintile								
lowest	18.9	24.3	19.0	24.5	35.3	11.1	23.4	20.0
next lowest	18.2	26.8	18.5	21.6	28.8	13.8	22.6	20.0
middle	10.0	31.0	18.6	29.7	15.3	22.3	20.4	20.0
next highest	22.2	14.4	20.8	15.2	11.1	24.3	18.3	20.0
highest	23.7	3.5	23.0	4.5	9.5	28.5	15.3	20.0
Total	100.0	100.0	100.0	100.0	100.0	100.0	100.0	100
Poverty rates:								
Poverty lines as percent of mean equivalence income								
40 %	2.5	1.1	2.6	0.7	0.7	1.5	3.1	2.3
50 %	4.3	3.1	4.5	2.7	2.8	3.3	5.2	4.2
60 %	10.8	12.6	11.0	12.0	16.5	6.4	13.6	11.2

Source: GSOEP 1991

Table 5aII Income distribution and Poverty rates in East Germany 1992 by socio-economic characteristics (2 years after transition began)

	Non-pensioners	Pensioners	Age of household head		one person households	other households without children	households with children	Population
			less than 60 years	aged over 60 years				
Quintile								
lowest	20.8	17.6	21.2	15.4	23.1	11.2	25.7	20.0
next lowest	17.4	28.5	17.9	29.2	23.6	17.7	20.9	20.0
middle	18.2	26.4	18.6	26.1	18.9	19.3	20.7	20.0
next highest	20.0	20.4	19.9	20.9	21.5	20.7	19.4	20.0
highest	23.6	7.1	22.4	8.4	12.9	31.1	13.3	20.0
Total	100.0	100.0	100.0	100.0	100.0	100.0	100.0	100
Poverty rates:								
Poverty lines as percent of mean equivalence income								
40 %	2.5	1.7	2.5	1.2	1.4	1.1	3.3	2.3
50 %	6.5	4.8	6.7	3.2	6.0	2.8	8.4	6.1
60 %	10.9	8.9	11.1	7.6	11.6	5.5	13.7	10.4

Source: GSOEP 1992.

Table 5bI: Income distribution and Poverty rates in Poland 1989 by socio-economic characteristics (1 year after transition began)

	Occupation of Head				Age of household head		one person households	other households without children	households with children	Population
	Workers	Farmers	Mixed	Pensioners	less than 60 years	aged over 60 years				
Quintile										
lowest	13.1	22.9	8.8	55.7	15.5	49.6	48.3	18.5	19.4	20
next lowest	21.2	14.4	14.8	26.0	19.3	24.8	21.9	16.7	25.0	20
middle	24.0	11.9	20.1	11.2	21.2	11.5	7.3	16.8	26.1	20
next highest	23.6	18.4	23.3	4.4	22.1	6.5	10.4	21.6	18.6	20
highest	18.6	32.5	33.0	2.7	21.9	7.6	12.1	26.4	10.9	20
Total	100.0	100.0	100.0	100.0	100.0	100.0	100.0	100.0	100.0	100
Poverty rates:										
Poverty lines as percent of mean equivalence income										
40 %	1.8	9.8	1.4	17.8	3.6	15.3	10.8	5.6	3.7	5.1
50 %	5.3	14.2	3.8	34.6	7.8	29.2	30.3	10.3	8.8	10.6
60 %	12.9	22.7	3.8	55.3	15.4	49.0	47.9	18.2	19.3	19.8

Source: Polish Household Panel 1989.

Table 5bII: Income distribution and Poverty rates in Poland 1990 by socio-economic characteristics (2 years after transition began)

	Occupation of Head				Age of household head		one person households	other households without children	households with children	Population
	Workers	Farmers	Mixed	Pensioners	less than 60 years	aged over 60 years				
Quintile										
lowest	17.9	21.1	9.0	37.0	18.0	32.4	36.2	15.1	25.9	20
next lowest	19.3	19.2	13.2	29.4	18.3	30.1	26.8	17.1	23.7	20
middle	20.9	19.6	18.6	18.5	20.2	18.3	15.2	18.9	22.1	20
next highest	21.5	15.6	27.9	10.7	21.7	10.3	9.7	22.9	16.6	20
highest	20.4	24.5	31.1	4.4	21.8	8.8	11.8	26.0	11.7	20
Total	100.0	100.0	100.0	100.0	100.0	100.0	100.0	100.0	100.0	100
Poverty rates:										
Poverty lines as percent of mean equivalence income										
40 %	2.0	5.9	0.7	5.5	2.5	4.6	3.1	2.6	3.2	2.8
50 %	8.0	12.7	3.7	15.1	8.4	12.5	11.5	6.8	12.4	9.0
60 %	15.4	19.8	7.6	31.8	15.6	28.0	32.0	13.0	22.6	17.4

Source: Polish Household Panel 1990.

Table 6: Income Distribution and Poverty in Poland and East Germany during the transition process: Mobility across quintiles

Poland

1989

	Quintile	lowest	next lowest	middle	next highest	highest
	lowest	50	25	9	4	2
1988	next lowest	22	36	27	11	4
	middle	10	22	34	26	8
	next highest	5	11	23	37	24
	highest	2	5	6	22	65

East Germany

1991

	Quintile	lowest	next lowest	middle	next highest	highest
	lowest	53	29	13	43	2
1990	next lowest	21	32	32	11	4
	middle	15	18	26	26	15
	next highest	8	15	24	32	21
	highest	5	4	9	27	55

Sources: GSOEP 1990, 1991; Polish Household Panel 1988, 1989.

Table 7: Poverty dynamics in Poland and East Germany in the transition process (1 year after transition began)

Poland 1988 - 1989

Poverty Experience	Occupation of Head				Age of household head		one person	other	households	Population
	Workers	Farmers	Mixed	Pensioners	less than 60 years	aged over 60 years	households	households without children	with children	
both years in poverty	2.0	2.9	1.2	13.3	2.8	10.0	12.3	3.6	3.1	3.7
out of poverty	1.9	6.4	1.0	6.4	2.6	5.8	6.8	2.6	3.2	3.0
in to poverty	3.8	11.3	3.2	18.4	5.1	18.6	19.9	6.9	5.4	6.8
both years not in poverty	92.3	79.4	94.6	61.9	89.5	65.6	61.0	86.9	88.3	86.5
Total	100.0	100.0	100.0	100.0	100.0	100.0	100.0	100.0	100.0	100

East Germany 1990 - 1991

Poverty Experience	Non-pensioners	Pensioners	Age of household head		one person	other	households	Population
			less than 60 years	aged over 60 years	households	households without children	with children	
both years in poverty	0.9	0.7	1.0	0.6	0.6	0.6	1.1	0.9
out of poverty	1.8	7.1	1.8	6.1	9.9	0.4	2.7	2.6
in to poverty	3.4	2.2	3.6	1.4	3.89	2.0	4.0	3.2
both years not in poverty	93.9	90.0	93.6	91.9	85.7	97.0	92.2	93.3
Total	100.0	100.0	100.0	100.0	100.0	100.0	100.0	100

Sources: GSOEP 1990, 1991; Polish Household Panel 1988, 1989.

Table 8: Poverty dynamics in Poland and East Germany in the transition process (2 years after transition began)

Poland 1989 - 1990

Poverty Experience	Occupation of Head				Age of household head		one person	other	households	Population
	Workers	Farmers	Mixed	Pensioners	less than 60 years	aged over 60 years	households	households without children	with children	
both years in poverty	2.8	4.5	1.3	10.9	3.3	8.3	7.2	3.3	4.7	3.9
out of poverty	2.6	9.8	2.5	23.7	4.5	20.9	23.1	7.1	4.2	6.6
in to poverty	5.6	6.4	3.1	4.3	5.1	5.0	4.2	3.2	8.1	5.1
both years not in poverty	89.0	79.3	93.1	61.1	87.1	65.8	65.6	86.5	83.0	84.4
Total	100.0	100.0	100.0	100.0	100.0	100.0	100.0	100.0	100.0	100

East Germany 1991 - 1992

Poverty Experience	Non-pensioners	Pensioners	Age of household head		one person	other	households	Population
			less than 60 years	aged over 60 years	households	households without children	with children	
both years in poverty	1.5	1.9	1.5	1.6	1.0	1.2	1.9	1.5
out of poverty	2.8	1.4	2.8	1.2	1.7	1.8	3.2	2.5
in to poverty	4.3	3.1	4.5	2.5	5.9	1.9	5.3	4.2
both years not in poverty	91.4	93.6	91.2	94.7	91.4	95.1	89.7	91.8
Total	100.0	100.0	00.0	100.0	100.0	100.0	100.0	100

Sources: GSOEP 1991, 1992; Polish Household Panel 1989, 1990.

Trends in the Income Distribution of Unified Germany Analyzed by Decomposable Inequality Measures

Johannes Schwarze

1 Introduction[1]

Since German unification, personal income distribution has been analysed especially with regards to East Germany. The first point of interest is how the income distribution within East Germany has changed during the transformation from a centrally planned to a market oriented system (cf. Mueller et al. 1994). A second aspect is the way in which incomes of households, wage earners, pensioners and others have changed with respect to comparable groups in West Germany. This "East-West" comparison can also be considered as a question of income distribution in a unified Germany.

Future analyses of the income distribution have to be focused more and more on the unified Germany. At the macroeconomic level the "statistical unification" - for example, the national accounting system - is now almost complete. Empirical economic research at the micro level is lagging behind. In most cases this is simply due to the fact that the objects of microeconomic research in the unified Germany are frequently still very heterogenous (e.g., labour force participation by women) thus reducing the sense of joint analyses for East and West.

In this context it is of minor importance to analyse the personal income distribution in unified Germany by means of a single measure. On the other hand, the income distributions in East and West Germany are interacting in particular ways, and that must also be taken in to account.

Even three years after unification about 70 percent of East Germany's national income is still financed by transfers from West Germany[2]. From the West German

---

1 Helpful comments by Richard V. Burkhauser, Syracuse University, by participants of a seminar at Syracuse University and participants of the seminar in Arnoldshain are greatfully acknowledged.

point of view a share of 7.7 percent of national income has to be transfered to the East; this figure represents more than the annual growth of the GNP. This, then, is a third distributive aspect of German unification: how and to what extent do West-East transfers influence the income distribution in West Germany. The public discussion, which preceded the adoption of a "Solidarity Pact", has increasingly put the spotlight on this special aspect of German income distribution.

For the time being, it seems to be unlikely to observe a significant change in the West German income distribution. Only a small share of the West-East German transfer volume is still financed by increasing income taxes and social security or by decreasing government expenditures for West German purposes. Increasing social security taxes lead to a more unequal distribution of after government income, because only employees (excluding the civil servants) are concerned. But this effect was particularly compensated by the so called "Solidaritätszuschlag" (solidarity surtax), which was collected from July 1991 to July 1992. The solidarity surtax was computed as a share of the monthly income tax load, resulting c.p. in a more equal income distribution.

Altogether, the income distribution has to be analyzed regarding three questions:

(1) How will the income distribution change during the transformation process in East Germany?

(2) How will the income distribution between East and West Germany change over time?

(3) What are the effects of the unification process on the income distribution in West Germany?

This paper provides a first attempt to analyse these three aspects. The approach is based on decomposable inequality measures. The data used is drawn from the German Socio-Economic Panel Study (GSOEP) from 1990 to 1992.

---

2 East Germanys national income will be estimated 242 billions DM in 1993. The estimated figure for West Germany is 2,119 billions DM. The West-East-German transfer volume will be 163 billions DM (Source: German Institute for Economic Research, Berlin).

2 Methodological Issues

Most analyses of personal income distributions use aggregated measures of inequality, such as variance, the coefficient of variation or the Gini-coefficient. All these measures are based explicit or implicit on a social welfare function, thus on a normative setting (cf. Blackorby and Donaldson 1978).

A well known measure, for example, is the class of inequality measures developed by Atkinson (1970), allowing integration of a wide range of economic and legal-philosophical considerations of social welfare and its distribution: It includes the utilitarian position as well as the criterion of John Rawls and the opposite criterion of Friedrich Nietzsche, according to which social welfare is at a maximum when the utility of the person who already enjoys the maximum utility cannot be increased any more.

Such a measure, however, is not suitable to our purposes because the Atkinson measure is not decomposable in a strict sense. Moreover, an explicit setting of a normative valuation would require a detailed theoretical analysis of the distributive relations between East and West Germany. The difficulty of this, can be shown by an example:

A number of conflicting positions can be identified when considering the development of the income distribution over time in transforming economies. One position, often formulated, is that the transition from planned to market oriented economies will increase efficiency, and therefore, in the context of the efficiency/equity discussion, increase the degree of inequality as well (cf. Atkinson and Micklewright 1992). This view is widely shared. The valuation of income distribution would then be measured by an utilitarian concept, although it remains unclear how this process would be initiated.

On the other hand, it is ambiguous how a market economy begins to work. What part is dominated during the transformation process by the implicit social structure that arise in Eastern Europe? Individuals are discovering difficulties - due to uncertainty and/or ignorance - in evaluating their own chances and opportunities within the market order. They are unaware of the "real" value of their own resources. This "veil of ignorance" (Rawls 1971) may induce behavioural patterns which prevent the development of market-economic structures, because certain distributional outcomes are not politically acceptable.

Such a view would lead to the application of the Rawlsian criterion, which is opposite to the position described before.

On account of these conceptual difficulties, no explicit welfare relation will be discussed further. Moreover, as will be shown later only one inequality measure can be used when decomposing overall German income inequality. Thus, the relating welfare function is defined a priori.

The overall German income inequality can be expressed as $I = I(I_e, I_w)$. I (the income inequality) is a function of I_e (the inequality within East Germany) and I_w (the inequality within West Germany). Relating this function to the three major questions formulated above, an additive relationship seems to be appropriate; in other words, inequality of the overall German income distribution can be expressed as the sum of I_e, I_{e-w} and I_w:

(1) $$I = I_e + I_{e-w} + I_w$$

And this is indeed a decomposed additive inequality measure. The income inequality between East and West (or the difference in welfare) is given here as I_{e-w}. Using this component, the process of harmonization between East and West Germany can be evaluated. The comparison of I_e and I_w allows us to describe differences between the income distributions in East and West Germany: how the transformation process induces changes in income distribution in East Germany, and how the "burden" of unification is distributed in West Germany.

Additively decomposable inequality measures can be expressed as the sum of the inequality existing between g subgroups of a population with n members and as a kind of 'weighted average' of the inequality within these groups (see for the following Bourguignon 1979 and Shorrocks 1980, 1984).

(2) $$I(y;n) = \sum_{g=1}^{G} w_g I(y_g; n_g) + B$$

I is an inequality measure, y an income vector of size n. w_g are coefficients for weighting the inequality within the sub-groups. B measures the inequality between the sub-groups and should be independent from the inequality within the sub-groups, depending only on their mean incomes. For the example considered in this paper, B denotes the welfare difference between East and West.

The same is required for the weights w_g. They should be independent from the level of inequality within the groups, being based on their mean values and population sizes only. If this restriction is not made, the choice of weightings is purely arbitrary, being based solely on normative decisions.

A further requirement is that the sum of the weights for the evaluation of the inequality within the sub-groups equals one. It can be shown that this is true only if the weights depend only on the mean income μ or on n.

Just two measures meet all the requirements for decomposability[3]: The mean logarithmic deviation $I(0)$ and the Theil index, here denoted as $I(1)$. Both measures belong to the generalized entropy class[4] and are computed as:

$$(3) \quad I(1) = \left(\frac{1}{n}\right)\sum_{i=1}^{N} \log\left(\frac{\mu}{y_i}\right)$$

$$(4) \quad I(1) = \left(\frac{1}{n}\right)\sum_{i=1}^{N} \left(\frac{y_i}{\mu}\right) \log\left(\frac{y_i}{\mu}\right)$$

$I(0)$ constitutes a "neutral" position in the sense of the normative perception of inequality, whereas $I(1)$ is a more "top-sensitive" measure. Both measures are not normalized, but in the case of equally distributed income the lower bound is zero.

$I(0)$ and $I(1)$ are decomposed in the following way:

$$(5) \quad I(0) = \sum_{g=1}^{G} p_g I(0)_g + \sum_{g=1}^{G} p_g \log\left(\frac{p_g}{v_g}\right)$$

$$(6) \quad I(1) = \sum_{g=1}^{G} v_g I(1)_g + \sum_{g=1}^{G} v_g \log\left(\frac{v_g}{p_g}\right)$$

---

3 Most of these special requirements are based on more general assumptions: the inequality measures should be continous and symmetric in y. Other assumptions are mean independence, population homogeneity and the principle of transfers (cf. Bourguignon 1979).

4 For several reasons most of the more popular inequality measures are not decomposable in a strict sense, e.g., the Gini-coefficient, the variance, or the class of Atkinson measures (cf. Bourguignon 1979 and Shorrocks 1980).

The first term denotes the "within" component of inequality; the second term measures the "between" component of inequality. The decomposition of both measures differ only in the different weights used. p_g is the share of the total population which is in subgroup g. v_g is the share of total income in subgroup g. Thus, $I(0)$ uses population shares for its decomposition weightings, whereas $I(1)$ makes use of the group shares of total income. In this case, the weighting of the within component is no longer independent from the weighting of the between component. If income of all persons in one group increases equally, only the mean income of this group increases but not the inequality. This may only be reflected in a change in the between component. But if the measure is weighted by income shares, the weights itself change too, and the significance of the within components shifts throughout the decomposition.

Therefore, a last requirement should be formulated: the weights should be depend on the population shares and not on the income shares. Thus, only $I(0)$ fulfill all the necessary requirements. For a demonstration concerning the sensitivity of decomposable inequality measures, the results for $I(1)$ will be briefly discussed.

3 Empirical Analyses of the German Income Distribution for 1990 to 1992

3.1 Data base, income concept, and population

The data base for the analysis is the German Socio-Economic Panel (GSOEP, cf. Wagner et al. 1993). The GSOEP is a longitudinal micro-database containing socio-economic information on private households in the United Federal Republic of Germany. The first wave of data was collected in 1984 including about 5,900 households with 12,000 persons. The first wave of a supplement was gathered in June 1990 in the German Democratic Republic, which became the New Bundeslaender in October 1990. In this analysis, GSOEP data from 1990 to 1992 is used for both the new and old states of Germany.

In a strict sense, the term "decomposition" is appropriate for 1991 and 1992 only, because the data for 1990 was collected before German unification. In a theoretical sense, however, it can be considered as an aggregation analysis of income distributions from two different countries. Because the aggregativity property is fulfilled by the decomposable measures used (cf. Bourguignon 1979), there is no difference between aggregation and decompositon in a methodological sense.

When comparing income distributions between countries with different political and economic systems, some theoretical and empirical problems have to be considered (cf. for the East-West German case, Hauser 1992). Prices and subsidies in the former GDR were extremely different from those in West Germany. But in the spring of 1990 just before unification the old subsidisation system in East Germany disappeared. And even though the level and structures of income have not changed significantly in East Germany, they have been correlated to the West German price and subsidisation system. Therefore, the analysis for 1990, just before the unification, is not as critical as it first seems to be.

The "before government income" and the "after government income" will be considered in the empirical analysis. The "before government income" makes it possible to analyze the "market" component of the transition process. It addresses the question of whether increased efficiency during transition from a centrally planned to a market oriented system in East Germany lead to greater inequality of market related incomes. "Before government income" is approximated by gross monthly income from employment[5]. It is evident that gross earnings from East Germany are not an optimal indicator for "market" income. A significant share of East German wage income is subsidized in different ways and therefore contains redistributive elements. This must be taken into account.

Redistribution within East and West Germany and between these regions can be studied by looking at "after government income". The GSOEP provides a proxy-measure by asking the head of each household for the value of disposable monthly household income including all received market and transfer income and deducting taxes and contributions to the social security system. Because the

---

5 Since the distribution of working hours is extremely different between East und West Germany, only the gross income from full-time employment is considered (e.g., the share of part-time workers in West Germany differs significantly from East Germany).

analysis is based on an individual rather than household level an equivalent personal income is computed[6].

Income, taking into account the extremely different developments in the cost of living in East and West Germany[7], is computed in real terms.

3.2 Decompositon of the income distribution for unified Germany for 1990 to 1992

The empirical results of the decomposition are depicted in Tables 1 and 2. Table A-1 and Table A-2 contain descriptive information on the data used, including the weightings used to decompose inequality.

The income measures not decomposed for unified Germany, and East and West Germany are shown in Table 1. The German unification process increased inequality of income significantly for both before and after government income. Compared to West Germany, income inequality rose by 120 percent in the case of gross wages and by 25 percent for after government income. In international comparison, however, even the "new" German inequality is not so extreme. In the United States of America the inequality of after government income is twice as high as in unified Germany. Burkhauser and Poupore (1993) computed a value of 0.287 (income year was 1988) for the inequality measure $I(1)$.

In 1990, the distribution of gross wages was more unequal than the distribution of disposable income. Inequality decreased significantly until 1992; this is especially true for gross income. As a result, in 1992 after government income became more unequal than gross wages. As will be shown later, this is not the result of a "perverted" redistribution policy, but the result of the different speed of adjusting wages and household income between East and West Germany[8].

---

6 The weights for each person are derived from the German Social Assistence Scheme.

7 Restricting 1990 to 100 the cost of living index was 107.9 for West and 128.7 for East Germany in 1992 (Source: German Institute for Economic Research, Berlin).

8 Moreover, Table 1 shows higher inequality for after government than for before government income for all years. This is due to the fact that the wage sample is restricted to fulltimers only.

Table 1: The Distribution of Personal Income for Unified Germany and its Components 1990 to 1992. Non-decomposed Inequality Measure $I(0)$.

Year	Total Inequality	Inequality East	Inequality West
Gross Monthly Income from Fulltime Employment			
1990	0.1719	0.0438	0.0784
1991	0.1317	0.0708	0.0780
1992	0.1192	0.0642	0.0750
After Government Monthly Household Income (adjusted for household size)			
1990	0.1473	0.0541	0.1175
1991	0.1369	0.0671	0.1103
1992	0.1322	0.0663	0.1124

Income in 1990 Deutsche Mark.
Source: GSOEP, 1990-1992.

For both types of income, inequality increased significantly in East Germany from 1990 to 1991 and decreased slightly in the following year. In West Germany, inequality of gross wages decreased over the whole period. The West German after government income became more unequal between 1991 and 1992. This can be interpreted as a result of increasing contributions to the Social Security system.

Table 2 presents the decomposition of $I(0)$ with regard to the three components: Inequality within East Germany, inequality between East and West Germany and inequality within West Germany. The additive characteristic of the measure provides the opportunity to express the components of inequality in terms of their share of total income inequality[9].

Before unification, overall inequality of gross wages was determined by the between component. More than half of the overall German inequality resulted

[9] The reason that only I(0) is used can be studied by looking at the results in Table A-3. This table presents the decomposed values of I(0) and I(1) for both, incomes in real and in nominal terms. Real incomes are computed by multiplying nominal incomes by a scalar for East and West Germany. As a result income inequality within East and West Germany should remain unchanged. But this assumption is fulfilled by I(0) only (for the methodological reasons see section 2).

Table 2: The Distribution of Personal Income for Unified Germany and its Components 1990 to 1992. Decomposed Inequality Measure $I(0)$

Year	Total Inequality	Inequality East	Inequality East-West	Inequality West
Gross Monthly Income from Full-time Employment				
1990	0.1719 100 %	0.0124 7,2 %	0.1033 60,0 %	0.0563 32,8 %
1991	0.1317 100 %	0.0155 11,8 %	0.0554 42.1%	0.0608 46,1 %
1992	0.1192 100 %	0.0147 12,3 %	0.0467 39,2 %	0.0578 48,5 %
After Government Monthly Household Income (adjusted for household size)				
1990	0.1473 100 %	0.0117 7,9 %	0.0435 29,5 %	
1991	0.1369 100 %	0.0142 10,4 %	0.0357 26,1 %	0.0869 63,5 %
1992	0.1322 100 %	0.0139 10,5 %	0.0294 22,2 %	0.0889 67,3 %

Income in 1990 Deutsche Mark.
Source: GSOEP, 1990-1992.

from the difference between East and West German wages. But the wage difference between East and West Germany was partly compensated by the higher female labor participation. In the GDR, on average, nearly two persons contributed earnings to the household income of couples. In West Germany this figure is on average 1.3 persons (cf. Schwarze et al. 1990). As a result the inequality of after government household income between East and West Germany was "only" 30 percent in 1990.

The inequality of after government income between East and West decreased from 1990 to 1992 in absolute terms as well as a share of the overall inequality. In 1992, inequality between East and West Germany contributed 22 percent to overall inequality. The share of between inequality of gross income shrunk from 60 percent in 1990 to 39 percent in 1992. Because of increasing unemployment, especially unemployment of women, the difference of wages between East and West affected the difference between household income to a larger extent. The variation of the inequality within East and West Germany will be discussed later in the form of a trend analysis.

Results from this first analysis should be able to affect social and income policy because they make it possible to integrate various problems of income distribution into a general pattern. The German public discussion is dominated by the East-West difference in income only. Social and policy aims can not allow increasing differences between East and West Germans after government income. It can be shown that even in the year of unification overall inequality was dominated by inequality within West Germany.

3.3 Analysing the trend in overall German income inequality

The previous analysis revealed the importance of inequality within East and West Germany and the inequality between those regions as shares of overall inequality. The development of the shares can also be studied over time. But looking at decomposition formula (5), it is obvious that changing inequality shares depend on several components, which can also vary over time. The main components are: mean income in East and West Germany, population shares, and inequality within East and West Germany.

Using a trend decompositon, these components and their contribution to overall German inequality can be separated:

- component k1 measures the influence of changing inequality within East and West Germany
- k2 indicates the effect of changes in the population shares on the inequality within East and within West Germany.
- k3 indicates the effect of changes in the population shares on the inequality between East and West Germany.
- k4 measures the contribution to the changing overall inequality due to relative changes in East and West German mean income.

As can be seen from Tables A-1 and A-2, it can be expected that component k4 contributes most to the reduction of overall inequality. From 1990 to 1992 mean gross wages rose at a rate of about 60 percent in East Germany. In contrast, this figure is only 4.6 percent for West Germany.

On the other hand, the economically active population of East Germany shrunk from 9 million at the end of 1989 to 6 million at the end of 1992. Registered unemployment averaged 1.2 million in 1992[10]. This development can also be considered from the changing population shares in Table A-1. Thus, there is also an impact of changing population shares on gross wage inequality to be expected. As a result, not only the smaller difference in the mean incomes between East and West Germany reduces overall inequality but so does the declining East German employment share. In other words, less people with a low income reduce c.p. overall inequality.

In contrast to gross wages, after government income is computed for the whole population. A declining population share can be observed for East Germany (and an increasing population share for West Germany, respectively, see Table A-2). This is due to the fact that a part of the East German population migrated to West Germany in the first years after unification[11]. This means the impact of East-West Migration on overall German income inequality can be measured by the components k2 and k3.

Changing overall German income inequality is decomposed as follows:

$$(7) \qquad I(0)_{t+1} - I(0)_t = k1 + k2 + k3 + k4$$

Taking first differences of the decomposition from $I(0)$, formula (5), k1 to k4 can be computed as follows (cf. Mookherjee and Shorrocks 1982):

$$(8) \qquad \mathrm{k1} = \sum_{g=1}^{G} \overline{p_g} \Delta I(0)_g$$

$$(9) \qquad \mathrm{k2} = \sum_{g=1}^{G} \overline{I(0)_g} \Delta p_g$$

---

10 Source: German Institute for Economic Research, Berlin.

11 From 1989 to 1992 1,2 Million East Germans or 7,2 percent of the 1989 East German population migrate to West Germany (Source: Central Statistical Office, Germany).

$$(10)\quad k3=\sum_{g=1}^{G}\left(\overline{\frac{\mu_g}{\mu}}-\overline{\log\left(\frac{\mu_g}{\mu}\right)}\right)\Delta p_g$$

$$(11)\quad k4=\sum_{g=1}^{G}\left(\overline{p_g\frac{\mu_g}{\mu}}-\overline{p_g}\right)\Delta\mu_g$$

where $\overline{p_g}=0.5(p_{t+1}+p_t)$. The other overlined elements are defined analogous. $\Delta I(0)_g$ is computed as $\left(I(0)_{t+1}-I(0)_t\right)$. All other elements signed by Δ are computed similarly.

When decomposing income inequality is associated with only a few subgroups, it may be of interest to consider some of the expressions (8) to (11) for each group seperately. Of special interest is the impact of changing inequality within East and West (k1e and k1w) on the overall inequality. The same is true for changing mean incomes (k4e and k4w).

The results of decomposing the trend of inequality are shown in Table 3. As can be seen from Table 2, overall German income inequality decreased from 1990 to 1993 for gross wages (-0.0528) more than for after government income (-0.0152). To make the effects of changing overall inequality comparable both values are standardized to -100.

According to this value, by changing inequality within East and West, the impact on overall inequality is very small. Considering gross wages, k1 contributes 5 points to increase overall German inequality. This effect is dominated by the increasing inequality within East Germany (k1e, nearly 10 points) compensated for by a declining inequality within West Germany. The question is whether this result can be interpreted as an effect of the beginning market economy. In the former GDR, wage dispersion was very low for ideological reasons, and it was to be expected that the wage structure would become more unequal during the transformation process. Surprisingly only the wage level changed significantly, but the overall structure of wages remained nearly the same (cf. Bird et al. 1994). What are the reasons for rising wage inequality? The dynamics of wages move much more in newly founded firms than

Table 3: Decomposition of Changing Inequality in Unified Germany 1990 to 1992

	Gross wages	After Government income
Change in total Inequality I	-0.0528 = -100	-0.0152 = -100
Contribution due to changes in[1]:		
Within group inequality		
- total (k1)	5.1	-9.4
- East (k1e)	9.9	17.1
- West (k1w)	-4.8	-26.5
Population shares on		
- within inequality (k2)	2.3	2.5
- between inequality (k3)	-22.4	-6.4
Mean group incomes		
- total (k4)	-85.0	-86.7
- East (k4e)	-95.4	-91.8
- West (k4w)	10.4	5.1

[1] The principal components k1 to k4 sum up to -100.
Source: GSOEP, 1990-1992.

in either privatized firms or in trust firms[12]. The return on human capital is nearly the same in newly founded firms as in western enterprises, whereas it still remains the same in privatized or trust firms. Furthermore, the monthly wages are on average significantly higher in newly founded firms than in others. Thus, both effects increase overall wage inequality in East Germany.

The k1 effect has, with respect to after government income, a negative impact on overall inequality. The results are clearly different for East and West Germany after decomposing for this effect. Rising inequality within East Germany contributes 17 points to the increased overall German inequality of after

12 Firms which belong to the *Treuhandanstalt*. The *Treuhandanstalt* was founded in 1989 by the government of the GDR. This trust owned most of industrial enterprises in East Germany. The aim of the trust is the restructuring and privatisation of those firms.

government income. This effect is overcompensated for by the reduced inequality within West Germany. This means that financing the unification process has not yet led to a more unequal distribution of after government income within West Germany, but as discussed before, it is to be expected that the process of "unequalisation" will start in 1994.

The effects of changing population shares on overall German income inequality is measured by k2 and k3. The positive effect of k2 is only small for overall inequality of both before and after government income. The increasing West German population shares shifted the weighted inequality upwards within West Germany.

Of more interest is the effect of k3, which measures the impact of changing population shares according to the inequality between East and West Germany. This effect is considerable for overall inequality of gross wages (-22 points) and can be interpreted in an interesting way: decreasing overall German inequality results, to a great extent, from decreasing employment in East Germany. In other words, a better employment situation in East Germany would lead to a more unequal overall German income distribution.

The impact of changing population shares on overall inequality is not so important in the case of after government income, although this effect is at least negative. Although this hyphothesis should be handled with caution, it can be assumed that this effect describes the impact of East-West Migration on overall German income inequality. The greater the migration from East to West Germany the lower the weight of income inequality between East and West Germany. Another question is whether the East emigrants lead to a greater inequality within West Germany. In this case, the "migration-effect" described by k3 is compensated for.

As expected, increasing mean income in East Germany contributed most to reducing overall German income inequality. For both before and after government income, the effect k4 is about -85 points. Considering this effect with respect to East (k4e) and West (k4w) seperately it can be seen that the advanced East German mean income lags behind a mean income for West Germany which has also increased.

4 Summary

This analysis of the income distribution for unified Germany has served to illuminate only certain aspects of the overall problem. Income distribution is far too broad a phenomenon to be dealt with in just one article. In addition, the "new" problems arising from the joint analysis of income distribution in two such heterogeneous economic areas must be addressed.

The use of additively decomposable inequality measures was discussed with regard to the analysis of income distribution in a unified Germany. The advantage of this method is to be seen in the fact that changes over time in the overall income distribution can be analysed within a consistent framework together with its most important aspects; distribution within the two areas and East-West income distribution. Given the current and future significance of West-East transfers, such analysis is of vital importance.

The discussed approach is not only of relevance in observing changes in income distribution ex post: using micro-simulation models, various policy programs can be evaluated with regard to their implications on income distribution. The public discussions surrounding the German "Solidarity Pact" have clearly revealed the need for such an instrument.

References

Atkinson, A. B. (1970): On the Measurement of Inequality. In: Journal of Economic Theory, 2, 244-263.

Atkinson, A. B. and J. Micklewright (1992): Economic transformation in Eastern Europe and the distribution of income. Cambridge.

Bird, E. J., J. Schwarze and G. G. Wagner (1994): Wage Effects of the Move Toward Free Markets in East Germany. In: Industrial and Labor Relations Review, 47, 390-400.

Blackorby, Ch. and D. Donaldson (1978): Measures of Relative Equality and Their Meaning in Terms of Social Welfare. In: Journal of Economic Theory, 18, 59-80.

Bourguignon, F. (1979): Decomposable Income Inequality Measures. In: Econometrica, 47, 901-920.

Burkhauser, R. V. and J. G. Poupore (1993): A Cross-National Comparison of Permanent Inequality in the United States and Germany. Cross-National Studies in Aging. Program Project Paper No. 10. Syracuse.

Hauser, R. (1992): Die personelle Einkommensverteilung in den alten und neuen Bundesländern vor der Vereinigung. Probleme eines empirischen Vergleichs und der Abschätzung von Entwicklungstendenzen. In: G. Kleinhenz (Ed.): Sozialpolitik im vereinten Deutschland II. Berlin.

Mookherjee, D. and A. F. Shorrocks (1982): A Decomposition Analysis of the Trend in UK Income Inequality. In: Economic Journal, 92, 886-902.

Mueller, K., G. G. Wagner, R. Hauser and J. Frick (1994): How Unemployment and Income Inequality Changed in East and West Germny Following Reunification. In:Vierteljahrshefte zur Wirtschaftsforschung, (1-2), 48-52.

Rawls, J. (1971): A Theory of Justice. Cambridge, Mass.

Schwarze, J., M. Gornig and M. Steinhöfel (1990): Die Bedeutung der Frauenerwerbstätigkeit für die Einkommensverteilung in beiden deutschen Staaten. In: Arbeit und Sozialpolitik, 44, 464-481.

Shorrocks, F. A. (1980): The Class of Additively Decomposable Inequality Measures. In: Econometrica, 48, 613-625.

Shorrocks, F. A. (1984): Inequality Decomposition by Population Subgroups. In: Econometrica, 52, 1369-1384.

Wagner, G., R. V. Burkhauser and F. Behringer (1993): The English Language Public Use File of the German Socio-Economic Panel. In: Journal of Human Resources, 28, 429-433.

Table A-1: Average Real Gross Monthly Income from Fulltime Employment and Decomposition Weightings in Percent

	1990	1991	1992
Unified Germany			
- Mean income	3004	3246	3375
East Germany			
- Mean Income	1223	1548	1760
- Share of total population	28.2	22.0	22.9
- Share of total income	11.5	10.5	12.0
West Germany			
- Mean Income	3705	3723	3856
- Share of total population	71.8	78.0	77.1
- Share of total income	88.5	89.5	88.0

Income in 1990 Deutsche Mark.
Source: GSOEP, 1990-1992.

Table A-2: Average Real After Government Personal Household Income[1] in D-Mark and Decomposition Weightings in Percent

	1990	1991	1992
Unified Germany	1395	1397	1435
- Mean income			
East Germany			
- Mean Income	727	775	842
- Share of total population	21.6	21.2	20.9
- Share of total income	11.3	11.8	12.3
West Germany			
- Mean Income	1579	3723	1592
- Share of total population	78.48	78.0	79.1
- Share of total income	88.7	89.5	87.7

[1] Size adjusted household income according to the German Bundessozialhilfegesetz.
Income in 1990 Deutsche Mark.
Source: GSOEP, 1990-1992.

Table A-3: The Distribution of Personal After Government Household Income in Nominal and Real Terms for the Unified Germany and its Components 1990 to 1992.

Decomposed Measures $I(0)$ and $I(1)$

Year	Total Inequality	Inequality East	Inequality East-West	Inequality West
I(0):				
1990[1]	0.1473	0.0117	0.0435	0.0921
1991:				
nominal	0.1292	0.0142	0.0280	0.0869
real	0.1369	0.0142	0.0357	0.0869
1992:				
nominal	0.1187	0.0139	0.0160	0.0889
real	0.1322	0.0139	0.0294	0.0889
I(1)				
1990[1]	0.1549	0.006	0.0365	0.1124
1991:				
nominal	0.1318	0.0084	0.0245	0.0989
real	0.1383	0.0078	0.0305	0.100
1992:				
nominal	0.1244	0.093	0.144	0.1007
real	0.1365	0.0080	0.0255	0.1030

[1] Real income is computed by setting 1990 equal 100.
Source: GSOEP, 1990-1992.

GPSR Compliance

The European Union's (EU) General Product Safety Regulation (GPSR) is a set of rules that requires consumer products to be safe and our obligations to ensure this.

If you have any concerns about our products, you can contact us on ProductSafety@springernature.com

In case Publisher is established outside the EU, the EU authorized representative is:

Springer Nature Customer Service Center GmbH
Europaplatz 3
69115 Heidelberg, Germany

Batch number: 10725973

Printed by Printforce, the Netherlands